Historical Studies in

INDUSTRIAL RELATIONS

——————— No. 36 2015 ———————

Edited by

Paul Smith and Dave Lyddon

Liverpool University Press
for the Keele University Centre for Industrial Relations

Correction
In 'Docks and Defeat: The 1909 General Strike in Sweden and the Role of Port Labour', *HSIR* 34 (2013), pp. 1–27, we succeeded in declaring dead the 'Amalthea man', Anton Nilsson, and one of his companions; presumably death occurred around 1910. This was quite an achievement on our part, not least considering that one of our colleagues met Nilsson in person in the 1980s. But in fact we wrote in several drafts to the journal (regarding the judicial aftermath to *Amalthea*) that: 'The two death sentences were, however, never executed.' In the published article, it is stated that the 'two death sentences were carried out' (p. 21). We did not notice the radically changed meaning when we did the final proofreading.
Jesper Hamark and Christer Thörnqvist.

Contents

Review Essays Symposium: The Winter of Discontent

Review Essay

Book Reviews

Abstracts

doi:10.3828/hsir.2015.36.1

German Codetermination without Nationalization, and British Nationalization without Codetermination: Retelling the Story

Rebecca Zahn

Codetermination – worker participation in management – forms part of the industrial relations traditions of a number of European countries.[1] Among these, the German system of parity codetermination (*paritätische Mitbestimmung*) – the focus of this article – provides the greatest level of involvement for workers by allowing for equal representation of employees and management on the supervisory boards of companies in certain industries and above specific size thresholds. This model of codetermination was first introduced in the iron and steel industries by the British military command after the Second World War and is widely regarded in

---

Thanks to Douglas Brodie for his advice, Peter Zahn for insightful discussions, and the editor for helpful comments. The author is grateful to the Society of Legal Scholars' Research Activities Fund for its financial support of the archival research that underpins this article, and to the Bundesarchiv Koblenz, The National Archives, and the People's History Museum. The usual disclaimers apply.

1 Workers' representation at the workplace can either take place through trade unions, works councils or at board level. Within the European Union, eighteen member-states make statutory provision for some form of board-level representation. Of these, the German system of equal representation of workers and employer representatives on the supervisory board of the coal, and iron and steel industries, provides the greatest level of involvement. See L. Fulton, *Worker Representation in Europe* (Labour Research Department and ETUI: 2013), available at http://www.worker-participation.eu/National-Industrial-Relations/Across-Europe/Board-level-Representation2. For a broader definition and discussion of the term 'Mitbestimmung – Codetermination' see M. Weiss, *European Employment and Industrial Relations Glossary: Germany* (Sweet and Maxwell: 1992), pp. 227–8.

the German literature as a successful trade-union achievement and a vital element,[2] even the most important 'socio-political innovation', of German post-war industrial democracy.[3]

A closer reading of the British accounts of the negotiations among the Allied powers over ownership of the coal and steel industries raises the question as to why codetermination was introduced when the ultimate goal of British policy was repeatedly outlined as nationalization of heavy industry.[4] One must therefore ask whether codetermination was intended as a form of industrial democracy or whether it was a British compromise and a first step on the road to the goal of nationalization of these industries (which was never completed). Parallels – which have largely been overlooked but which help to explain the reasons for the introduction of codetermination – can be drawn with the debates taking place in the UK with regard to the programme of nationalization initiated by the new Labour government, elected in July 1945.

However, there were repeated attempts to delay the nationalization of the iron and steel industries for economic reasons until at least after the general election in 1950. Yet any postponement was seen as irreconcilable with the British insistence on the nationalization of the German iron and steel industries,[5] lending weight to the argument that the introduction of codetermination in Germany should be considered a stepping stone to nationalization. This article considers not only why codetermination was not introduced in the UK when similar debates on codetermination and nationalization were taking place at the same time, but also whether the failure to institute a system of workers' participation in management in the UK should be considered a missed opportunity.

---

2 There is only limited archival material and historical literature documenting the negotiations that resulted in the adoption of *Mitbestimmung*. The most detailed and influential account was written by E. Potthoff, *Der Kampf um die Montanmitbestimmung* (Bund-Verlag, Köln: 1957) who as head of the West German trade-union confederation's (*DGB*) economic research institute (*Wirtschaftswissenschaftliches Institut*) between 1946 and 1949 played an influential role in the elaboration and implementation of the concept. See also H. Thum, *Mitbestimmung in der Montanindustrie* (DVA, Stuttgart: 1982) and G. Müller, *Mitbestimmung in der Nachkriegszeit* (Schwan, Düsseldorf: 1987).

3 *Ibid.*, p. 7: 'die bedeutsamste sozialpolitische Neuerung in der Geschichte der Bundesrepublik.'

4 See A. Bullock, *The Life and Times of Ernest Bevin, Vol. 3: Foreign Secretary 1945–1951* (Heinemann: 1983), ch. 11.

5 See H. Pelling, *The Labour Governments 1945–51* (Macmillan: 1984).

Iron and steel in post-war Germany: attempts at nationalization

Codetermination in the form of some sort of employee representation in German enterprises had existed in different forms since the 1890s.[6] It was formally provided for in legislation with the introduction of the Works Council Act (*Betriebsrätegesetz*) in 1920.[7] However, as Helga Grebing points out,

> the double task imposed on the works councils [during this period] proved extremely difficult, if not altogether impossible; they were to 'look after the common economic interests of the employees vis à vis the employer', and at the same time, 'support the employer in the fulfilment of the establishment's purpose'.[8]

The Act was repealed by the Nazi government in 1934 and replaced with an Act for the organization of national labour (*Gesetz zur Ordnung der nationalen Arbeit*) which abolished any kind of codetermination.

After the Second World War and the unconditional surrender and military occupation of Germany by the four Allied powers,[9] economic production – especially in the German coal, and iron and steel industries – was at the heart of much of the Allied discussions.[10] France objected fundamentally to the restoration of German industry to its old levels of production

---

6 For an overview of the history of the German system of workers' representation see R. Dukes, 'The Origins of the German System of Worker Representation', *Historical Studies in Industrial Relations (HSIR)* 19 (2005), pp. 31–62.

7 L. F. Neumann and K. Schaper, *Die Sozialordnung der Bundesrepublik Deutschland* (Bundeszentrale für politische Bildung, Bonn: 2008), p. 33.

8 H. Grebing, *The History of the German Labour Movement* (Oswald Wolff: 1969), p. 107.

9 After its unconditional surrender on 7/8 May 1945, Germany was divided into four occupation zones which were governed by the Allied Control Council, set up as an overarching control body able to issue laws, directives, orders, and proclamations. The Council was run by the UK, the USA, France, and the Soviet Union. The four occupation zones were controlled at an administrative level by the *Gouvernement militaire de la zone française d'occupation* (*GMZFO*) (France), the Control Commission for Germany (British Element) (UK), the Office of Military Government, United States (OMGUS) (USA), and the Soviet Military Administration in Germany (Soviet Union). For a detailed overview see Bundeszentrale für politische Bildung, *Errichtung der Besatzungsherrschaft* (2005), available at http://www.bpb.de/izpb/10048/errichtung-der-besatzungsherrschaft?p=1.

10 For an overview of the rationale behind British military and economic policy, particularly with regard to the denazification of large enterprises, see Thum, *Mitbestimmung*, pp. 26–31 and the references at pp. 27–8.

which it saw as a renewed threat to its own and Europe's security.[11] Its representatives argued instead for the separation of the Rhineland and the Ruhr from Germany, or at least for the internationalization of the Ruhr so that its coal resources could be used to build up the heavy industry of Germany's neighbours and so avoid recreating Germany's former industrial domination. The US, on the other hand, did not have a common position. The War Department proposed that ownership should be vested in German trustees until a German central government was established, and the German people could vote on the issue of nationalization in more 'normal' conditions after five years. By contrast, the State Department supported the French position that German industry should be included in a European recovery programme. From the outset the decentralization of German industry formed a key part of Allied policy.[12]

In the British sector where most heavy industry was located, the initial focus was decentralization of industry, combined with a process of denazification. Thus the 'British policy in denazifying German industry was two-pronged: first, to investigate and, where a case existed, to dismiss management; second, to strengthen the role of the trade unions.'[13] From an economic point of view, the British were keen for German industry to play a vital role in ensuring German economic recovery so as to lessen the financial pressure on the UK as an occupying power. Heavy industry, particularly iron and steel which was controlled by a handful of companies, was to be restructured and broken up into smaller entities. In July 1946, Sholto Douglas, Commander of the British Zone in Germany, on the basis of plans outlined by Ernest Bevin, the British Foreign Secretary, to the Cabinet early in 1946, announced plans for the eventual nationalization (or socialization as it was referred to) of the main German industries. There is doubt in the German literature as to whether the British were serious in their pursuit of nationalization[14] as the policy did not seem to correspond with the UK's economic priorities of increasing German production.[15]

Nationalization implied a change in management which would initially lead to a fall in output rather than making Germany less reliant on British

---

11 Bullock, *Bevin: Foreign Secretary*, ch. 7.
12 See the Potsdam Agreement in *Mitteilungen über die Dreimächtekonferenz*, Europa-Archiv, pp. 216–17.
13 F. Taylor, *Exorcising Hitler* (Bloomsbury: 2011), p. 308.
14 See W. Rudzio, 'Die ausgebliebene Sozialisierung an Rhein und Ruhr: Zur Sozialisierungspolitik von Labour-Regierung und SPD 1945–1949', *Archiv für Sozialgeschichte* (1978), pp. 1–39; H. Lademacher, 'Die britische Sozialisierungspolitik im Rhein-Ruhr-Raum 1945–1948', in C. Scharf and H. J. Schröder (eds), *Die Deutschlandpolitik Großbritanniens und die britische Zone 1945–1949* (Steiner Franz Verlag, Wiesbaden: 1979), pp. 51–92.
15 Müller, *Mitbestimmung*, p. 31.

financial support. Moreover, the British made few attempts in practice to pursue nationalization.[16] Following this line of reasoning, the seizure of the iron and steel companies in August 1946 and their placement under the control of the British-administered North German Iron and Steel Control Authority (NGISC) should be seen as a temporary measure in order to better organize the industry's decentralization rather than as an act of nationalization.[17] While the British did pursue decentralization of the sector from 1946 onwards, this occurred in parallel to ongoing negotiations between the UK, the USA, and France over possible nationalization.[18]

A different picture emerges from the British literature, where Bevin's commitment to nationalization becomes obvious. In an article written for *The Times* in 1977, William Harris-Burland, the British official in Germany responsible for the decentralization of German industry, recalled:

> In 1946 I was appointed controller of the steel concerns in the British zone of control, with instructions to reorganize and deconcentrate them in fulfilment of a requirement in the Potsdam agreement. To this was later added a quasi-secret instruction to prepare the steel industry for nationalization.[19]

There is also clear evidence that in proposing nationalization, Bevin was heavily influenced by the UK government's domestic approach to industrial planning,[20] and in particular by left-wing supporters of the British Labour Party.[21] This is not surprising as Bevin had been active in British industrial relations before the war as general secretary of the Transport and General Workers' Union (TGWU) from 1922 to 1940, and held the position of Minister for Labour and National Service from 1940 to 1945,[22] before becoming Foreign Secretary in 1945, and he continued to be involved in British domestic politics.

In April 1946, Bevin recommended first the creation of 'a new German province' and, second, that the heavy industries should 'be made into a socialised German corporation whose relation to the Provincial Government would be the same as that of the National Coal Board in this country to

---

16 W. Adelshauser, 'Die verhinderte Neuordnung? Wirtschaftsordnung und Sozialstaatsprinzip in der Nachkriegszeit', *Politische Bildung* (1976), pp. 53–72.
17 Müller, *Mitbestimmung*, p. 32.
18 For an overview of decentralization see Thum, *Mitbestimmung*, pp. 31–7.
19 W. Harris-Burland, 'Workers' Role in German industry', *The Times*, 27 January 1977.
20 See Pelling, *The Labour Governments*, ch. 5.
21 See E. Schmidt, *Die verhinderte Neuordnung 1945–1952* (Europäische Verlagsanstalt, Frankfurt a.M.: 1971), p. 84.
22 See A. Bullock, *The Life and Times of Ernest Bevin, Vol. 1: Trade Union Leader 1881–1940* (Heinemann: 1960).

HMG [His Majesty's Government]'.[23] This proposal was not accepted by the USA and France, both of which favoured the internationalization of the Ruhr. Nonetheless, later that year, in August, Bevin 'committed the British Government to the public ownership of German heavy industry',[24] and confirmed the British intention 'that these industries should be owned and worked by the German people'.[25] The transfer of the iron and steel industries to the control of the NGISC should therefore be considered a first step towards nationalization. This is supported by the reaction of the German metalworkers' union to the creation of the NGISC when it described the transfer 'as the first step towards the socialization of heavy industry' and called for the active involvement of German trade unions in the NGISC's work if a democratization of the economy through nationalization were to succeed.[26]

Disputes between the Allied powers over the nature and form of nationalization continued into the autumn of 1947. In the hope of appeasing the *Gouvernement militaire de la zone française d'occupation* (*GMZFO*) which was vehemently opposed to any form of nationalization, Bevin repeatedly clarified that he did not advocate the transfer of the industries to a German government,[27] but argued in favour of decentralization and the vesting of industry ownership in the new Land Nordrhein-Westfalen. Bevin's main political supporters over this issue were the British trade unions which 'were completely wedded to the idea of public ownership and were afraid that, if measures of socialisation were not carried out quickly, there was a danger of the ownership of these industries with their dangerous war potential reverting to the large combines'.[28] British trade unions were of course also heavily influenced by the domestic debate taking place in the UK over the nationalization of heavy industry, which they actively endorsed (see below).

French and, especially, American opposition to nationalization were pivotal in securing its eventual failure.[29] From an American perspective,

23 Memorandum by the Secretary of State for Foreign Affairs on the Ruhr and West Germany circulated to the Cabinet, 15 April 1946, CAB 129/8/39, The National Archives (TNA), Kew, London.
24 Bullock, *Bevin: Foreign Secretary*, p. 320.
25 Memorandum by the Secretary of State for Foreign Affairs on Germany, 17 October 1946, Conclusions and Recommendations, CAB 129/13/33, TNA.
26 Schmidt, *Die verhinderte Neuordnung*, p. 76.
27 This would have not only upset France which was fearful of the recreation of a strong German state but there was also a perceived danger of a future German government falling under Communist-Russian control. See Bullock, *Bevin: Foreign Secretary*, pp. 340–3.
28 Lew Douglas (US Ambassador) report to US Secretary of State, 4 July 1947. Foreign Relations of the United States (FRUS) 1947 (3), p. 312.
29 Bullock, *Bevin: Foreign Secretary*, ch. 11.

nationalization would hamper the Ruhr's industrial output, an increase of which was perceived as vital for broader European economic recovery. The French, on the other hand, 'objected fundamentally to the restoration of German industry to its old levels of production which they saw as a renewed threat to their own and Europe's security', arguing instead for 'the separation of the Rhineland and the Ruhr from Germany, or at least for the internationalization of the Ruhr'.[30] In August 1947, during tripartite talks between the British, Americans and French, which took place at a time when the UK could no longer afford to financially support its German zone and was heavily indebted to the USA, Bevin eventually agreed to an American compromise:

> The joint communiqué issued at the end of the coal talks, on 10 September, transferred responsibility for coal production to German hands under the supervision of a joint US/UK control group. The question of ownership of the mines was left open, but when the two military governments published their Law No. 75 for the reorganization of both the German coal and steel industries, two months later, ownership, in both cases, was vested in German trustees pending a final decision by 'a representative, freely-elected German government.'[31]

Whereas the compromise kept open the possibility of future nationalization, it took the process out of British hands, and plans for nationalization were eventually shelved. What remains of the aim of socialization is *Mitbestimmung*, or, as Bullock writes, 'the legacy of the British occupation was not, as Bevin had hoped, the nationalization of the German coal and steel industries but the institution of *Mitbestimmung* (codetermination) between management and trade unions, a practice which, despite its success in Germany … has still to be introduced in Britain itself'.[32] Similarly, Harris-Burland suggests that 'those in the Labour Government who had been advocating nationalization of the German steel industry, when they saw their aim to be unattainable, were prepared to console themselves with codetermination as a substitute'.[33]

---

30 *Ibid.*, p. 431.
31 *Ibid.*, p. 435, citing the text of the communiqué in Royal Institute of International Affairs, *Documents 1947–48*, pp. 622–3, and of Law No. 75, pp. 637–45.
32 *Ibid.*, pp. 435–6.
33 Harris-Burland, *The Times*, 27 January 1977.

Iron and steel in post-war Germany: the introduction of codetermination

Reconstituted German trade unions[34] had begun to call for the institution-alization of *Mitbestimmung* – which they associated with the equal status of workers and employers in the management of enterprises – as early as March 1946 at their first post-war congress.[35] Influenced by plans for a reorganization of the German economy drawn up by exiled German trade-unionists based in the UK during the Second World War,[36] German trade unions supported codetermination to control the employers, and to obtain a role in the regulation of workers' terms and conditions of employment. It was unclear, however, whether rights of codetermination should be granted to works councils or trade unions. While the general tenor of the congress spoke of works councils being granted rights of 'codetermination in all social and labour law related matters of the enterprise and of responsible collaboration and codetermination in the areas of production and distri-bution of profits',[37] Hans Böckler – president of the German trade-union confederation in the British Zone – firmly argued in favour of trade unions taking on such a role:

---

34 As a result of military restrictions on the right to freedom of association in the early post-war years (Industrial Relations Directive No. 1, 1945), trade unions were initially concentrated at a local level. The first trade-union confed-eration within the British Zone was not formed until April 1947. In parallel, a group of former union leaders from the Weimar Republic had come together to form a committee (*Siebener-Ausschuß*) led by Hans Böckler in March 1945. This committee operated as the voice of local trade unions and acted as principal contact for the British government and military leaders. See Müller, *Mitbestimmung*, p. 68. For an overview of the state of German trade-unionism in the late 1940s see Grebing, *History*, pp. 172–82.

35 Protokoll der ersten Gewerkschaftskonferenz der britischen Zone vom 12.–14. März 1946, Hannover.

36 Schmidt, *Die verhinderte Neuordnung*, p. 67. See also G. Stuttard, 'Book Review of C. Dartmann, *Redistribution of Power: Joint Consultation or Productivity Coalitions? Labour and Postwar Reconstruction in Germany and Britain, 1945–1953* (Brockmeyer, Bochum: 1996)', *HSIR* 15 (2003), pp. 147–51, who references the document at p. 149. For an overview of the rationale behind German trade unions' reasoning see C. Dartmann, *Re-Distrbution of Power, Joint Consultation or Productivity Coalitions?* (Brockmeyer, Bochum: 1996), pp. 94–147.

37 Protokoll der ersten Gewerkschaftskonferenz der britischen Zone vom 12.–14. März 1946, Hannover. Entschließung Nr. 6, p. 56: 'Diese Rechte [des Betriebsrats] bestehen in der Mitbestimmung der Betriebsräte in allen sozialen und arbeitsrechtlichen Angelegenheiten des Betriebes und der verantwortlichen Mitarbeit und Mitbestimmung bei der Produktion und der Verteilung des Ertrags.'

We really cannot leave the employers alone together in a room by themselves for a moment and if we have separate chambers [for the employer and the workers], then I can tell you exactly what will happen … We have to be directly involved in the economy and be equals … So I suggest the following: representation on the management boards and supervisory boards of industry.[38]

A resolution calling for 'the right to codetermination for trade unions and works councils in industry'[39] was passed at the second trade-union congress held in December 1946.

In parallel, German trade unions called for a reorganization of the economy in which heavy industry should become 'communal property' (*Gemeineigentum*) rather than outright nationalization.[40] Codetermination was conceived as an integral part of such a reorganization, particularly by the Metalworkers' Union (*IGMetall*) which represented workers in the iron and steel industries.[41] The British Labour government was seen as an ally, and its plans for the decentralization of the iron and steel industries were considered to open up the possibility for trade unions to participate in industrial reorganization.[42] In a statement on the socialization of German industry, German trade unions called for equal participation of workers and management on the supervisory boards of industry.[43] Harris-Burland recalls that Böckler approached the NGISC in 1946 to request 'that the appointments to [the decentralized iron and steel] companies' supervisory and management boards should include representatives of the trade unions and workers'.[44] In negotiating over the future of the iron and steel industries, German trade unions adopted a conciliatory approach, offering their support for British plans for industrial reorganization and economic

---

38 *Ibid.*, Hans Böckler at p. 33: 'Wir dürfen aber eigentlich die Unternehmer keinen Augenblick unter sich alleine lassen, und bei getrennten Kammern weiß ich genau, wie es kommt … Wir müssen in der Wirtschaft selber sein, also völlig gleichberechtigt vertreten sein … Also der Gedanke ist der: Vertretung in den Vorständen und Aufsichtsräten der Gesellschaften.'
39 Schmidt, *Die verhinderte Neuordnung*, p. 71.
40 While nationalization involves the transfer of private property to state ownership, communal property implies public ownership of industry which is also publicly available. This can only be achieved through a democratization of an industry and its production processes through, for example, codetermination.
41 Thum, *Mitbestimmung*, p. 20.
42 *Ibid.*, p. 25.
43 B109/144 'Niederschrift über die Zusammenkunft mit den Vertretern der Gewerkschaften' at Anlage 2: 'Stellungnahme der Gewerkschaften zur Sozialisierung', 11 December 1946, p. 3.
44 Harris-Burland, *The Times*, 27 January 1977.

growth in return for organizational reform, including the introduction of codetermination.[45]

After Böckler's initial request, from October 1946 the NGISC involved German trade unions in the decentralization of the iron and steel industries. In addition, Harris-Burland appointed Rennie Smith – a former Labour MP and trade-unionist fluent in German[46] – as a mediator between the NGISC and the German trade unions. At a meeting between Harris-Burland for the NGISC, Heinrich Dinkelbach and Günter Max Paefgen as representatives of its German trustees (*Treuhandverwaltung*) and six trade-union representatives (including Böckler) on 14 December 1946, Dinkelbach outlined a plan, which had already been approved by the relevant British authorities in London and by the British military government in Berlin, to reorganize the iron and steel industries.[47] Its principal objectives were to limit the sphere of influence of the current owners while also guaranteeing workers' involvement in the management of the industries.[48] The underlying aim was to guarantee 'true industrial democracy'.[49]

While Dinkelbach indicated that future negotiations with trade unions would clarify the extent of workers' involvement in management, he suggested equal representation for workers and management on the supervisory boards of the iron and steel industries.[50] The detailed framework for this unprecedented form of codetermination was subsequently negotiated between trade unions[51] and the *Treuhandver-waltung*, and finalized in January 1947. The management board was to include a 'labour director' (*Arbeitsdirektor*) as one of its three members who could only be appointed with the agreement of the trade unions, and supervisory boards were to consist of eleven members, five of whom were to represent the employer and the workers respectively,[52] with the neutral chairman appointed by the *Treuhandverwaltung*. Industry owners were

45 Thum, *Mitbestimmung*, p. 26.
46 See M. Ceadel, *Semi-Detached Idealists: The British Peace Movement and International Relations 1854–1945* (Oxford University Press: 2000), pp. 298–9, and B109/144. 'Niederschrift über die Zusammenkunft mit den Vertretern der Gewerkschaften' at Anlage 1.
47 Schmidt, *Die verhinderte Neuordnung*, p. 76.
48 B109/144 'Niederschrift über die Zusammenkunft mit den Vertretern der Gewerkschaften' at Anlage 1, p. 2.
49 *Ibid.*, p. 4: 'Im Sinne einer wahren Wirtschaftsdemokratie werden die Rechte der Arbeiter in jeder Hinsicht gewahrt.'
50 *Ibid.*, p. 3; see Schmidt, *Die verhinderte Neuordnung*, p. 77.
51 Led by E. Potthoff and K. Strohmenger.
52 Among the five worker representatives two would be nominated by the works council, two by the trade unions and one from another source. See Thum, *Mitbestimmung*, p. 36.

not involved in the negotiations and were only officially informed of the outcome in January 1947. Equal representation on supervisory boards was extended beyond the British military zone in April 1951 by an Act of the German Parliament (*Gesetz über die paritätische Mitbestimmung in der Montanindustrie*) to cover the coal, and iron and steel industries, and paved the way for the Works Constitution Act 1952 (*Betriebsverfassungsgesetz*) which reintroduced works councils and extended workers' representation on supervisory boards to other industries.[53]

Gloria Müller argues that the owners, despite not being officially involved in the negotiations over the future of heavy industry, were prepared to accept far-reaching workers' involvement in management in order to garner trade-union support against British plans for the break-up of the coal, and iron and steel industries.[54] Here it has been argued that codetermination was the result of Anglo-German co-operation that fostered solidarity between employers and workers, leading to the implementation of a union policy with the agreement of the relevant employers.[55] This thesis is not supported by all writers on the subject. For example, Jürgen Nautz and Peter Hüttenberger argue that the British were not supportive of codetermination and, indeed, were pushing instead for the reform of German industrial relations to model the British system of free collective bargaining.[56]

The introduction of codetermination should therefore be seen as a strategic mechanism to alter the role of trade unions. Regardless of the underlying British aims, the central role played by the British in the creation of codetermination should not be overlooked. Harris-Burland, in particular, appears to have played a vital role. Rennie Smith writes that Harris-Burland was convinced that 'the Trade Unions had an important part to play. As far as he was concerned, he wanted to see them play it.

---

53 The 1952 Act provides for codetermination on the supervisory boards of companies with more than 500 employees. Employee representatives make up one-third of the members of the supervisory board in such cases. The 1951 Act provides for parity codetermination on the supervisory boards of the coal, and iron and steel industries.

54 Müller, *Mitbestimmung*. See also Thum, *Mitbestimmung*, p. 35, where he summarizes letters between industry owners and trade unions offering trade unions shares and information and consultation rights in return for their support against British decentralization plans.

55 W. Hirsch-Weber, *Gewerkschaften in der Politik* (Verlag für Sozialwissenschaften, Köln: 1959), pp. 82–4.

56 J. P. Nautz, *Die Durchsetzung der Tarifautonomie in Westdeutschland: Das Tarifvertragsgesetz vom 9.4.1949* (Peter Lang, Frankfurt a.M.: 1985); P. Hüttenberger, 'Die Anfänge der Gesellschaftspolitik in der britischen Zone', *Vierteljahreshefte für Zeitgeschichte* 21 (1973), pp. 171–6.

He was willing to take them fully into confidence.'[57] Moreover, Harris-Burland viewed the trade unions 'as one of the chief stabilising influences in the political, social and economic life of the British Zone'.[58] On a broader level, Walther Bernecker, Volker Berghahn, and Müller emphasize the positive British attitude towards the very idea of workers' involvement in management, as well as their natural affinity with the social-democratic leadership of the German trade unions.[59] This is perhaps not surprising as similar discussions over nationalization and codetermination were taking place in the UK at the same time (see below). Arguably, therefore, British intervention created the necessary framework and sufficient pressure so that agreement over the concept of codetermination could be reached. As Eberhard Schmidt explains: 'the introduction of parity codetermination in the iron and steel industries in February 1947 is therefore the result of trade-union pressure for the democratization of the economy, as well as fulfilling the interests of the British.'[60] While the introduction of *Mitbestimmung* can be celebrated as an achievement of the German trade unions, it is unlikely that the idea would have come to fruition without the positive support of the British Labour government which was no stranger to the idea of workers' involvement in the management in nationalized industries.

Parallel debates: nationalization and codetermination in UK politics

Nationalization formed a major part of the election manifesto – *Let Us Face the Future*[61] drafted by Herbert Morrison with the assistance of Michael Young – of the 1945 Labour government. Between 1945 and 1950, it 'was responsible for nationalising the Bank of England, coal mining, electricity and gas, the whole railway system and a section of road transport, civil aviation and telecommunications, and finally, though ineffectually, the

---

57 Rennie Smith, diaries III, entry for 16–31 December 1946, Bodleian Library, Oxford.
58 'Interim Report upon the progress made in carrying out Operation "Severance"', 21 March 1947, FO 1039/816, TNA.
59 Müller, *Mitbestimmung*; W. L. Bernecker, 'Die Neugründung der Gewerk-schaften in den Westzonen 1945–1949', in J. Becker, T. Stammen and P. Waldmann (eds), *Vorgeschichte der Bundesrepublik Deutschland* (Fink, München: 1979), pp. 261–92; V. Berghahn, *Unternehmer und Politik in der Bundesrepublik* (Suhrkamp, Frankfurt: 1985).
60 Schmidt, *Die verhinderte Neuordnung*, p. 82: 'Die Einführung der paritätischen Mitbestimmung in den entflochtenen Werken der Eisen-und Stahlindustrie im Februar 1947 ist also das Resultat des gewerkschaftlichen Drängens auf Demokratisierung der Wirtschaft, ebenso wie des Interesses der britischen Besatzungsmacht.'
61 Labour Party, *Let Us Face The Future* (1945).

major part of the iron and steel industry'.[62] Nationalization statutes were passed in 1946, 1947, and 1948, with little political or public opposition;[63] the only real opposition occurred in relation to the Iron and Steel Bill as 'the industry, unlike coal or the railways, was profitable; for another, it had a tradition of good public relations, and its trade union leaders were themselves understood to be lukewarm about public ownership'.[64] Nationalization of iron and steel was first proposed in 1946 by John Wilmot, Minister of Supply,[65] but was met with considerable controversy and opposition. It was suggested that 'in order to "retain the willing co-operation of the industry", the Government should not nationalise but should impose a "permanent statutory control"'.[66] Such a compromise was favoured by Wilmot and by Morrison, who as Deputy Prime Minister supervised the implementation of the nationalization programme. It was vehemently opposed by the Minister for Health, Aneurin Bevan, who argued in early summer 1947 that 'it would be difficult for the Government to insist on nationalising the industry of the Ruhr while retreating from the same policy inside Britain'.[67] A renewed attempt at nationalization was made in 1948 when a Bill prepared by Wilmot's successor – George Strauss – was introduced. Bevin, who spoke out in favour of the Bill, adopted a similar argument to Bevan: failure to nationalize the British iron and steel industries would be 'inconsistent with the policy of seeking to promote the socialisation of the Ruhr steel industry'.[68] The Iron and Steel Act was eventually passed in 1949,[69] receiving Royal Assent on 24 November but, as a compromise,

---

62 E. Eldon Barry, *Nationalisation in British Politics* (Jonathan Cape: 1965), p. 369. For a detailed account of the various nationalization statutes see R. A. Brady, *Crisis in Britain: Plans and Achievements of the Labour Government* (University of California Press, Berkeley, CA: 1950). For a critique of the policies see W. A. Robson, *Nationalised Industry and Public Ownership* (Allen and Unwin: 1960); S. Pollard, *The Development of the British Economy, 1914–1950* (Edward Arnold: 1962); R. Miliband, *Parliamentary Socialism* (Allen and Unwin: 1960).

63 Nationalization statutes include, *inter alia*, Bank of England Act 1946, Coal Industry Nationalisation Act 1946, Civil Aviation Act 1946, Electricity Act 1947, Transport Act 1947, and Gas Act 1948. See Eldon Barry, *Nationalisation*, at pp. 374–6, for a discussion of reactions to nationalization.

64 Pelling, *The Labour Governments*, p. 83.

65 For a more detailed account see *ibid.*, p. 83 onwards. Nationalization of iron and steel was considered highly complicated 'owing to the difficulty of separating out the manufacture of iron and steel from the other activities of the companies concerned.'

66 *Ibid.*, p. 84.

67 *Ibid.*, p. 85.

68 *Ibid.*, p. 87.

69 For a detailed analysis of the Act see S. Langley, 'The Iron and Steel Act 1949', *Economic Journal* 60 (1950), pp. 311–22.

vesting day did not occur until 15 February 1951, after a general election which was won by the Labour Party with a small majority. Unlike the coal industry, the organization of the iron and steel industries was largely left intact, but the undertakings were transferred to, and vested in, the Iron and Steel Corporation of Great Britain.

The Labour government's programme of nationalization was based largely on the party's 1934 programme, *For Socialism and Peace*,[70] and consolidated in the Trades Union Congress (TUC)'s 1944 *Interim Report on Post-War Reconstruction*.[71] The issue of labour representation had featured heavily in the debates preceding adoption of the 1934 programme. The TUC's economic committee – composed of a dozen trade-unionists, including Bevin – together with Hugh Dalton and Morrison as represent-atives of the Labour Party, had drafted a report in 1931 on 'Public Control and Regulation of Industry and Trade' which considered the question of labour representation on the boards of nationalized industries.[72] The report adopted Morrison's vision of nationalization – a public corporation where members of the board were appointed by the relevant minister from among suitably qualified individuals – which he had attempted to put into practice in the London Passenger Transport Bill, proposed during the last year of the 1929 Labour government in 1931.[73] Morrison objected to any form of statutory worker representation on management boards:

> I was not convinced that the statutory right of the representation of labour in the industry would necessarily provide the best man from the ranks of labour; it would involve a difficult and embarrassing business of selection from the names submitted by the various Trades Unions in the industry; and if I conceded the statutory right of representation to labour in the industry, I should ... inevitably be involved in almost irresistible demands for the right of representation from other elements of interests.[74]

His approach to labour representation had been heavily criticized in 1931 by the TGWU, where Bevin, as general secretary, was 'insistent that the Board should include representatives of labour chosen by the unions concerned,

---

70 Labour Party, *For Socialism and Peace* (1934).
71 Trades Union Congress (TUC), *Interim Report on Post-War Reconstruction* (1944).
72 TUC, *Report on Public Control and Regulation of Industry and Trade* (1932), submitted to the TUC Congress at Newcastle, 1932.
73 The Bill was never adopted but a similar Bill – the London Passenger Transport Act – was passed by Ramsay MacDonald's National government in 1933.
74 H. Morrison, *Socialisation and Transport* (Constable: 1933), p. 191.

or at least statutory provision for consultation of the unions before the appointments were made'.[75]

The same criticism arose again in relation to the TUC's 1931 report, where Bevin alone spoke out against the public corporation as being 'positively the worst form of public control'.[76] In doing so, he followed a TUC tradition of advocating workers' representation in management. Until 1932, the TUC's standing orders had called for 'the General Council [to] endeavour to establish ... public ownership and control of natural resources and of services with proper provision for the adequate participation of the workers in the control and management of public services and industries'.[77] From 1932, however, reference was instead made to the public corporation and the 1931 report was adopted by the Congress.[78] Nonetheless, the issue of workers' representation on the boards of nationalized industry continued to arise at subsequent conferences of both the TUC and the Labour Party,[79] with Morrison and Bevin adopting opposing views. Even writing in 1944, Bevin criticized boards without workers' representation as 'unrepresentative, unresponsive and unlikely to pay much attention to the public interest'.[80] As Alan Bullock explains:

> Bevin's antagonism towards Morrison was unconcealed ... Socialism to Bevin meant something more than planning and public ownership; it meant a change in the status of the worker, the end of that exclusion from responsibility, the stigma of inferiority, which he had always regarded as the key to improving industrial relations.[81]

In arguing in favour of statutory representation of workers on management boards, Bevin was supported not only by the TGWU but also by the Associated Society of Locomotive Engineers and Firemen and the National Union of General and Municipal Workers, whose general secretary, Charles Dukes, proposed that worker representatives should have a statutory right to

---

75 Bullock, *Bevin: Trade Union Leader*, p. 459.
76 Note circulated to members of the Committee, 21 December 1931. See Bullock, *Bevin: Trade Union Leader*, p. 510.
77 See, for example, TUC, Annual Report, 1932, TUC Standing Orders, Appendix B, p. 450.
78 See *ibid.*, p. 206. The shift which occurred within the TUC between 1931 and 1932 is described in Eldon Barry, *Nationalisation*, pp. 320–4 and Bullock, *Bevin: Trade Union Leader*, p. 459.
79 For an overview of the debates see Eldon Barry, *Nationalisation*, pp. 320–2.
80 Letter from Bevin to Attlee in response to the draft paper on 'The Immediate Future of Financial and Industrial Planning', 22 November 1944, Bevin papers II 4/12, Churchill Archive Centre, Churchill College, Cambridge.
81 Bullock, *Bevin: Trade Union Leader*, pp. 514–15.

fill 50% of the members of the boards of management.[82] As a compromise, in its final version, the 1934 programme contained the principle 'that wage earners of all grades and occupations have a right which should be acknowledged by law to an effective share in the control and direction of socialised industries which their labour sustains'.[83]

The same questions over labour representation arose after the Second World War but the position adopted by the TUC and the Labour Party remained virtually unchanged from its pre-war position. As Christoph Dartmann points out:

> In the end ... in spite of the fact that the discussion of labour's position regarding the control and administration of industry had started with economic and industrial developments, and in spite of the fact that therefore economic and industrial development, control of industry, and labour participation were generically linked, this link was argumentatively reduced to the question of efficient management. Efficiency became the major yardstick for the eventual success of nationalisation and socialist policies. 'Efficiency' was once again reduced to the managerial and technical skills of the persons in charge, and consequently became the slogan with which the promoters of the public corporation rejected any claim for labour participation.[84]

In its *Interim Report on Post-War Reconstruction*, the TUC confirmed that nationalized industries were to take on the legal form of public corporations and that 'trade unions shall maintain their complete independence. They can hardly do so if they are compromised in regard to Board decisions which are not considered to be in their members' interests by the fact of their representatives' participation in them'.[85]

With hindsight it is clear that 'the question of trade union and workers' participation in the management of the nation's industries had been an issue on which the TUC had differed from the Labour Government's nationalisation proposals'. This contradiction is also obvious in the TUC's 1944 report when, at the same time as rejecting workers' participation in management, it called for the 'democratisation of economic life' which required 'the trade union movement to participate in the determination of all questions affecting the conduct of an industry'.[86] Nationalization legislation

---

82 TUC, Annual Report, 1933, p. 369.
83 Labour Party, Annual Conference Report, 1933, p. 205.
84 Dartmann, *Re-Distribution of Power*, pp. 58–9.
85 TUC, Annual Report, 1944, p. 411. See also D. N. Chester, 'Management Accountability in the Nationalised Industries', *Public Administration* 30 (1952), pp. 27–47, p. 35.
86 TUC, *The History of the TUC, 1868–1968* (1968), p. 131; TUC, Annual Report, 1944, p. 439. See also R. Dahl, 'Workers' Control of Industry and the British

fell short of this aim and, in effect, adopted Morrison's policy: governing boards of nationalized industries were appointed by a minister 'from amongst persons ... having had experience of, and having shown capacity in, industrial, commercial or financial matters, applied science, administration or the organization of workers'.[87] Any board members drawn from the trade-union movement were required to 'surrender any position held in, or any formal responsibility to, the Trade Union'[88] in order to preserve trade-union independence,[89] which would in turn ensure freedom of action in collective bargaining.

While nationalized industries were under a duty to establish machinery for the settlement of terms and conditions of employment, the wording of the relevant provisions was so vague that the obligation should be considered as good practice rather than a legal requirement to engage in effective collective bargaining.[90] As such, 'the only real claim to innovation in industrial relations in the nationalized industries can be found in the field of joint consultation'[91] in the form of joint production boards, which were under a statutory obligation to consult with relevant trade unions on the establishment of permanent consultation machinery for safety, health, and welfare issues. Paul Davies and Mark Freedland suggest that 'this form of participation was acceptable to the TUC since the machinery was under the control of the unions, did not embrace the matters that were central to collective bargaining and did not commit the unions to the decisions reached'.[92] Apart from failing to guarantee the involvement of workers or their representatives in the regulation of nationalized industry, the proposed legal form – the public corporation – 'ruled out ... any direct accountability of the board members (or even of some of them) to the workers employed in the industry, let alone any election by the workers of directors to the board of the nationalized corporation'.[93]

Signs of discontent among trade unions and some Labour Party members over the absence of workers' representation in the nationalized industries resurfaced after 1946,[94] when 'a minority continued to press the claim

---

Labor Party', *American Political Science Review* (*Am. Pol. Sc. Rev.*) 41 (1947), pp. 875–900, p. 875.

87 Coal Industry Nationalisation Act 1946, s. 2(3).

88 TUC, Annual Report, 1944, p. 412.

89 *Ibid.*, p. 411.

90 See, for example, Coal Industry Nationalisation Act 1946, s. 46.

91 P. Davies and M. Freedland, *Labour Legislation and Public Policy* (Clarendon Press, Oxford: 1993), p. 70.

92 *Ibid.*

93 *Ibid.*, p. 68.

94 Sixteen motions presented at the 1948 Labour Party conference, and eighteen motions submitted to the 1949 Labour Party conference, dealt *inter alia* with issues of democratic control of nationalized industries and workers'

for direct worker participation in the management of these industries'.[95]
A resolution, remitted to the TUC general council, at the TUC's Brighton
congress in 1946 pressed upon 'the Government the desirability of making
provision for workers' participation at all levels in the management of the
industry'.[96] At the 1947 congress, a resolution was passed unanimously which
demanded full participation by workers, through their trade unions, in the
management of nationalized industries.[97] At the Labour Party conference in
1948, a resolution was proposed which called for 'the principle of workers'
participation through their trade unions in the direction and management of
nationalized industry at all levels [to] be firmly adopted in practice'[98] on the
basis that 'it is the negation first of all of Socialism and secondly of sanity
itself to nationalise an industry and then leave the control of it in the hands
of the Tories'.[99] Moreover it was argued that:

> Something more than consultation must be given to the men. They should
> have the opportunity of appointment to managerial and supervisory positions.
> Only in that way are we going to get co-operation between the managerial and
> supervisory side and those who are supervised.[100]

The Association of Engineering and Shipbuilding Draughtsmen, in
seconding the resolution, argued that:

> [T]o nationalise an industry is not the same thing as socialising it … We believe
> that the extension of the principle of industrial democracy is just as important
> as the extension of political democracy … In urging that workers employed
> in nationalized industry should participate in management we do so because
> we believe that that is fundamental for industrial democracy and will increase
> production.[101]

Morrison expressed the views of the government when he disagreed with
the tenor of the resolution by calling for ministers to be given 'adequate time
to consolidate, to develop, to make efficient or more efficient the industries

participation on boards of nationalized industries: Agendas of Labour Party
conferences, 1948, pp. 18–19; 1949, pp. 15–17: Transport House Library,
London.

95 N. Chester, *The Nationalisation of British Industry, 1945–51* (HMSO: 1975),
    p. 844.
96 *Ibid.*, pp. 844–5.
97 TUC, Annual Report, 1947, pp. 472–7, 519–24.
98 Labour Party, Annual Conference Report, 1948, pp. 167–72.
99 *Ibid.*, pp. 166–7.
100 *Ibid.*, pp. 168–9.
101 *Ibid.*, p. 168.

which have been socialised in the present Parliament'.[102] Thus the National Union of Mineworkers argued that:

> We as a miners' organisation do not want to have people in the ridiculous position that we see on the Continent where the president or secretary of a miners' organization is also on the Coal Board running the industry, so that he has on occasion to pass a resolution to ask himself to give himself something.[103]

Similarly, the TGWU followed Morrison's line of reasoning by pointing out that 'we have had eighteen months' experience of the running of socialised industry ... With the ultimate purpose of the resolution I am in full sympathy and full support, but you have to walk before you can run.'[104] It was agreed instead that the matter would be remitted to the Labour Party's executive for 'further consultation with the Trades Union Congress'.[105]

The issue of codetermination in management of nationalized industries was also raised by a number of trade unions with various government departments, and directly with the Prime Minister. A letter written by the National Union of Railwaymen in 1950 to the Minister of Transport opined that 'it is essential that the actual workers in the industry should have a greater participation in the management of the Railways'.[106] The TGWU – which had originally opposed the 1948 resolution – in a letter dated 21 September 1951 reiterated 'the view that in giving effect to the principle of public ownership full advantage should be taken of the knowledge, skill and experience of the workers and that in all appointments made in the nationalized industries proper regard should be had [to suitably qualified workers]'.[107] In response, it was suggested that 'under present circumstances no action is necessary, but that after the Election whoever is Secretary of the Socialisation of Industries Committee might then consider whether this is a matter to be placed on the agenda'.[108] The 1951 general election was won by the Conservative Party, and the new government privatized the iron and steel industries in 1953.

---

102 *Ibid.*, p. 122. The National Union of Mineworkers and the Transport and General Workers' Union (TGWU) agreed, and it has been suggested that they were 'too loyal to the Government to agree with the critics': Pelling, *The Labour Governments*, p. 92.

103 Labour Party, Annual Conference Report, 1948, p. 170.

104 *Ibid.*

105 *Ibid.*, p. 170–1. See also Pelling, *The Labour Governments*, p. 92.

106 Letter from J. B. Figgins, National Union of Railwaymen, to Alfred Barnes, Minister of Transport, 30 October 1950, CAB 21/2757, TNA.

107 Letter from Arthur Deakin, general secretary TGWU, to Clement Attlee, 21 September 1951, CAB 21/2757, TNA.

108 Letter from the Chancellor of the Duchy of Lancaster to the Cabinet Office, 11 October 1951, CAB 21/2757, TNA.

Industrial democracy – different meanings

Thus codetermination was introduced without nationalization in Germany, whereas in the UK nationalization was implemented without codetermination. This contrast was in part the result of a difference in the understanding of industrial democracy and of the role of trade unions.[109] The concept of industrial democracy was first explored by Beatrice and Sidney Webb who argued that it should be understood in a twofold manner:[110] first, it has an internal dimension which refers to trade-union democracy,[111] and, second, it has an external dimension which they understood as effective collective bargaining.[112] Although the Webbs later included an element of workers' representation in management in their understanding of industrial democracy,[113] this was merged with the idea of public ownership. As Ewan McGaughey points out, the Webbs' approach 'envisaged one model of governance for all types of enterprise, as if one size might fit all. To socialise economic participation, they thought it necessary to socialise ownership.'[114]

Hugh Clegg later elaborated three principles underpinning industrial democracy which, he argued, crystallized in the inter-war years: first, trade unions must be independent of the state; second, trade unions can only represent the industrial interests of workers; and, third, the ownership of industries is irrelevant to good industrial relations.[115] Similar to the Webbs, Clegg argued that workers' representation in management or their involvement in the control of industry does not therefore form a fundamental underpinning of industrial democracy and is indeed 'unacceptable' as it threatens trade-union independence.[116] Such a view clearly underpins the arguments for and against nationalization and the introduction of codetermination in the UK throughout the 1940s. Thus the main argument in favour of workers' or trade unions' participation in management in the UK 'was not that the Unions in the industry would thereby take their share of managerial responsibility for the industry but that those involved in making

---

109 For an overview of ideological developments in British and German trade-union movements see Dartmann, *Re-Distribution of Power*, ch. 2.
110 See S. Webb and B. Webb, *Industrial Democracy* (Longmans, Green and Co.: 1897).
111 *Ibid.*, part 1.
112 *Ibid.*, part 2.
113 S. Webb and B. Webb, *The History of Trade Unionism* (Longmans, Green and Co.: 1920), p. 760.
114 E. McGaughey, 'British Codetermination and the Churchillian Circle', *UCL Labour Rights Institute On-Line Working Papers* 2/2014, p. 22.
115 H. A. Clegg, *A New Approach to Industrial Democracy* (Blackwell, Oxford: 1960), pp. 21–5. For a broader overview see *idem, Industrial Democracy and Nationalization* (Blackwell, Oxford: 1951).
116 Clegg, *New Approach to Industrial Democracy*, p. 22.

the managerial decisions would have a sympathetic understanding of the problems, needs and viewpoints of the individual workers'.[117] This would, however, threaten trade unions' independence from the state and thereby restrict their ability to engage in free collective bargaining. As Sir Norman Chester explained:

> The Unions did not want this, any more than did management, for their basic purpose was to bargain about wages and conditions. If they were part of management they would be bargaining with themselves, in other words, so far as the men were concerned they would be indistinguishable from management.[118]

Martin Francis has, more recently, argued in a similar vein by suggesting that:

> Union leaders saw nationalization as a means to pursue a more advantageous position within a framework of continued conflict, rather than as an opportunity to replace the old adversarial form of industrial relations. Moreover, most workers in nationalized industries exhibited an essentially instrumentalist attitude, favouring public ownership because it secured job security and improved wages rather than because it promised the creation of a new set of socialist relationships in the workplace.[119]

Codetermination in any form was not therefore seen as a desirable option for many in the Labour Party or among the majority of trade-unionists. Only Bevin seemed to approach industrial democracy from a different perspective when he argued in favour of workers being given increased responsibility in the management of their place of work. For the majority of the Labour Party, nationalization was regarded as sufficient to guarantee workers' involvement in the governance of companies.

The concept of industrial democracy was translated in Germany as *Wirtschaftsdemokratie* by Fritz Naphtali writing in the 1920s. It was understood as the equivalent of the Webbs' concept of industrial democracy; in substance it was in fact very different. Thus *Wirtschaftsdemokratie* was defined as 'a form of economic constitution, a democratic constitution in the economy as opposed to economic autocracy ... The nature of this democracy presumes codetermination.'[120] German trade unions

---

117 Chester, *Nationalisation of British Industry*, p. 848.
118 *Ibid.*
119 M. Francis, *Ideas and Policies under Labour, 1945–1951: Building a New Britain* (Manchester University Press: 1997), p. 82.
120 F. Naphtali, *Wirtschaftsdemokratie – Ihr Wesen, Weg und Ziel* (Verlagsgesellschaft des ADBG, Berlin: 1928), p. 14/1. *Wirtschaftsdemokratie* is defined as 'eine Form der wirtschaftlichen Verfassung, die demokratische Verfassung

understood this as turning industrial servants into industrial citizens,[121] which meant that capital and labour should be equals in the running of businesses. The reason given for this approach was that 'the interests of the worker in the success and proper organization and management of his employer are at least as important as those of the employer and certainly more important than those of mere shareholders'.[122] German trade unions thus associated codetermination with equality of workers and employers in the management of enterprises, as well as offering the possibility of control of the employers coupled with the need to be involved in the regulation of workers' terms and conditions of employment. Codetermination was considered as separate from and in addition to nationalization.[123] Historical factors also played a role in German trade unions' embrace of codetermination after the war. As Dartmann explains:

> [T]he development of codetermination ... owed its development mainly to the interpretation of the rise of Hitler the unions arrived at immediately after the war, in which they blamed big business alone and therefore uncritically failed to provide an assessment of their own roles in the critical period leading to the Third Reich.[124]

The introduction of codetermination in and of itself was therefore considered a success by German trade unions, whereas from the perspective of the British military government, influenced by a different understanding of industrial democracy, it was a stepping stone on the road to nationalization which, in Germany, was never completed.

Against this background, one must question whether the failure to institute a system of codetermination in the UK should be considered a missed opportunity for British trade unions. Frances O'Grady, current TUC general secretary, writing in 2013 appears to answer this question in the affirmative when she argues that:

---

in der Wirtschaft im Unterschied und im Gegensatz zur wirtschaftlichen Autokratie ... Das Wesen der Demokratie setzt ... Mitbestimmung voraus.'
121 F. Naumann, *Neudeutsche Wirtschaftspolitik* (n.p. Berlin: 1911), p. 294.
122 E. Jaffé, 'Die Vertretung der Arbeiterinteressen im neuen Deutschland', in F. Thimme and C. Leigen (eds), *Die Arbeiterschaft im neuen Deutschland* (Hirzel, Leipzig: 1915), p. 111: 'Das Interesse der Arbeiter an dem Gedeihen und damit an der richtigen Organization und Führung der Betriebe [ist] mindestens ebenso groß wie das der Unternehmer, sicher (aber) größer und lebenswichtiger als das der lediglich mit ihren Kapitaleinschüssen beteiligten Aktionäre.'
123 See H. Böckler, *Die Aufgaben der deutschen Gewerkschaften in Wirtschaft, Staat und Gesellschaft* (DGB, Düsseldorf: 1949), p. 23.
124 Dartmann, *Re-Distribution of Power*, p. 17.

Arguably unions in this country [in the 1980s] were reaping the consequences of a strategic error made in failing to seize the opportunity of the European model of codetermination and industrial democracy. Ernest Bevin was acutely aware of the German system. As Foreign Secretary he played a large part in creating it. But alas not here. In 1945, we had an important opportunity to lift our gaze beyond the immediate task of improving terms and conditions and play a different role within the emerging mixed economy: giving workers a voice and a stake in strategic decision making, in the newly nationalised industries and the new welfare state. But it was one that we squandered. Rather than rising to the profound challenge of collective ownership – not just redistributing power to workers, but also to those who depended on the goods and services we produced – we chose instead to take the easy option.[125]

Indeed, the absence of codetermination is increasingly bemoaned in the UK. O'Grady emphasizes that trade unions should 'embrace industrial democracy and take up every chance to re-shape economic relationships'. She argues that 'economic strength demands economic democracy, a recalibration of the relationship between capital and labour'. In suggesting such reforms, she reverts to the German trade unions' understanding of industrial democracy:

[I]ndustrial democracy poses a challenge to us in the trade union movement. It implies a role that is not just more ambitious, but more demanding, than the one we usually have now. It means accepting responsibility, moving out of a comfort zone of short-termism, to taking the long view and championing the greater good.[126]

With hindsight, British unions' unwillingness to embrace codetermination can be considered a short-sighted, if not necessarily surprising, approach to industrial relations. As Alan Fox pointed out, the British labour movement was 'a reformist labour movement that, with its own deep interests in the existing order, constitutes one of the major blockages to radical social transformation'.[127] Acceptance of codetermination would have necessitated a 'fundamental shift' in the thinking of the labour movement which significant numbers of trade-union and Labour Party leaders were not prepared to undertake, preferring a 'conflictual' to a

---

125 F. O'Grady, *Attlee Memorial lecture*, 26 April 2013, available at http://www. tuc.org.uk/union-issues/frances-ogradys-atlee-memorial-lecture.
126 *Ibid.*
127 A. Fox, 'Corporatism and Industrial Democracy: The Social Origins of Present Forms and Methods in Britain and Germany' (Paper given at the SSRC International Conference on Industrial Democracy, Churchill College, Cambridge, 4–8 July 1977), p. 19.

'co-operative' strategy.[128] Ultimately, it is clear that Labour, in its nationalization programme in the 1940s, was 'unable to agree on what the ultimate purpose of nationalization should be: ... a means to facilitate greater industrial efficiency and modernisation, or ... a tool to achieve a fundamental transformation in the balance of class power.'[129]

From an ideological perspective, there was a clash within the Labour movement throughout the 1930s and early 1940s between, on the one hand, Fabianism[130] – represented by large parts of the Labour Party – and, on the other hand, Guild Socialism[131] – dominant among a number of trade unions. The lack of enthusiasm for direct workers' control in nationalized industries by the Labour Party in its 1945 manifesto represented a clear 'swing away from the syndicalist content of socialist thinking in the direction of Fabian ideas'.[132] As a result, '[t]he justifications for each of the individual acts of nationalization specified in *Let Us Face the Future* were all based primarily on the need to release productive energies which had remained dormant under private ownership.'[133] The only exception to this was found in the iron and steel industries which had performed well under private ownership, thus making nationalization on purely economic grounds difficult to justify. The rationale was instead given as power,[134] the argument being that 'steel represents the largest concentration of power in the economic system'.[135] Nonetheless, nationalization of these industries faced considerably more opposition. It must be questioned whether this would have been different

---

128 *Ibid.*, p. 21. According to Fox, the '"conflictual" strategy aims at improving membership welfare through unrestricted collective bargaining and the maintenance of a high level of mobilization of membership, while the "co-operative" strategy is pursued through constructive collaboration with employer and government, and depends less upon mobilization and the threat of conflict.'

129 Francis, *Ideas and Policies under Labour*, p. 65.

130 Fabianism rejected direct workers' control of nationalized industry, favouring instead exclusive parliamentary control. See Dahl, 'Workers' Control of Industry', *Am. Pol. Sc. Rev.*, pp. 876–82.

131 Guild Socialism aimed to 'strengthen social and economic institutions against the over-riding power of the state' and favoured some form of workers' participation in management. See *ibid.* While guild socialism was not advocated by all trade-union leaders (see Clegg, *Industrial Democracy and Nationalization*, pp. 99–112), it was the preferred form of organization of a group of active trade-unionists and socialists including C. Dukes, H. Cliff and G. D. H. Cole. See Eldon Barry, *Nationalisation*, p. 323.

132 Dahl, 'Workers' Control of Industry', *Am. Pol. Sc. Rev.*, p. 875.

133 Francis, *Ideas and Policies under Labour*, p. 72.

134 See W. Fienburgh and R. Evely, *Steel is Power: The Case for Nationalization* (Gollancz: 1948).

135 *Socialist Commentary* 12:15, December 1948, pp. 338–9.

had nationalization been justified on the grounds of empowering workers to share in certain responsibilities for the management of these industries.

British trade unions, for the most part, also did not share the same level of distrust of employers and the state as German trade unions after the Second World War. This is partly explained by British Guild Socialism which bore little resemblance to 'the extreme anti-state views of Continental [European] syndicalist movements'.[136] The state was perceived in the UK, unlike in Germany, as being 'an instrument of freedom and progress'.[137] Nonetheless, trade unions' narrow vision first became obvious when industries were privatized after the change of government in 1951, leaving workers with no role in the management of industry. Even in those industries which were not immediately privatized, the selection of board members was left to the individual minister concerned, thereby providing no guarantee that workers' interests would be recognized. Such a scenario had been foreseen by those in the union movement arguing in favour of workers' participation in management,[138] considered as 'partial insurance against [untold harm coming to workers]' in the case that 'bureaucratic control over industry were to fall into the hands of an anti-trade union government'.[139] Such arguments were, however, routinely defeated.[140]

Finally, the central role of collective *laissez-faire*[141] in the historical development of British labour law undoubtedly played a role in trade unions' continued preference for collective bargaining as the mechanism to regulate worker–employer relations. In order for such an approach to succeed, industrial autonomy of employers and trade unions, and equilibrium between both parties, must be guaranteed. Once the autonomy of either party is undermined, through, for example, state intervention in

136 Dahl, 'Workers' Control of Industry', *Am. Pol. Sc. Rev.*, p. 879.
137 *Ibid.*
138 For a more detailed overview see Labour Party, Annual Conference Report, 1932, pp. 215 and 219; Labour Party, Annual Conference Report, 1933, pp. 206–7; TUC, Annual Report, 1932, p. 380; TUC, Annual Report, 1933, pp. 373 and 376; H. Clay, 'Workers' Control', in C. Addison *et al.*, *Problems of a Socialist Government* (Gollancz: 1933), p. 216; and G. D. H. Cole and W. Mellor, *Workers' Control and Self-Government in Industry* (Gollancz and New Fabian Research Bureau: 1933).
139 Dahl, 'Workers' Control of Industry', *Am. Pol. Sc. Rev.*, p. 889.
140 For a more detailed overview of argument against workers' control see Labour Party, Annual Conference Report, 1932, pp. 212–14 and 221–3; Labour Party, Annual Conference Report, 1933, p. 208; Morrison, *Socialisation*, chs 10–13; and G. D. H. Cole, *The Next Ten Years in British Social and Economic Policy* (Macmillan: 1929), chs 7 and 8.
141 O. Kahn-Freund, 'Labour Law', in *idem*, *O. Kahn-Freund: Selected Writings* (Stevens: 1978), p. 8; Davies and Freedland, *Labour Legislation*, ch. 1; see also K. D. Ewing, 'The State and Industrial Relations', *HSIR* 5 (1998), pp. 1–31, p. 1.

industrial relations, collective bargaining as an effective mechanism for the governance of workplace relations can no longer exist. The changes in, *inter alia*, industrial structure and increasing regulation of industrial relations through law during the second half of the twentieth century has illustrated the weakness of the voluntarist approach:[142] without an institutionalized role in the management of industry, such as in Germany, British trade unions rely primarily on industrial strength in order to represent workers. Although union density[143] is higher today in the UK (26%) than in Germany (18%), German trade unions have greater influence in the regulation of the individual employment relationship through, *inter alia*, alternative mechanisms to collective bargaining,[144] such as codetermination, which are guaranteed by legislation.[145]

In conclusion, the nationalization programme of the British post-war Labour government had a profound effect on German industrial relations, creating the necessary framework within which parity codetermination could be introduced. While nationalization in the German iron and steel industries was never achieved, codetermination has had a lasting and substantial impact on German trade unions and on the German labour law system. Parallels can be drawn with debates taking place at the same time in the UK over nationalization and workers' participation in management.

---

142 This is also argued in C. Howell, *Trade Unions and the State: The Construction of Industrial Relations Institutions in Britain, 1890–2000* (Princeton University Press, NJ and Oxford: 2005), ch. 5.

143 Union density – defined as the proportion of employees who are union members – is only one way of measuring union strength but is a key indicator. For data on German union density, see *ICTWSS: Database on Institutional Characteristics of Trade Unions, Wage Setting, State Intervention and Social Pacts in 34 countries between 1960 and 2012* compiled by J. Visser, Amsterdam Institute for Advanced Labour Studies (AIAS), Version 4, April 2013, University of Amsterdam (see http://www.uva-aias.net/207). For comparable figures in the UK see BIS, *Trade Union Membership 2012: Statistical Bulletin*, 2013, where it stood at 26%.

144 Due to industry-level bargaining Germany has a higher level of collective-bargaining coverage than the UK, where collective bargaining takes place at company level. See L. Fulton, 'Worker representation in Europe' (Labour Research Department and ETUI: 2013) available at http://www.worker-participation.eu/National-Industrial-Relations/Across-Europe/Collective-Bargaining2.

145 In addition to their involvement in the collective-bargaining process, German trade unions have a role in codetermination in the enterprise through works councils which is guaranteed by legislation. See, further, W. Müller-Jentsch, 'Germany: From Collective Voice to Co-management', in J. Rogers and W. Streeck (eds), *Works Councils: Consultation, Representation and Cooperation in Industrial Relations* (University of Chicago Press: 1995), pp. 61–5.

However, historical differences between the British and German trade-union movements, as well as differences in the understanding of industrial democracy, resulted in the nationalization of the major industries in the UK without workers' involvement in the management of these industries. With the benefit of hindsight and in light of the changes that occurred in the regulation of British industrial relations in the second half of the twentieth century, the failure to institute a system of codetermination in the UK in the late 1940s must be considered a missed opportunity for British trade unions.

Law School
University of Strathclyde
Glasgow G1 1XQ

HSIR 36 (2015) 29–57

doi:10.3828/hsir.2015.36.2

Spheres of Justice in the 1942 Betteshanger Miners' Strike: An Essay in Historical Ethnography

Ariane Mak

The strike at Betteshanger colliery, Kent, in January 1942, has often been attributed the limited role of the 'standard illustration' of the difficulty encountered by the British government in implementing Order 1305.[1] The Conditions of Employment and National Arbitration Order (Order 1305) operated from July 1940 to August 1951 and was the cornerstone of special legislation regulating wartime industrial relations.[2] Part one of the Order was devoted to the creation of the National Arbitration Tribunal, designed to intervene as a last resort, if other means of settlement failed. Part two famously outlawed all strikes, except where the Ministry of Labour and National Service failed to refer the dispute for settlement within twenty-one days. Order 1305 thus strengthened compulsory arbitration and potentially criminalized strikers. During the war, 109 prosecutions involving nearly 6,300 individuals were filed.[3]

I wish to thank the two referees, whose insightful comments and suggestions have significantly improved this article, Jim Phillips for his thoughtful contributions, and Alain Cottereau for his pivotal role.

1 The term used by N. Fishman, '"A Vital Element in British Industrial Relations": A Reassessment of Order 1305, 1940–51', *Historical Studies in Industrial Relations* (*HSIR*) 8 (1999), pp. 43–86, at p. 47.
2 The Order was drafted on the recommendations of the National Joint Consultative Committee at the Ministry of Labour and National Service (which grouped together the representatives of the British Employers' Confederation and the Trades Union Congress) and came under the Defence Regulation 58aa (SR&O 1217, 1940).
3 Ministry of Labour, 'Prosecutions of Strikers under Order 1305', LAB 10/173, The National Archives, Kew, London (hereafter TNA).

The Betteshanger strike occupies a central role within a historiography in which, from the late 1950s, the prevailing idea was the inefficacy of the Order. Indeed, with three strike leaders imprisoned and more than a thousand strikers fined, that mass sanctions could not be enforced. Based on the written evidence of Sir Harold Emmerson (former Permanent Secretary to the Ministry of Labour and the Chief Industrial Commissioner in 1942), the strike was cited in the 1968 Donovan Report to demonstrate the 'fruitlessness … of penal procedures' in regulating strikes.[4] His testimony would have a lasting influence on future studies of the Order, which to some extent explains why these tended to concentrate on the difficulties encountered by administrators, describing the disagreements between departments and ministries and the technical, practical and strategic problems of applying mass sanctions.

Studies reassessing Order 1305 and the Betteshanger strike have been published in *Historical Studies in Industrial Relations*. In the article that re-launched interest in the issue, Nina Fishman questioned the supposedly voluntarist nature of British industrial relations. According to the voluntarist paradigm, the compulsory arbitration forced on the miners by Order 1305 was simply an extraordinary measure in the extraordinary circumstances of wartime, and thus hardly representative of British industrial relations in general.[5] Through analysing the use of Order 1305 in the immediate post-war years, Fishman strove to return it to its rightful position as a 'vital element in British industrial relations'.[6] She also exposed the electoral and political motivations behind the Order's sudden revocation in 1951. Another interpretation was proposed by James Jaffe, who examined the ambiguities of Order 1305 within the historical context of the common-law practice of civil and industrial arbitration.[7] By focusing on the paradoxes of the legal text (the failure to include any enforcement mechanisms, among other things), Jaffe identified the many difficulties encountered by the National Arbitration Tribunal. He maintained that the 'compulsory' aspect of 'compulsory arbitration' under Order 1305 was mainly a 'mirage' purposely nurtured by the Ministry of Labour in an effort to hide the Order's weaknesses.

The second part of Order 1305, outlawing strikes and lockouts, has also been the subject of lively debates. Fishman questioned the wisdom of judging it on the sole basis of its failure to ban strikes.[8] By concentrating

---

4 Royal Commission on Trade Unions and Employers' Associations, 1965–68 (Donovan), *Report*, Cmnd 3623 (1968), para. 486 and pp. 340–1 (appendix 6).
5 Fishman, 'A Reassessment of Order 1305', *HSIR*.
6 *Ibid.*, p. 46, quoting Otto Kahn-Freund.
7 J. A. Jaffe, 'The Ambiguities of Compulsory Arbitration and the Wartime Experience of Order 1305', *HSIR* 15 (2003), pp. 1–26.
8 Fishman, 'A Reassessment of Order 1305', *HSIR*.

more on the everyday use of the Order, and the on-site role of the Regional Industrial Relations Officers, she demonstrated its contribution to the relative continuity of production. She also claimed that, by facilitating union recognition and rapid intervention in conflicts, before attitudes could polarize, Order 1305 had not been without benefits for both union leaders and activists. John McIlroy and Alan Campbell contested this; by exploring Scottish coalmining strikes affected by Order 1305, they concluded that it should be depicted more as a catalyst of conflict than a tool of reconciliation. They also stressed the importance of not dissociating Order 1305 from the arsenal of other wartime measures, particularly the Essential Work Orders, in order to remain as close as possible to the holistic perception of the Order held by miners.[9] Our understanding of the Betteshanger strike has benefited from these new frameworks of analysis. Adrian Tyndall's study offered one of the most complete descriptions of the strike,[10] though he was criticized for according too little attention to the motivations of the strike leaders – and, one could add, to the stakes of the strike and the meaning of the prosecutions from the viewpoint of the miners themselves.[11] Indeed, as McIlroy and Campbell have pointed out, what is ultimately missing is an analysis of the reactions of 'ordinary' miners to the implementation of Order 1305. They called for 'thick-textured, empirical, historical studies', and stressed that 'understanding requires incursions into sociology, politics and economics and moves towards total history'.[12]

One highly detailed and illuminating source are the wartime industrial relations surveys undertaken by Mass Observation (MO). These have not been widely used by historians of industrial relations, yet they exactly answer the call for thick-textured empirical studies. MO, a British social-sciences research organization, was created for the purpose of transposing the anthropological methods used in the Trobriand Islands to contemporary English society.[13] From 1937 to 1949, MO engaged in several activities: numerous field surveys, collections of directive replies provided by a national panel of 3,000 volunteers to monthly questionnaires, and a large collection of personal diaries. While the majority of historical studies have

9 J. McIlroy and A. Campbell, 'Beyond Betteshanger: Order 1305 in the Scottish Coalfields during the Second World War, Part 1: Politics, Prosecutions and Protest', *HSIR* 15 (2003), pp. 27–72; *idem*, 'Beyond Betteshanger: Order 1305 in the Scottish Coalfields during the Second World War, Part 2: The Cardowan Story', *HSIR* 16 (2003), pp. 39–80.

10 A. Tyndall, 'Patriotism and Principles: Order 1305 and the Betteshanger Strike of 1942', *HSIR* 12 (2001), pp. 109–30.

11 McIlroy and Campbell, 'Beyond Betteshanger, Part 1', *HSIR*, p. 30.

12 McIlroy and Campbell, 'Beyond Betteshanger, Part 2', *HSIR*, p. 79.

13 J. Hinton, *The Mass Observers: A History, 1937–1949* (Oxford University Press: 2013).

focused on the national panel and the diaries, the ethnographical surveys are a valuable resource. The investigators' notes, which have been usually neglected in favour of internal reports and publications, can be compared to anthropologist's field notes and are invaluable sources.

When the Betteshanger strike started, MO sent an observer, Veronica Tester, to investigate. Her interviews with miners, their wives, and the conciliators sent to the colliery, and her observations and descriptions of the mining village of Mill Hill and the neighbouring town of Deal, constitute a rich source of information, which has not been exploited before. The strike is seen over the shoulder, so to speak, of the investigator who was present at the time. Instead of encountering the rank and file only for the purpose of invoking an elusive legitimacy of representation, these primary source documents allow for the analysis – in real time, and not just retrospectively – of the perception and evaluation of the events from the viewpoint of all the groups concerned. Indeed, we operate on the phenomenological premise that acts are the result of several types of comprehensions, both internal and external, taking place in the course of an action or retrospectively. In that sense, this article proposes a historical ethnography of the Betteshanger strike, shifting the focus from the difficulties facing Whitehall to the local attitudes and interpretations of the conflict. This allows us to examine the strike from the miners' and their representatives' point of view, that is to use American anthropologist Clifford Geertz's famous turn of phrase, 'from the native's point of view'.[14] Their framing of the strike developed in answer to the accusations they faced, a dialogical aspect that has not been covered by previous studies.

Furthermore, eschewing heroic or managerial approaches to the conflict, the MO survey allows us to explore the impact of the war and Order 1305 on the normative worlds[15] and moral economy[16] of the Betteshanger miners. How were strikes legitimated during the war? To borrow Michael Walzer's term, which 'spheres of justice' were featured and how were they connected or kept apart?[17] Thus this article will outline ethnographically the ongoing arguments over legitimacy and legality during the Betteshanger strike. It will shed light on how the conflicting definitions linked together or split

---

14 C. Geertz, 'From the Native's Point of View: On the Nature of Anthropological Understanding', in *idem*, *Local Knowledge: Further Essays in Interpretative Anthropology* (Basic Books, New York: 1983), pp. 55–70.

15 See, in particular, A. Cottereau, 'Sens du juste et usages du droit du travail: une évolution contrastée entre la France et la Grande-Bretagne au XIXe siècle', *Revue d'histoire du XIXe siècle* 33 (2006), pp. 95–115.

16 E. P. Thompson, 'The Moral Economy of the English Crowd in the Eighteenth Century', *Past and Present* 50 (1971), pp. 76–136.

17 M. Walzer, *Spheres of Justice: A Defence of Pluralism and Equality* (Basic Books, New York: 1983), p. 345.

apart three main 'spheres of justice': patriotism, social justice, and legality. The transformations in the arguments about legitimacy and equity will be taken into account and their dialogical process emphasized. The article argues that the conflicting framing of these three spheres of justice is of central importance in a reappraisal of the failure to enforce Order 1305 at Betteshanger. Indeed, as Alvin Gouldner's seminal study established, unveiling 'the divergent emphasis and meaning which management and workers gave to the issues involved' is essential, for 'if the way in which the conflicting parties saw the strike is known, it may help to explain how they later sought to cope with it. For the solutions they adopted derived in part from the ways in which they looked upon the strike.'[18] For Betteshanger, they have been neglected in favour of the technical and political difficulties facing the authorities in applying sanctions.

First, an analysis of the conflicting definitions of the initial Betteshanger dispute will examine two divergent frameworks of reference in explaining the mine's low productivity. The second part will examine the conflict between two spheres of justice – patriotism and social justice – focusing in particular on accusations that the miners were unpatriotic. In the final part, the debate about the criminalization of the strikers will be analysed through the confrontation between legality and legitimacy.

Conflicting definitions of the situation in the initial Betteshanger dispute

Two divergent frameworks of reference in explaining low productivity and the arbitrator's decision

The Betteshanger strike, which began on 9 January 1942, had its origins in the opening of a new coalface in November 1941. Output on this was particularly low: whereas the managers expected at least four tons of coal to be extracted daily, barely half of that amount was brought out. This would be the subject of conflicting descriptions.

The managers accused the miners on no. 2 coalface of undertaking a go-slow (ca'canny), a deliberate reduction in the pace of work. The coal getters' piecework wages were cut, by only paying them for the coal actually extracted. This unilateral decision clashed with a collective agreement, between the company and the Kent Mineworkers' Association (KMWA), that coal getters received 1*s.* 11½*d.* (10p) per ton of coal or, with percentage addition, 2*s.* 7*d.* (13p) per ton, and various war additions (amounting to 3*s.*

---

18 A. W. Gouldner, *Wildcat Strike* (Antioch Press, Yellow Springs, OH: 1954), p. 53.

8*d.* (18p) per day at the time) were also paid. But most importantly, the 1933 Kent County agreement gave a minimum wage of 10*s.* 4½*d.* (52p) per shift and a supplementary allowance taking into account abnormally difficult working conditions that could increase wages to 15*s.* 3*d.* (76p).[19] This was the principle that was challenged by the management, which wanted to force the 'recalcitrant' miners to return to a 'normal' rate of production. The mine manager reported that he had addressed the miners' union leaders in these terms: 'I said that [no.] 2's men had been paid every penny that they had earned, and, as they had deliberately ca'cannied, they were not entitled to receive anything in addition to what they had earned.'[20]

The miners hotly rejected accusations of ca'canny and opposed a very different frame of reference. For them, the low productivity was a result of geological conditions. First, the new coalface was much harder; a miner with thirty years' experience said that the coal there was 'as hard as iron'.[21] The face also contained some exceptionally low-lying deposits. While underground seams can run at different heights, from 1.5 to 30 feet (46cm–9.1m), one of the miners explained that 'there's some men working on a very low cliff (indicated about 2 feet [60cm]). You can see they can't swing a pick or shovel properly.'[22] Of the 87 yards (80 metres) of coalface, 32 yards (29 metres) were between 2 feet 5½ inches and 3 feet 1 inch

---

19 According to the Mines Department and the regional controller, at Betteshanger colliery 'the seam is undulating and changes take place in the working conditions week by week and sometimes every other day, and when some of these difficulties arise, the agreed piece rates are not adequate to meet the extra work entailed and the loss of output they create'. None of the eighteen faces was working to the normal price list fixed in 1933 in very different conditions. This supplementary allowance to meet conditions on the various faces was thus 'the rule rather than the exception': Ministry of Labour, 'Strike at Pearson & Dorman Long Ltd. over reduction in temporary increases of wages involving Kent Mine Workers Association', letter from the Mines Department to Ernest Bevin, 9 March 1942, and letter from the regional controller to the Ministry of Labour, 22 January 1942, LAB 10/204, TNA. See H. M. Parker, *Manpower: A Study of War-time Policy and Administration* (HMSO: 1957), pp. 460–1; Tyndall, 'Patriotism and Principles', *HSIR*, p. 114.
20 Ministry of Labour, 'Strike at Pearson & Dorman Long Ltd', LAB 10/204, TNA.
21 Mass Observation, 'Survey of a Strike at Betteshanger Colliery, Kent, 1942', 16 January 1942, SxMOA1/2/64/2/A, Mass Observation Archives, Special Collections, University of Sussex, Brighton (hereafter MOA).
22 *Ibid.* 'M30D' grouped three elements of identification: the gender of the person; his or her approximate age; and his or her social category. The last was designated with a letter (upper class, A; middle class, B; artisan or skilled working class, C; unskilled working class, D).

(75–94cm).[23] Mining the J seam required the miners to work on their knees, with limited freedom of movement, and on an extremely hard face. Further, the coalface had a faulty installation requiring constant repair, creating extra workload: 'each shift coming on takes about an hour repairing it. Of course that reduces their output.' The miners felt that blaming low productivity on an intentional slowdown was fundamentally unfair; and the pay cut for the miners working on no. 2 coalface was seen as illegal.

The negotiations between local union leaders and management failed, resulting in the resignations of the branch president and secretary, who were replaced by Tudor Davies and William Powell.[24] An arbitrator, Sir Charles Doughty, was then sent to Betteshanger by the Department of Mines. He was accompanied by W. L. Cook, a mining specialist and department conciliator, who acted as assessor. On 19 December, Doughty announced his decision: the employers were right to expect the miners, 'with goodwill', to extract at least four tons of coal per day, instead of the average one to three tons they had been bringing out. He supported every point of the management's proposal, which he described as generous and awarded a 1s. 1d. (5.5p) per ton allowance to no. 2 men. The arbitrator also ruled that the miners had adopted a ca'canny policy.[25] Although the conclusions of this report are often cited, few studies have examined the circumstances surrounding their reception.

The strikers challenged the validity of the arbitrator's decision and even his legitimacy to judge these questions. They pointed out that he had made only a fleeting visit, as his inspection was cut short when he fainted shortly after descending into the mine. The MO investigator reported a discussion, in the Mill Hill village pub, that took place less than a week after the strike began:

> M45D said 'You know that solicitor man they got down from Sheffield – he fainted just walking round the pit. We have to work in it. He was just walking round and he fainted.' Inv. [Investigator] expressed surprise so M40D corroborated the statement and said 'What's he know about working conditions when he faints just walking.'[26]
>
> 'They say the men are ca'cannying but what do they know when the arbitrator faints just walking round?'[27]

23 Ministry of Labour, 'Strike at Pearson & Dorman Long Ltd', Arbitrator Award, Charles Doughty, LAB 10/204, TNA.
24 Tyndall, 'Patriotism and Principles', *HSIR*, p. 115.
25 Ministry of Labour, 'Strike at Pearson & Dorman Long Ltd', Arbitrator Award, LAB 10/204, TNA.
26 Mass Observation, 'Survey of a Strike at Betteshanger Colliery, Kent, 1942', 14 January 1942, SxMOA1/2/64/2/A, MOA.
27 *Ibid.*, 17 January 1942.

How, then, could the arbitrator possibly have judged the working conditions in the mine, and especially on no. 2 coalface? On what observations did he base his estimate of the capacity of production and how could he set the figure of four tons per day? Although the arbitrator claimed to have seen the coalface in question, a doubt was cast not only on the process involved in the expertise, but also on the individual and his role as expert (in practice, Cook would have provided the necessary expertise). Doughty was also described by the miners as being doubly foreign to Betteshanger: his reaction down the mine automatically made him an outsider to the coalmining industry – and not a particularly manly one – and he was not from the area, but a solicitor from Yorkshire. Both of these points underestimated Doughty's actual standing.[28]

Backed up by the arbitration, Betteshanger's management decided to reduce no. 2's colliers' wages from 8 January 1942. The Labour Supply Officer, W. Twigger, was warned by Charles Magee, Betteshanger's agent:

> [Magee] would not tell me what it was but said I should get a shock within the next 24 hours. When I did hear something he would like to have my reactions. Well the shock I got was that when [no.] 2s got their Dockets on Thursday afternoon, he had only paid them the exact amount they had earned on their Piece rates plus the addition of the Arbitration Award. The men naturally went to the Union Officials claiming they had not been paid the Kent District Day Wage Rates, which is generally the minimum wage. The Union Officials were told that the men had got what they earned, and they would get no more.[29]

The next day, 2,000 Betteshanger miners were on strike.[30]

Early accusations of anti-patriotism from both sides

These divergent framings of the initial disputes were complicated by accusations of anti-patriotism by management and miners. Indeed, the first days of the strike saw the intervention of the public authorities and, with

---

28 Although Betteshanger miners might have been unaware, Sir Charles Doughty was not unfamiliar with coalmining and was an experienced conciliator and arbitrator. He was chair of the Lancashire and Cheshire Coal Mining Minimum Wage Board from 1935. He was also a King's Counsel and the Recorder for Canterbury from 1929 to 1937, so not unfamiliar with the area. I am very grateful to one referee for this information.

29 Ministry of Labour, 'Strike at Pearson & Dorman Long Ltd', report on Betteshanger position by W. Twigger, Labour Supply Officer (LSO), 12 January 1942, LAB 10/204, TNA.

30 These figures only take into account the underground workers, as the Ministry of Labour considered that the stoppage by the surface workers was simply a technical consequence of the strike.

them, the emergence of the anti-patriotism accusations. In accordance with official procedure, the mining company informed the Mines Department of the strike and located its consequences within the broader sphere of the national war effort:

> The Company submits that the payment of a wage of 15*s*. 3*d*. per shift to men who are withholding their labour *would be detrimental to the National Output* and would also be prejudicial to Local Agreements, as the men concerned could with reasonable effort easily produce a substantially greater output and thereby earn much higher wages than the 15*s*. 3*d*. per shift claimed.[31] (added emphasis)

In other words, the financial interest of the company, Pearson & Dorman Long, was not the only thing under threat: the national output of coal, an essential part of the war effort, was also at risk. From this point, the strikers were depicted by the mine's management as men devoid of patriotism. The mine manager refused to meet miners' representatives, who were asking for the reinstatement of the minimum wage: 'I said I was not going to be blackmailed by men who had so little thought for their country that they could stoop to this policy of ca'canny.'[32]

In the mining village of Mill Hill, different rumours circulated about the lack of patriotism by the mine's management. In this case, too, the accusation was put in a communication addressed to a government representative. The labour supply officer for Kent County, present during the first days of the strike, was taken into the confidence of several miners. The rumours concerned suspicious manoeuvres by the management. Why would they close a coalface with one of the highest outputs in the mine, and then open another that was difficult to work? The managers had claimed the manpower shortage led them to close the eastern section of the mine and concentrate on the J seam. Nevertheless, rumours suggested that management was manoeuvring to close the easily mined coalfaces to save all the profits until after the war. More or less directly, this suggested that the managers (and owners) were war profiteers. The Ministry of Labour officer (a former miners' checkweighman himself) reported back to his superiors:

> Did you notice in the Arbitrators' Report the reference to resentment that may have been felt by the men of being shifted from one district to another? Well from what I gather the men at Betteshanger are of the opinion that this change

---

31 Ministry of Labour, 'Strike at Pearson & Dorman Long Ltd', letter from the directors of Pearson & Dorman Long Ltd to the Mines Department, 10 January 1942, LAB 10/204, TNA.

32 Ministry of Labour, 'Strike at Pearson & Dorman Long Ltd', letter from the director of the Betteshanger colliery, 8 January 1942, LAB 10/204, TNA.

was made for ulterior motives, and there is a deep rooted conviction that the only idea is to reserve a good Panel of Coal until after the War, where the same men who are now only producing about 3 tons per man would be able to fill 7 or 8 tons per man. I cannot express my opinion about it … but it does appear a little strange that at a time when the maximum output is required, a good panel of coal is abandoned, to work what has proved to be a bad one.[33]

These suspicions were also confided to the MO correspondent who arrived a few days later:

It started when the company opened up a fresh coalface which was very difficult to work. We've all been getting a good lot out from a big face that's easy to work, but they've closed that now because the government pays subsidies in war for a new one to be opened. After a bit they'll open the other one again to get another subsidy.[34]

Whether it was saving the best coal seams for after the war, or taking advantage of subsidies, these suspicions reverse the accusations of anti-patriotism.[35]

---

33 Ministry of Labour, 'Strike at Pearson & Dorman Long Ltd', LSO's report, 12 January 1942, LAB 10/204, TNA.

34 Mass Observation, 'Survey of a Strike at Betteshanger Colliery, Kent, 1942', M50D, 17 January 1942, SxMOA1/2/64/2/A, MOA.

35 Although no documents can be found confirming these rumours in the few archives kept by Pearson & Dorman Long, they cannot be disregarded as unfounded. At the time when the management decided to close the mine's eastern section and open a new coalface, Betteshanger colliery was in the midst of an assessment procedure carried out under the Coal Act 1938. This law, disparaged by legal experts, authorized the newly created Coal Commission to become owner, as of 1 July 1942, of any colliery or coal seam that was not being worked. A sum of £66,450,000 was divided up among the different colliery owners, according to the value of coal seams not worked up to that time. The evaluation of Betteshanger sparked off debates within the Southern Regional Board. Several civil engineers disagreed with the figures presented by A. C. Pickering, secretary of Pearson & Dorman Long. The evaluation of the H and J seams, a central issue in the strike, was particularly problematic. When the Central Valuation Board reviewed the work of the Southern Regional Board, alarmist letters about the many irregularities that had been discovered started circulating. One of the mine's mineral agents was strongly suspected of having manipulated the evaluations in a way that 'would result in values about three times the normal, and has been trying to force this down the Board's throat in the supposed interests of his clients'. See National Coal Board, correspondence of the Southern Regional Valuation Board, 'Correspondence mostly relating to Betteshanger Colliery, Kent, 1941–1942', NCB 2/5/334–396, Nottinghamshire Archives, Nottingham; Ministry of Power, correspondence relative

The interplay of two spheres of justice: patriotism and social justice

Safeguarding the minimum wage: social justice and the Betteshanger strikers

The MO survey allows us to delve beyond the conflict over no. 2 coalface to explore what was at stake to the miners. Conversations recorded over several days by the investigator, in a Mill Hill pub, reveal the strikers' fears that a wage reduction for those working on no. 2 coalface would only be the first blow against the minimum wage, and would be extended to all the workers in the colliery. She describes, for example, the following scene:

> On the evening of Friday, January 16, when the men had all been paid, M20D came into the pub and said: 'Do you know what the men got today? 6s. 8½d. [33.5p] a day. Not even 7s. [35p].'

> M35D: 'The buggers. What do you think of that? 6s. 8½d. a day. It's only starting, they'll do it to all of us.'[36]

The idea that 'it was only starting' was shared by the miners and their wives. What mattered was maintaining the minimum wage. Securing it was all the more important at Betteshanger because, as even the colliery management's solicitors admitted, not one of the eighteen coalfaces operated in accordance with the official wage scale.[37] If the employers won this time, the security net provided by the 1912 Coal Mines (Minimum Wage) Act, and the 1933 Kent County agreement, would dissolve and leave the field open for wage reductions for everyone:

> M50D: 'We'll go on fighting. If they get us this time it's the thin end of the wedge. They'll put the wages down all through. It's the management that's wrong. They're breaking a definite contract and they can't do that.'[38]

> F25D: 'The men have got to do it. They must stick it out. If the manager beats them this time he'll lower the wages all round the pit. And it's him that's in the

---

to Southern Regional Board, letter from H. W. Naish to W. G. Nott-Bower, 2 July 1942, POWE 22/147, TNA.

36 Mass Observation, 'Survey of a Strike at Betteshanger Colliery, Kent, 1942', 17 January 1942, SxMOA1/2/64/2/A, MOA.

37 Ministry of Labour, 'Strike at Pearson & Dorman Long Ltd', Officer report, 29 January 1942, LAB 10/204, TNA.

38 Mass Observation, 'Survey of a Strike at Betteshanger Colliery, Kent, 1942', 15 January 1942, SxMOA1/2/64/2/A, MOA.

wrong – he's going against the minimum wage agreement. It's rotten – a miner's a hard job and they don't get a lot for it now, without making it worse.'[39]

Specialized studies have recently pointed out that the personalities of colliery managers were important variables in miners' decisions to go on strike rather than to follow the arbitration procedures. This role has too often been neglected in the monographs on strikes.[40] At Betteshanger, the fears provoked by the mine's agent, Magee, reinforced the general apprehension that this was only the first blow in a wider attack against wages and the union.[41] Magee appears to have been greatly feared and the MO investigator recorded several rumours circulating about him. A miner of about forty years old reported that, in his former mine, Featherstone, Yorkshire, Magee had kept the men on strike for two-and-a-half years 'and even gone round turning the women and children from their homes into the street. Nothing could move him.' Two others added that 'he kept them out up there and let them starve, the women and children went and pleaded with him but he didn't care'. Arriving at Betteshanger from a non-union mine, it was said that he swore to see the unions on their knees. The supposed dark intentions of Magee contributed to the Betteshanger miners' conviction that the minimum wage was at stake.[42]

Indeed, one of the assumptions considered as evident in the miners' discussions was the idea that the wage level was a collective good, and that they had to fight for a hard-won principle: the minimum wage. This interpretation is a far cry from what a *Daily Express* article summed up as '9,000 tons of coal lost, all for just £15 a week'.[43] The only aspect of the strike touched on was the few shillings' difference in wage and the small number of men directly concerned, those on no. 2 coalface. Moreover, while the article adopted a short-term perspective, the miners gave priority to the long-term risks to the mining community as a whole. These issues of social justice were the ones the miners hoped to see discussed in the press.

---

39 *Ibid.*, 14 January 1942.
40 R. Church and Q. Outram, *Strikes and Solidarity: Coalfield Conflict in Britain 1889–1966* (Cambridge University Press: 2002), p. 217.
41 The negative role played by Magee in the conflict was also mentioned by the officials from the Ministry of Labour, who were surprised that the Mines Department did not consider the possibility of a change of personnel: Ministry of Labour, 'Strike at Pearson & Dorman Long Ltd', letter from Emmerson, LAB 10/204, TNA.
42 A song written by the strikers and posted on the walls of the Mill Hill pub implored the Ministry of Labour: 'So, Mr Bevin, we ask you please / To take our case before Magee's. / We know the country's short of coal / But 6/9 [6s. 9d.]'s worse than the dole.'
43 *Daily Express*, 17 January 1942.

Instead, it was their supposed anti-patriotism that focused the attention nationally and locally.

The strikers' patriotism in question

Media accusations of sabotaging the war effort

A *Daily Express* article on the strike provoked much commentary in the pubs of Mill Hill. It gave the reasons for the strike, stressed the patriotism of the Betteshanger 'front line miners' and published a long interview with a miner.[44] Most other newspaper articles were less sympathetic to the miners, who were accused of defying Order 1305 and sabotaging the war effort. This was the stance taken by the *Daily Telegraph*, for example, and the miners kept an especially close watch on its reporting. To take one example, at the end of the first week of the strike, this newspaper stated:

> What it means to the nation's war effort is a simple and complete demonstration of the purpose with which the order was made. Each day of idleness has deprived the war industry of nearly 2,000 tons of coal ... How, it may well be asked, is it possible that at a time like this a body of workers should act in flat defiance of a legal prohibition, as well as in utter disregard of their country's need?[45]

The same day, two short articles in local newspapers quoted the Betteshanger manager's statement about miners deliberately withholding work, to the detriment of the national interest.[46] This accusation was reproduced in several national newspapers. As the strike became more publicized, the attacks against the miners multiplied, spreading doubts about their patriotism. The *Daily Mirror* and *Daily Express* regularly published updates on the number of tons of coal lost in the strike.[47] During the days after the trial, these same newspapers openly supported the view that the miners on coalface no. 2 had engaged in a go-slow, even though this question had been neither examined nor judged during the trial.

---

44 *Ibid.*, 14 January 1942.
45 *Daily Telegraph*, 16 January 1942. For an in-depth analysis of the similar position adopted by the Communist Party after the Nazi invasion of the Soviet Union, see McIlroy and Campbell, 'Beyond Betteshanger, Part 1', *HSIR*, pp. 40–51.
46 *Kentish Express* and *Dover Express*, 16 January 1942.
47 With estimates ranging from 9,000 tons lost on 17 January to 20,000 on 27 January 1942.

In the nearest town: rumours and suspicions of war-profiteering

Mill Hill, built during the inter-war years, counted 1,500 mining families among its inhabitants in 1939. The miners' wives did their weekly shopping in Deal, even though 'nobody says they're going into town to shop, they always say going into Deal [...] rotten little place'.[48] The miners' arrival in the area fifteen years earlier had been fraught with tension, and miners were still looked down on in Deal.[49] The MO investigator's visit to Deal coincided with the publication of the first newspaper accounts of the strike. One grocer, worried about the effects on business, confided that: 'You hear so many rumours. Some say the managers aren't paying up the money, others say the miners aren't working properly.'[50] Most people the investigator met seemed to have made up their mind.

> F55B (proprietress of hotel): I've heard that the miners aren't thrusting out enough work. They should all be sent into the army. That's my opinion. The poor boys in the Forces don't get much. What about the Air Force. You don't feel like fighting and losing lives for that sort. That's what it means. The Air Force boys are losing their lives for these men at home. It makes me sick. Send them all in the army.

> M45BC (landlord of pub): Three quarters of the miners are very uncouth – of course I can't say much of them here, but I hear plenty and keep my mouth shut. Some of them earn £8 a week the ones that work. They go off on the morning shift, from 6 a.m.–2 p.m., and then they go back in the evening at 10 or the night shift. That gives them overtime money, filling in the extra shifts. But a lot don't work their full time at all. You often get them in here at 9 o'clock, before they go on the night shift. They'll be drinking hard and not little about the time, and then they don't go at all – just stay drinking till closing time and go home.[51]

Whether relying on rumour or observation, these two Deal traders repeated accusations of a lack of miners' contribution to the war effort. Behind the lamentations about the soldiers on the front lay another image: miners tucked safely away from the war. The pub landlord contributed a personal (and clichéd) explanation of miners' absenteeism: their love of drink. He

---

48 Mass Observation, 'Survey of a Strike at Betteshanger Colliery, Kent, 1942', 18 January 1942, SxMOA1/2/64/2/A, MOA.
49 G. Harkell, 'The Migration of Mining Families to the Kent Coalfield between the Wars', *Oral History* 6:1 (1978), pp. 98–113.
50 Mass Observation, 'Survey of a Strike at Betteshanger Colliery, Kent, 1942', 17 January 1942, SxMOA1/2/64/2/A, MOA.
51 *Ibid.*

also introduced the opposite to the absentee miner: the miner who worked several shifts a day, pocketing overtime pay. Many of the testimonies collected by the investigator indicated the difficulty of evaluating the miners' earnings, while voicing the suspicion that they were quite high.

> M55C (bus conductor): You don't know whether to sympathize or not – miners are always discontented. Some of them say they get £3 a week but then they don't tell you all the extras they get on top of that. The war bonus and so much on each ton they get out. There's a girl works here with her father at the pit and she told me he only gets £3. Well I don't believe it. He's not counting in all the excesses … The miners are a rough lot – some of them are alright, but they're always grumbling.

> M50C (bus driver): Some of them are getting plenty of money. A woman today pulled out a £5 note and said to their neighbours: 'He's had a good week this week – look what he's given me.' Some of them do more shifts I suppose.

> M55C: That's what I said – if one man can bring home £5 there's others can too.[52]

The whys and wherefores of the strike appeared relatively hazy to Deal inhabitants, whose opinion was close to newspaper articles, which saw the movement as nothing other than an attempt to get 'a few more shillings'. The strikers thus appeared unpatriotic. But while they were accused of sabotaging the war effort, in Deal they were suspected of war-profiteering.

Accusations of anti-patriotism during the trial

The accusations of citizen disloyalty reached a symbolic climax during the trial on 23 January 1942. It was a key moment in the confrontation between legality and legitimacy, as the third part of this paper will show. First, though, we must note that the strikers and their three union branch leaders appeared before the Petty Division of Wingham Magistrates Court in Canterbury, charged with two offences: the original (civil) summons for breach of contract issued by the colliery company was eventually withdrawn at court, while the other charge, the (criminal) infringement of Order 1305, was maintained. Yet, the solicitor for Pearson & Dorman Long was allowed to formulate the first case without giving the miners a chance to defend themselves. George Daughtrey, KMWA president and former Betteshanger branch secretary, protested:

---

52 *Ibid.*

When the miners appeared in Court the Company solicitor stated the case against the men, alleging that they were unpatriotic, etc. – and then he withdrew the case. The men faced the second charge, during which the prosecution maintained that the merits of the strike were quite irrelevant; 21 days' notice of the dispute had not been given to the Ministry and the law had been broken. *Thus the men were ruled out from replying to the allegations made by the company solicitor.*[53] (added emphasis)

The mine management's accusations and the company solicitor's indictment, pronounced within a legal framework (even if they were legally withdrawn) and revisited in part by the media, constituted a public renewal of the doubts cast over the miners about their patriotism. The miners and their leaders would respond in turn to these accusations. An analysis of their responses may shed some light on the different objects of discussion that drew attention in each sphere of justice.

Feelings of injustice and dialogical responses in the mining community

The strike as a patriotic act? Public responses on the part of the miners' representatives

Faced with these accusations of anti-patriotism, the miners' representatives, in turn, seized the media. There were newspaper interviews with miners who spoke out in the name of the Mill Hill community, with public officials and union representatives. It was mainly during the trial that newspapers that had previously hardly followed the strike gave the miners and their representatives a chance to speak out.

These communications in the press were opportunities to set out the initial conflict that had had such sparse newspaper coverage, most just reporting the suspicion of a go-slow without further details. The miners' frame of reference was anchored in a technical understanding of underground work which their representatives had to explain to readers unfamiliar with mining. Thus, when a journalist interviewed Mrs Mantle, a Deal town council member and a miner's wife, she used graphic imagery to stress the excessive hardness of the coalface: 'It is as if a woman were to take a pick and shovel to dig concrete.'[54]

---

53 G. W. Daughtrey, 'Truth about Betteshanger', *New Leader*, 31 January 1942, in personal archives of Di Parkin. Thanks to Di Parkin for giving access to her archives on Betteshanger, and an interview, 24 April 2012. D. Parkin, *Sixty Years of Struggle: History of Betteshanger Colliery* (Betteshanger Social Welfare Scheme, Deal: 2007), casts light on the local dynamics of the 1942 strike.
54 *Evening Standard*, 26 January 1942.

What the miners considered to be essential introductory remarks were clearly explained to an *Evening Standard* journalist:

> Here are some of the points which the miners made to me. I give them as I got them:
> 1. The new coalface which was opened on November 8 replaced another wall which the employers decided to close. This older wall was among the most productive in the mine, and there was no sign of ca'canny there.
> 2. Equally there was no ca'canny on the new face. Production was low because of difficulties of working.
> 3. The result of the Ministry of Mines arbitration inspired no confidence among the men in the official machinery for settlement. Sir Charles Doughty went down the mine but he had to be assisted to the surface shortly afterwards because he was overcome by the atmosphere.[55]

In answer to the accusations of a go-slow and the misconceptions surrounding these accusations, the miners explained the situation within a longer time-frame. The drop in productivity was not sudden and did not take place on a coalface that had formerly known a normal level of productivity. In their rejection of the arbitration, it was the illegitimacy of the arbitrator that the miners wanted to make public. In other words, the union representatives spoke out against labelling the miners as saboteurs of the war effort, and put forward several points to prove their patriotism. Daughtrey summed it up in the *New Leader*, an Independent Labour Party publication:

> All the talk about the Betteshanger miners being 'unpatriotic' is Boss-Class Ballyhoo, an attempt to create prejudice in the mind of the public. These men are on the most exposed part of the coast, nearest to the German planes from the Continent, and during the Battle for Britain they remained at their posts and kept the colliery at full production, even when bombs were actually dropping in the pit yard [...] Moreover, about 250 of the strikers are in the Home Guard ... [D]uring the third week in December the Betteshanger pit exceeded the Ministry of Mines' 'target figure' of 9,500 tons.[56]

Daughtrey denounced the patriotic rhetoric that was used for the employers' own purposes – and the dialogical nature of the discourse is evident here – echoing the accusations recently reformulated during the trial and relayed throughout the conflict by the media. His response took the form of a demonstration of the miners' patriotism. The miners interviewed by the *Evening Standard* also pointed out: 'There was no desire to sabotage the

---

55 *Ibid.*
56 'Truth about Betteshanger', *New Leader*, 31 January 1942.

war effort. Home Guard miners continued to guard the pit.'[57] The miners thus differentiated between two spheres: that of social justice on the one hand, and that of patriotism on the other. By establishing separate domains for the things that have connections with one another and those that do not, they removed judgement of what was fair from the sphere of patriotism.[58]

Other members of the community claimed there were strong connections between the ongoing strike and war duties. This was the case for Mrs Mantle, interviewed by the *Evening Standard*: 'I questioned Mrs Mantle on the principle of striking in time of war. She replied: "Most of us older mining families have sons serving in the Forces. They are fighting for democracy and freedom. So are we".'[59] The strike was understood as a patriotic act, in a different way, by a miner originating from Durham: 'We are fighting to retain the minimum wage. We are accused of betraying the war effort; but if we did not fight we should be betraying *the miners in the Army* and the other coalfields.'[60] While public opinion differentiated and opposed miners and soldiers to each other, he stressed that the army counted many miners within its ranks. The dilemma facing the miners was: betraying miners and soldiers by 'not fighting' for the minimum wage, or appearing to sabotage the war effort by striking. The strike was one way to support the soldiers fighting on the front, in accordance with the principle of miners' solidarity.

In-group reactions: miners' discussions in the village pub

Miners seemed to have been particularly attentive to the way in which the strike was presented to the public. On the fifth day of the strike, the *Daily Express* published a long article:

> *14 January. The Mill pub, lunchtime.*
>
> M45D: There's nowt about it in *News Chronicle* or *Telegraph*.
>
> M50D: No, only in the *Express*.
>
> Landlady produces *Express* with heading about 'Unhappy Miners'. This gets a laugh …
>
> M45D: Unhappy? Not us. Do we look it? We can manage alright.

---

57 *Evening Standard*, 26 January 1942
58 Walzer, *Spheres of Justice*.
59 Mrs Mantle, interviewed by *Evening Standard*, 26 January 1942.
60 *Daily Telegraph*, 15 January 1942.

M30D: We can always go to the bank. (laugh) If you've got it in what's it for but to take it out?

M45D: Oh some money'll turn in from somewhere. It always does. You see.[61]

15 January. The Mill Pub, lunchtime.

A group of M20D were sitting round the fire laughing continually.

1M20D: Look at my white hands.

2M20D: You'd almost pass for a gentleman.

3M20D: This suits me fine. I had 25*s*. [£1.25p] at the beginning of the week and there's 4*s*. 6*d*. [22.5p] left. When I've spent all my wages me mother will have to keep me till it's over.

2M20D: Did you see that in the *Express* about unhappy miners?

3M20D: Unhappy miners – don't we look it. (loud laughter from all of them and others)[62]

Very quickly, and perhaps, in the first case, because they had not read the entire article, the miners' comments focused only on the headline: 'Danger Zone. Strikers are unhappy'. The jokes were meant to refute the characterization of the unhappy miner, an image that undermined the culture of *joie de vivre* that had been proclaimed throughout the strike, but their purpose was also to defuse anything that might undermine the community's morale, and hasten a return to work. The 'danger zone' was as much their area of Kent, at the front line of the bombings, as it was the risk of the strike running out of steam.

The words (below) of a miner interviewed by the *Daily Express* were also discussed by several groups of miners in the main pub at Mill Hill.

But, as one man (a Scot) told me: 'We didn't want to strike: we want to work for a total war against Hitler. We are fighting now for the principle of a minimum wage. We say that our agreement with the company does not allow them to make a wage cut, although they say there was ca'canny in the pit.'

---

61 Mass Observation, 'Survey of a Strike at Betteshanger Colliery, Kent, 1942', 14 January 1942, SxMOA1/2/64/2/A, MOA.

62 *Ibid.*, 15 January 1942.

Faults

'I've been working as a miner for 48 years. I don't like being idle. I like this pit. Back in the North, where I come from, I worked harder for less money. This is an old man's pit. The seam I've been working is never less than 2ft 6ins [76cm] thick, and widens to 7ft or 8ft [2.1–2.4m]. In the north, I worked a seam only 8ins [20cm] thick – the rest was stone. Some of the younger ones here think they can act the goat. There are faults on both sides.'[63]

Even though his account appeared to demonstrate the importance of fighting for the minimum wage, despite the demands of war, it did not meet the unanimous approval of the miners:

14 January. The Mill pub, lunchtime.

M50D: (looking at *Express* article): See this old man here moaning? One of the Scots. I bet he got 2*s*. 6*d*. [12.5p] for that …

M45D: Or maybe a few pints.

Landlady: Can't we send something to the papers and get half a crown [12.5p]. We could split the money on beer.

M65D: Yes. I expect he did alright for saying that bit.

M45D: You never get the proper thing in the press. They'll be calling us the "scums of the earth" again. You see.[64]

15 January. The Mill pub, lunchtime.

M30D: Did you see those reporters today?

M60D: I don't think they should talk to the press.

M30D: Oh no – if they tell them proper things it's alright.

M35D: They can only put in what the paper lets them – that's the matter.

M30D: That's wrong – a good reporter gets it in alright. He knows how to put his story so they do put it in.

---

63 *Daily Express*, 14 January 1942.
64 Mass Observation, 'Survey of a Strike at Betteshanger Colliery, Kent, 1942', 14 January 1942, SxMOA1/2/64/2/A, MOA.

M35D: But you need to be careful what you say to press. Like that in the *Express* – one man says a bit and they thrust it and make it everybody's opinion. You can't trust papers to have truth.[65]

The spectre of the man who 'sells out' to the press appeared. Even if the miner who was interviewed did not directly challenge the idea of difficult working conditions on the new coalface, he revealed several snags in it. He described a mine with favourable geological conditions and suggested laying some of the blame on certain younger miners who were guilty of 'acting the goat'. The miners distanced themselves from him. First, he was described as 'this old man'. This echoes the rumours observed by the MO investigator, who reported that some older miners had not been inclined to go on strike. He was also described as 'a Scot'. Such typification was important in Betteshanger, and is recurrent in the oral histories collected through interviews with former miners: each person mentioned is defined in terms of his or her regional origins. The Kent collieries were well known for having absorbed mining families from Yorkshire, Scotland and Wales after the months-long mining lockout of 1926.[66]

On 23 January, when the union leaders were sentenced to prison and other strikers fined, the strike was thrust into the media. The MO investigator made this important observation:

> Reports in the press were eagerly scanned and there was a good deal of satisfaction because at last the strike had become real news. There has been a great deal of annoyance about the inadequacy of the press reports, and the men still feel that their side of the case has never been properly put before the public. They know that miners are looked upon as a rough lot and always grumbling and they resent the way the press talk about a wage dispute without stating the rights and wrongs of it clearly. 'People think we want more money, not that we only want our minimum' is frequently said when men are explaining the situation.[67]

Beyond the miners' dissatisfaction with the way the press reported the strike, their remarkable knowledge of the misconceptions and misunderstandings

---

65 *Ibid.*, 15 January 1942.
66 Terry Harrison, a former Betteshanger miner, confirmed that regional origins were the major criteria for distinguishing between miners and an important obstacle to solidarity. Hence the colliery's former union leaders' nickname of 'the Yorkshire mafia', while those who were active during the 1942 strike had a definite Welsh bias: interview, 28 July 2012. Thanks to Terry Harrison for two very useful interviews and I hope to see his book on the history of Betteshanger colliery published. See, also, Harkell, 'The Migration of Mining Families to the Kent Coalfield between the Wars', *Oral History*.
67 Mass Observation, 'Survey of a Strike at Betteshanger Colliery, Kent, 1942', 24 January 1942, SxMOA1/2/64/2/A, MOA.

that were spreading within the out-group should also be noted. Each of the points mentioned echoed one of the miscomprehensions circulating in the press or in the nearest town. The image of the miner as coarse and crude was widespread at the time, and the interviews with locals in Deal provide an excellent sample of this. The narrow view that the strike was simply another attempt to get more money reminds us as much of the views expressed by the citizens of Deal as of the article in the *Daily Express* that referred to 'a strike for £15'. What people were not informed about was precisely the central issue in the miners' frame of reference: the preservation of the minimum wage.

Legality and legitimacy

The strike on trial: prosecution for offences under Order 1305

Before Betteshanger, Order 1305 had been invoked infrequently and union leaders were unfamiliar with it.[68] Ministry of Labour regional officers noted a general ignorance and confusion about it – the Order had been hastily drafted and was strewn with vague phrasing. It was not unusual for articles on Betteshanger to get the name of the Order wrong. We may well wonder how well known Order 1305 was to the miners when the strike started on 9 January. For example, Powell, the branch secretary, declared in court that they did not know about the Order; one miner, interviewed by the investigator early in the strike, compared the banning of strikes to Nazi policies. Even if some or all Betteshanger miners were unaware of Order 1305 at the beginning of the strike, they did not claim to be ignorant of it during the strike. The strike's legality was hotly discussed and challenged on grounds of legitimacy.

The illegality of the strike *was explained* to all the miners at the end of the first week, 16 January, during a meeting with the two conciliation officers from the Department of Mines, Cook and Farrow, when the matter of possible prosecutions came up. One conciliation officer confided to the MO investigator that discussion about the legitimacy of the strike was to be avoided, the only important matter was getting the miners back to work:

The Mines officials seemed quite confident of success when addressing the main body of the men the following morning.

---

68 See in particular, Tyndall, 'Patriotism and Principles', *HSIR*; N. Stammers, *Civil Liberties in Britain during the 2nd World War: A Political Study* (St. Martin's Press, New York: 1983); E. Wigham, *Strikes and the Government 1893–1974* (Macmillan: 1976).

M44BC [Farrow] said: 'I'm coming to let Father do the talking – he's the one to tackle them – I'm keeping in the background.' He explained to inv. that their job was to get the mines working again, not to arbitrate. 'When the men ask us what we think of the management's action we don't answer that – we try to give them another bone to gnaw by saying "why can't you go on working while the matter is being threshed out". I suppose in a way it's not quite honest but we have to do it.'[69]

Cook explained Order 1305 and 'emphasized the fact that they had incurred the risk of serious penalties by calling the strike without giving notice to the Government'.[70] The Order provided for prison sentences and fines for strikers, or any other person who provoked a strike.

On 23 January 1942, the strikers appeared in court at Canterbury. Once again, the trial was not the occasion where the legitimacy or illegitimacy of the strike could be settled. Its causes were not relevant objects of discussion in this legal arena. The official representing the Ministry of Labour made it clear that

the Ministry was not concerned as to why there should be this dispute; nor was the Bench concerned as to the rights of any party – whether the miners should have had more money or less money, more work or less work. The summonses were simply taken out because these people had broken the law and gone on strike without giving the 21 days' notice, to give a chance of the dispute being dealt with.[71]

The declarations made by the union leaders, when they were called before the court, reflected the tensions between legality and legitimacy:

Powell declared from the dock: 'We took action to defend our hard-won minimum wage. We did not know of the Regulation. We felt justified in our action, and whatever is done today will not bring peace to Betteshanger Colliery.'[72]

Tudor Davies said there had been contravention of what the miners held sacred – the minimum wage agreement. Many of their people in the past had died so that they could have some security. The minimum wage they held to be their security, and if the management would pay the proper rates he could give his word that the men would go back to work that night.[73]

---

69 Mass Observation, 'Survey of a Strike at Betteshanger Colliery, Kent, 1942', 15 January 1942, SxMOA1/2/64/2/A, MOA.
70 *The Times*, 17 January 1942.
71 *Ibid.*, 24 January 1942.
72 Daughtrey, 'Truth about Betteshanger', *New Leader*.
73 'The strike ended', newspaper article, 31 January 1942, personal archives of Di Parkin.

Both defendants raised another principle of legality – the agreement on the minimum wage – and indexed it to a moral constraint: that of preserving an agreement that is considered to be sacred, one gained at the expense of tough battles fought by past generations. In the judicial arena, the two union leaders felt that a transcription of these principles was necessary.

For that matter, their statements made it obvious that the little the court knew about the causes of the conflict were swept under the carpet at the beginning of the trial, and in no uncertain terms: it was of no consequence 'whether the miners should have had more money or less money, more work or less work'. This reminds us of the words of the Betteshanger miners who lamented that 'People think we want more money, not that we only want our minimum.' The authorities had no more knowledge of the case than 'the man in the street'.[74]

At the end of the trial, the three union leaders, considered to be the instigators of the strike, were sentenced to hard labour in prison. Powell (branch secretary) received a two-month sentence, Davies and Isaac Methuen (respectively, branch president and vice-chairman) a one-month sentence. The 35 miners on no. 2 coalface were fined £3 each and 1,050 other miners fined £1, for having 'unlawfully taken part in a strike in connection with a trade dispute not reported to the Minister of Labour and National Service in accordance with Article 2 of the Conditions of Employment and National Registration Order, 1940, contrary to Article 4 of the said Order and Regulation 58AA of the Defence (General) Regulations, 1939'.[75]

Understanding the miners' reactions to the sentences

The prison sentences, especially for Davies, a Justice of the Peace (JP) and a much respected man in the mining community, were seen as an enormous injustice by the Betteshanger miners. The impression was that everything had been decided in advance. The MO investigator recorded the following comments overheard in the crowded pub at the Welfare Centre:

---

74 Cf. the three ideal-types of knowledge defined by Alfred Schutz: the expert, the man in the street, and the well-informed citizen. Among other things, the man in the street is characterized in terms of his knowledge in all categories that are not related to immediate practical purposes, for which he 'establishes a set of non-clarified convictions and views to which he adheres as long as they do not interfere with his pursuit of happiness'. Here, the reasons for the strike are assumed to be self-evident, not requiring any investigation: A. Schutz, 'The Well-informed Citizen. An Essay on the Social Distribution of Knowledge', in *idem, Collected Papers, 2: Studies in Social Theory* (Martinus Nijhoff, The Hague: 1964), pp. 121–34.

75 *Dover Express and East Kent News*, 23 January 1942 ; Ministry of Labour, 'Strike at Pearson & Dorman Long Ltd', LAB 10/204, TNA.

M40D: Tudor Davies is a fine man. They say his speech made tears run down the faces of some people sitting in the court, but it's no good. They've got it fixed. He's never been in before.

M35D: Neither's Methuen. Billy Powell has, that's why he's got it worst I expect.

M40D: He's a rotten judge. He's always got it in for miners, he hates them.[76]

The trial's outcome hardened opinions. A week earlier many miners were talking about the possibility of returning to work; now there was no question of doing so, for this would mean abandoning those miners now in prison. Two days after the trial, the colliery management wrote to each striker asking them to return to work. One said: 'They think we'll go back now they've locked up our leaders, but they'll have to think again.'[77] The same day, a meeting with the strikers turned into what those who were present described as a 'mutiny'. Two representatives were booed and roughly pushed away from the rostrum when they enjoined the strikers to return to work. The next day, a second ballot confirmed the strike's continuation, even though the strike was entering its third week and many families were having a hard time, as the MO reports reveal. In the middle of winter, the lack of coal, usually bought at reduced prices from the colliery, was cruelly felt. The MO investigator described the straits of one family:

> During the last couple of weeks they had chopped up the two chairs from their Anderson shelter, torn up the whole floor and used it board by board, done the same to the door and on Sunday night were removing the final doorpost. Inv. asked what they would use next; they laughed and said they'd come by something or start on the fence or the furniture.[78]

The main subject of conversation throughout Mill Hill was the fines, to be paid under pain of two to four weeks' imprisonment. The day after the trial, the investigator noticed that 'the frequent greeting all day, both among men and women was: "You getting ready to go down the line?" F25D: "Your man going to pay the fine?" F50D: "My man's bloody going down bloody line with rest".' No one seemed to be willing to pay the fine. 'Joking remarks about prison cells and food, and wives taking lodgers were made, but the

76 Mass Observation, 'Survey of a Strike at Betteshanger Colliery, Kent, 1942', 23 January, report on 'Reactions to events', dated 26 January 1942, SxMOA1/2/64/2/A, MOA.

77 *Ibid.*

78 Mass Observation, 'Survey of a Strike at Betteshanger Colliery, Kent, 1942', report on 'General Morale', dated 26 January 1942, SxMOA1/2/64/2/A, MOA.

serious idea behind all this was the fact that they are kept in prison, and then their wives can scrape along better alone on the relief money.'[79]

The jokes provide a glimpse of the miners' real preoccupations. At the same time, alarming rumours were circulating: several miners, for example, feared that a prison sentence could be extended indefinitely. Imprisonment would have been extremely disadvantageous, for a miner with such a record would not be able to find employment in other collieries. 'It goes against you moving jobs if they hear you've been in, you're marked', confirmed one of the strikers.[80]

A crucial point for understanding the refusal to pay fines was that this sanction seemed to be linked less to Order 1305 than to the initial causes of the movement, which had not been heard by the bench. To pay the fines was to accept the accusations of anti-patriotism and the loss of the minimum wage. Subsequent interviews with two of the miners involved throw light on this:

> Well I would've called up to the first Sergeant Major and ask him that he might shoot me or send me to prison, that would have been my answer to that because I didn't consider myself or my mates unpatriotic at all! They weren't unpatriotic! We were all very sincere in this effort and the first concern was coal, the second concern was our homes.[81]

and

> Well of course I would have gone, I mean, the principle was there. *If I'd paid the fine I'd concede it*, that I was in the wrong, and I wasn't prepared to do that at any stage.[82] (emphasis added)

---

79 Mass Observation, 'Survey of a Strike at Betteshanger Colliery, Kent, 1942', 23 January, report on 'Reactions to events', dated 26 January 1942, SxMOA1/2/64/2/A, MOA.

80 Mass Observation, 'Survey of a Strike at Betteshanger Colliery, Kent, 1942', report on 'General Morale', dated 26 January 1942, SxMOA1/2/64/2/A, MOA.

81 Oral history interview no. 2738, Bill Roberts, 1972, Imperial War Museum, London (hereafter IWM). Bill Roberts, a Betteshanger miner who participated in the 1942 strike and was fined, was interviewed for a Thames Television programme.

82 Oral history interview no. 2735, Dick, 1972, IWM. Dick was one of the Betteshanger miners transferred on no. 2 coalface. His family name is not mentioned but his answers indicate that this might be Dick Hill, a 'monkey puffler' in charge of negotiating rates according to conditions on behalf of the men.

Epilogue and conclusion

In the aftermath, a record number of letters was sent to the Ministry of Labour and the Home Office to denounce the sentences, which were judged excessive, and several collieries struck in protest. The company was very eager for the men to return, to the extent that it was prepared to agree to the original demands. On 28 January 1942, an agreement was reached to end the strike. The negotiations took place in Maidstone prison, in the presence of the three strike leaders, David Rhys Grenfell (Secretary for Mines) and Ebby Edwards (secretary of the Mineworkers' Federation of Great Britain). The management agreed to guarantee the minimum wage at 15s. 3d. per shift, as long as it could call in an arbitrator in cases of ca'canny. The miners agreed to these terms after a meeting at the Welfare Club in Mill Hill during that afternoon. As the Ministry of Labour conceded, 'the settlement at Betteshanger amounted, practically, to a complete surrender to the men, even though there may be apparently safeguarding words in the agreement. We had hoped and had been led to believe, that no concessions would be made unless and until the men returned to work'.[83]

Grenfell undertook to obtain the release of the three leaders, Powell, Davies and Methuen, emphasizing in communications with the Home Office that, although there was no question about the validity of the sentences, 'it would promote good relations and the maintenance of a cooperative spirit amongst the workers'.[84] On 2 February, after eleven days in prison sewing mail bags, the three were released, after a pardon from King George VI. The Ministry of Labour never again during the war imprisoned workers directly because of their defiance of Order 1305; any going to prison would be for non-payment of fines.[85]

Despite the risk of two to four weeks' imprisonment, only nine miners had paid their fines four months after the strike. Nothing happened. Correspondence between the Mines Department, the Home Office and the local JPs reveal the embarrassment caused by this 'thorny question'. The Home Office said it could not turn a blind eye to the 'serious practical difficulties or the possible effect on coal production if men were imprisoned' and feared they would take up arms again if they were to be imprisoned

83 Ministry of Labour, 'Strike at Pearson & Dorman Long Ltd', memorandum of the Secretary for Ministry of Labour, 29 January 1942, LAB 10/204, TNA.
84 Home Office, 'Illegal strike at Betteshanger Colliery, Deal, Kent', HO45/25091, TNA.
85 McIlroy and Campbell, 'Beyond Betteshanger, Part 1', *HSIR*, p. 32, Table 1, and pp. 62–3, Table 6.

just months after their leaders were released.[86] In July 1943, the Home Office Minister agreed to remit the fines, 'because of the importance of maintaining harmonious industrial relations, especially with the miners during this time of war'.

This article has demonstrated that the MO ethnographic surveys are essential sources for such episodes of industrial relations history. They allow for three important shifts. First, a change of scale which gives priority to a local analysis of the process of the strike in the mining villages rather than the discussions it provoked in Whitehall. Second, they allow for the confrontation of a multiplicity of descriptions of the conflict and frames of references involved: the strikers, their families and neighbours, union representatives and rank and file, coal owners and colliery managers, conciliation officers from various departments, and the press. The sources also avoid presenting a monolithic account of the strikers' views, stressing the differences and divisions within the mining community. Last, MO sources present the ongoing action at the time, rather than retrospectively. This enables us to analyse the dialogic aspect of reactions in the conflict: there are no more fixed accounts and legitimations of the strike, but a process of responses to opposing views, reformulations and new framing.

These shifts allow for an essay in historical ethnography exploring the complex connections between three spheres of justice – patriotism, social justice, and legality. The spheres are connected very differently in the accounts of the conflict by miners and their representatives, by the colliery company, the press, and neighbouring non-miners. The strikers are not the only ones accused of anti-patriotism and they sometimes invoke patriotism themselves in order to legitimate the strike. To the illegality of the strike as per Order 1305, the strikers oppose the infringement of the local agreements by the colliery company.

The discrepancy in the connection of these spheres of justice has been neglected to date. Yet it is an important factor in the failure of mass sanctions at Betteshanger, more than just the difficulties of applying them. The MO documents enable us to grasp the reason behind the escalation of the conflict and the miners' obstinate resistance. Two of the central issues to the miners – the infringement of the minimum wage and the accusations of anti-patriotism – were not understood by the public and deemed secondary by the press and the court. Indeed, at every step of the procedure, Order 1305 and the illegality of the strike have eclipsed a judgement on the strike's legitimacy and on the initial conflict. The arbitrator's decision

---

86 Home Office, 'Illegal strike at Betteshanger Colliery, Deal, Kent', HO 45/25091, TNA; Ministry of Labour, 'Strike at Pearson & Dorman Long Ltd', memorandum of the Secretary for Ministry of Labour, 29 January 1942, LAB 10/204, TNA.

had no validity to the miners; the conciliation officers did not discuss the legitimacy of the initial conflict; the trial did not examine the legitimacy of the strike, only its illegality. Nevertheless, in court, the miners were faced with accusations of anti-patriotism, to which they were not allowed to reply. To the miners, the fines and imprisonment were not so much linked to Order 1305 as to the legitimacy of the strike. In their view, the prison sentences and fines countenanced both an infringement of the law (minimum wage) and a judgement of their failure to do their duty as citizens (patriotism). These are essential in re-evaluating the failure of Order 1305 at Betteshanger.

École des Hautes Études en Sciences Sociales (EHESS)
190–198 avenue de France, 75244 Paris cedex 13, France

doi:10.3828/hsir.2015.36.3

Arms'-Length or Nose to Nose?
Eric Batstone and Bargaining in 1970s France

Steve Jefferys

Eric Batstone (1944–87) did much of his best work in the transitional period at the end of the post-war boom around forty years ago. In the UK his capacity for detailed observation of work and his ability to generalize analytical insights of real value to the whole employment relations system is well known. *Shop Stewards in Action: The Organization of Workplace Conflict and Accommodation* (1977) and *The Social Organization of Strikes* (1978), both written with Ian Boraston and Stephen Frenkel, are classic examples of this.[1] Their vivid observations on workplace life at what was probably the height of shop stewards' influence in the Coventry Massey–Ferguson plant gave rise to major understandings of the nature of bargaining.

What is less known is that Batstone also researched in France and more widely in Europe, although only a few comparative papers were published.[2] The study that follows is titled 'Arms'-Length Bargaining',[3] and while it

---

1 E. Batstone, I. Boraston and S. Frenkel, *Shop Stewards in Action: The Organization of Workplace Conflict and Accommodation* (Blackwell, Oxford: 1977), and *idem, The Social Organization of Strikes* (Blackwell, Oxford: 1978).

2 E. Batstone and P. L. Davies, *Industrial Democracy: European Experience: Two Research Reports* (HMSO: 1976); *idem, Industrial Democracy and Worker Representation at Board Level: A Review of the European Experience.* E. Batstone, 'Organization and Orientation: A Life Cycle Model of French Co-operatives', *Economic and Industrial Democracy* 4:2 (1983), pp. 139–61; *idem,* 'International Variations in Strike Activity', *European Sociological Review* 1:1 (1985), pp. 46–64.

3 Batstone's title includes a different apostrophe position than in the American usage, which refers to 'arm's-length bargaining'. Perhaps this is a typo, or perhaps he was trying to suggest several more lengths of arms between the parties than in the American context?

was circulated within the Industrial Relations Research Unit at Warwick University in 1978, it was never given a wider airing.

Batstone conducted the research through interviews with the company personnel manager and union activists in two French Chrysler–*SIMCA* (*Société Industrielle de Mécanique et de Carrosserie Automobile*) car plants.[4] He also had access to many internal documents and conducted a significant literature review. The largest Chrysler–*SIMCA* plant was a former Ford one, at Poissy, on the Seine at Yvelines to the north-west of Paris. The Périgny La Rochelle factory, built in the Charente–Maritime department between Nantes and Bordeaux under France's 1960s regional relocation policy, doubled in size between 1968 and 1975 by when it also employed over 3,000 workers, making suspensions and transmissions for the whole *SIMCA* range.

Ironically, his research took place in 1977 and 1978, the last years in which the *SIMCA* brand had a clear identity. Established initially in 1935 by Fiat to escape import duties through building its cars in France, *SIMCA*'s post-war history had seen Ford taking a 15% stake in the company in 1954. Henry Ford II was initiating an exit strategy from France, driven by his paranoia that the country would be taken over by the Communists and his factory nationalized. Four years later he sold the entire holding to Chrysler, which was then only starting its European expansion. In 1963 Chrysler became the majority shareholder and soon after it bought out the Fiat stake to take complete ownership. In 1978, when Chrysler Europe collapsed, *SIMCA* was acquired by *PSA* Peugeot–Citroën.[5] The new owners rebranded the Chrysler France plants and cars as Talbot, but by the mid-1980s both the names *SIMCA* and Talbot had disappeared. Today, only the Poissy plant, now fully integrated into *PSA* Peugeot–Citroën, survives making cars.

The 1970s had seen the end of nearly thirty years of post-war economic growth in both France and the UK. Industrial relations in the two countries were remodelled during the Second World War and the boom years, displacing the systems dominated by unitary management that had marked the pre-war era.[6] After such a lengthy period of unprecedented employment

---

4 While Batstone concealed the firm's identity at the time, his description of it as a 'foreign-owned' car company in France tends to pinpoint Chrysler– *SIMCA*. The two factories I mention are possibly, but not certainly, the two researched.

5 At the same time as it acquired Chrysler UK (formerly Rootes).

6 Alan Fox coined the description of a significant part of British management ideology as being 'unitary', based on the assumption that the interests of workers and owners were the same or identical: A. Fox, *Industrial Sociology and Industrial Relations: Research Paper 3, Royal Commission on Trade Unions and Employers' Associations* (HMSO: 1966). In France, where the military term 'cadre' emerged from the mid-nineteenth century to describe

security, workers had become more confident in their capacity to introduce economic democracy into the workplace. They did so by pressing employers to institutionalize systems of employment regulation that gave greater space to workers' voices than ever before, albeit in quite contrasting forms in the two countries.

Even today those boom years are still described in France as '*les trente glorieuses*'.[7] Over the period 1951–73 French unemployment had averaged 1.2%. At the same time it was at a low average of just 1.6% in the UK. The 1971 collapse of monetary stability sustained by the Bretton Woods system,[8] and the 1973 oil crisis,[9] marked the end of that global boom. Unemployment in the UK leapt to average 7.4% between 1980 and 2009, while in France it rose to average 9.5% over the same three decades.[10]

The 1970s began the transition between the periods of boom and of much slower growth. Nonetheless these transitional years witnessed the continuing institutionalization of many of the gains made in the earlier period, as well as signs of an employers' ideological realignment with American 'free market' managerialism.[11] In this decade many groups of workers still saw that collective action and organization could be used effectively to respond to the absence of workplace democracy and rights. They joined unions more readily, often taking industrial action, unaware

---

the distinct caste of managers, as late as the 1990s nearly a quarter of French employers opposed employee representation on principle. Paternalist unitarism there was often influenced by the corporatism of Social Catholicism (on which see footnote 15).

7 The term believed to be coined by the *Le Figaro* editorialist and economist Jean Fourastié in his 1979 book, *Les Trente Glorieuses, ou la Révolution invisible de 1946 à 1975* (Fayard, Paris: 1979). He was playing on references to the July 1830 '*Trois glorieuses*': the three revolutionary days that saw the monarchy passing from the Bourbon Charles X to Louis-Philippe, Duke of Orléans.

8 The Bretton Woods international monetary system was established by the soon-to-be victorious wartime Allies in 1944. It established fixed-exchange rates based on the US dollar and gold. In 1971 the US stopped guaranteeing a fixed-exchange rate between the dollar and gold, and by 1973 the system had effectively been replaced by the current free-floating exchange rate system.

9 The 1971 end of the Bretton Woods system led to the depreciation of the dollar. Oil was priced in dollars, and as a result the twelve principal oil-exporting countries decided collectively to demand a higher price by lowering output. Their resolve to act was finally triggered by the 1973 Yom Kippur war, after the US started to send arms to Israel. The price of oil quadrupled, the West's stock markets crashed and an economic recession set in.

10 R. Skidelsky, *Keynes: The Return of the Master* (Allen Lane: 2009).

11 M. Carpenter and S. Jefferys, *Management, Work and Welfare in Western Europe: A Historical and Contemporary Analysis* (Edward Elgar, Cheltenham: 2000).

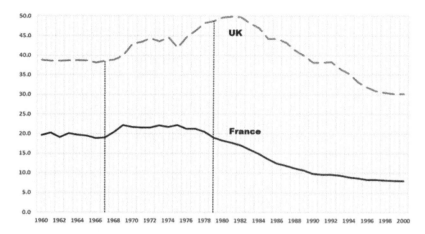

Figure 1: Trade-union density (as a % of all employees) in the UK and France, 1960–2000

that economic power in their relations with capital was slowly starting to shift against them.

Reflecting this greater confidence, union density rose in both France and the UK in the 1970s. It remained at or above its 1967 levels through the whole decade right up to 1979 in France and for a decade longer in the UK. Figure 1 shows union density grew more dynamically in the 1970s in the UK, to its highest-ever level of around half all employees.

In France in the 1970s, if density remained at less than half the British level, it also increased. Table 1 shows that membership rose by a million above its average for the 1960s. This 30% increase was inspired directly by the success of the mass strike wave of 1968, and by subsequent industrial and political gains.[12]

---

12 S. Jefferys, *Liberté, Egalité and Fraternité at Work: Changing French Employment Relations and Management* (Palgrave Macmillan, Basingstoke: 2003).

Table 1: Estimated average annual trade-union membership (excluding retirees) (000s), 1950s–90s[13,14]

	1950–59	1960–69	1970–79	1980–89	1990–99
CGT	2,046	1,321	1,500	768	420
CFDT		507	684	486	500
CFTC	360	150	200	185	160
FO	1,000	800	1,000	500	300
CGC	100	200	300	225	180
FEN/UNSA	200	300	500	300	100
FSU					150
CFT/CSL		50	50	100	50
G10 (Sud)				250	100
Others	100	200	300	250	140
Rounded total	3,800	3,500	4,500	3,100	2,100

While it grew, French union membership never recovered the five million members of the immediate post-war period. That peak had been achieved at a moment when the Communist Party polled 28% in the first round of the 1946 Assembly elections, making it France's biggest political party. The participation of the Communist Party in government between 1945 and 1947 enabled the nationalization of the Renault works, the mines and several banks, and formalized the presence of works councils in most of France's large firms. But by the 1970s, if in dues-paying workers it could not rival British numbers, the French trade-union movement nonetheless did share the heady experience of membership growth with its British equivalents.

The much lower levels of union membership in France than in the UK (and elsewhere) need some explanation. The main reasons for this French

---

13 Sources: S. Jefferys, 'Down but not out: French Unions after Chirac', *Work, Employment and Society* 10:3 (1996), pp. 509–27; *Le Monde*, various dates, for 1995–2001.

14 The acronyms stand for the following union confederation names: *CGT* (*Confédération générale du travail*); *CFDT* (*Confédération française démocratique du travail*); *CFTC* (*Confédération française des travailleurs chrétiens*); *FO* (*CGT–Force ouvrière*); *CGC* (*Confédération générale des cadres*); *FEN* (*Fédération de l'éducation nationale*); *UNSA* (*Union nationale des syndicats autonomes*); *FSU* (*Fédération syndicale unitaire*); *CFT* (*Confédération française du travail*); *CSL* (*Confédération des syndicats libres*); *G10* (*Le groupe des dix*); *Sud* (*Solidaires Unitaires Démocratiques*).

'exceptionalism' relate to the motivations for members' adhesion, and to the extremely high levels of hostility shown to union membership on the part of French employers. The total absence of an influential 'reformist', Liberal current among French employers in the nineteenth and twentieth centuries is quite remarkable when compared with the UK. This is clearly related to the frequency with which employers' property rights were challenged – not least in the revolutions of 1789, 1830, 1832, 1848, and 1870. It is also linked ideologically with the significant presence of strongly paternalist Social Catholicism.[15] But it is also a consequence of the greater weight of micro, small and medium-sized firms in a society where in 1962 some 40% of the population still lived in towns with less than 2,000 people.[16]

It is a mistake, however, to assume that low total numbers means proportionately fewer numbers of committed union activists. And it is also a mistake to assume that that 'commitment' means the same in both countries. Intense hostility by French employers to the 64,000 union

---

15 Jefferys, *Liberté, Egalité and Fraternité at Work*, pp. 73–4, describes Social Catholicism as 'a major source of French employer ideology [that] can be seen as a blend of Catholic paternalism with utopian nineteenth century Saint-Simonian ideology. The Saint-Simonians favoured the unity of all productive and industrious elements (bourgeoisie, peasant and worker) against the useless aristocrats and rentiers (money lenders and landlords) in the interests of a functional administrative structure and a commitment to aggregate wealth and welfare. Alongside this, but not necessarily in contradiction, French paternalism represented a powerful unitary appeal to the *patron*'s inalienable *liberté* to do as he pleased within his family or *patrie*, provided he "looked after his people". For many employers this was an ethical responsibility. The influential early sociologist Frédéric Le Play, whose views carried considerable weight with Napoleon III, considered it the moral duty of the wealthy to provide "patronage" for the less fortunate. In 1889 a Catholic industrialist drafted this "Catechism of the *Patron*": "*The authority of the employer should be as close as possible to parental authority ... (The employer) must aid with all his power larger families, thereby honouring the Law of God ... he must facilitate marriages between well-behaved young people, he must end illicit relationships, and, if unfortunately, children are the consequence, he must work to get them legitimated*" (cited in Jean Savatier, "La liberté dans le travail", *Droit social*, 1 janvier 1990, p. 52). Although proactive paternalism was regularly switched on and off according to the extent of labour shortage and the availability of substitute immigrant labour, it remained the dominant managerial ideology ... although in response to the emerging socialist movement and the increase in average workplace size, the earlier "industrial patronage" that was based largely on Christian morality and the metaphor of the family in employment relations tended to make way [in the twentieth century] for a "paternalism" motivated primarily by ideological anti-unionism and union-avoidance strategies.'

16 Jefferys, *Liberté, Egalité and Fraternité at Work*.

members estimated in 1880, shortly before unions were finally legalized, had the unintended consequence of radicalizing the meaning of union membership in France.[17] Direct action by a determined unionized minority became viewed as a democratic way of offering all workers the possibility of participating in struggles to improve working and living conditions, as well as to change society.[18] The Fourth (1946) and Fifth Republic Constitutions (1958) thus both included a constitutional protection for the individual worker to take strike action.

Fear of dismissal and of victimization by the employer for union membership remained (and remains) a huge factor in the reluctance to join unions. Many French employers actively supported 'yellow' company unions. One of the most well known of these was based at *SIMCA*, where management sponsored the company union at the expense of the *Confédération générale du travail* (*CGT*). This *SIMCA* union formed the core of the *Confédération française du travail* (*CFT*), a grouping of similar company unions founded in 1959 and known for its support of management and 'traditional values'. Thus in 1968 the large *SIMCA* Poissy factory was one of the very few in the car industry that did not come out on strike or occupy.[19] A contemporary poster (Figure 2) highlighted its exceptionalism: *May 1968: 9 million workers on strike. SIMCA is not striking!*

Other tactics included creating 'commando' groups to attack strike pickets and factory occupations. This 'union' was forced to change its name in 1977 after one of the members of a *CFT*–Citroën commando group shot at and killed a *CGT* strike picket in Reims.[20] The bad publicity that resulted then led most employers to distance themselves from these unions and to stop the practice of providing fictional jobs for local *CFT* leaders.[21] Despite 'trade-union discrimination' being added to the list of illegal forms

---

17 M. Dreyfus, *Histoire de la C.G.T.* (Éditions complexe, Paris: 1995).
18 J.-D. Reynaud, *Les Syndicats en France*, 2 Vols (Éditions du Seuil, Paris: 1975).
19 J.-L. Loubet and N. Hatzfeld, 'Poissy: de la CGT à la CFT', *Vingtième Siècle: Revue d'histoire* 1:73 (2002), pp. 67–81.
20 Nonetheless the strength of the extreme right in France meant that the new trade union, the *CSL*, survived and even prospered somewhat until 2002. When it was dissolved the most significant membership remained within the former *SIMCA* in what is now the *PSA* Peugeot–Citroën group. Some of its Citroën activists joined *FO*, but most of its factory sections formed the *SIA* (*Syndicat indépendant de l'automobile*), which is recognized only by *PSA*'s management. The *SIA* is affiliated to other former company trade-union sections based at Renault and elsewhere in an organization called the *Groupement des syndicats européens de l'automobile* (*GSEA*), which won 14,000 votes in the French industrial tribunal elections in 2002.
21 H. Rollin, *Militant chez Simca–Chrysler* (Éditions sociales, Paris: 1977).

Figure 2: 1968 strike poster

of discrimination along with age, sexuality, ethnicity, and gender in the French transposition of the 2000 Employment Rights Directive, French employers still regularly played (and play) on workers' fears of losing their job or career opportunities to deter union membership.

Other explanations for the low levels of union members include the pluralism of French unions: while not all unions are present in all workplaces, the fact that up to the 1980s there were six main confederations, of which five were in very active competition with each other, made such competition a plausible reason for many workers not to join. Yet for those who supported the unions but did not wish to take the risk of becoming a committed activist there was also a logic to non-membership. Workers benefited from sector and national collective bargaining through the system of the nearly automatic extension of agreements by the Ministry of Labour, whether or not they were union members. As such the vast majority of workers constituted 'free-riders'. But unlike the 'classic' anti-union 'free-rider', in most workplaces these non-members were also consulted informally on a regular basis by those who were union members and who they regularly elected to represent them on works councils.[22] From 1954,

22 S. Contrepois, *Syndicats: La nouvelle donne: Enquête sociologique au cœur d'un bassin industriel* (Syllepse, Paris: 2003).

unions also secured a significant degree of legitimacy through their being entitled to run lists in the election of the worker judges who would sit on employment tribunals, with about two-thirds of eligible full- and part-time workers participating.[23]

During the ten years after the 1973–75 recession, industrial relations in both the UK and France became increasingly tense. Workers responded combatively to rising inflation and the reappearance of job insecurity. In Britain, the 1972 and 1974 miners' strikes were both won. They gave an important boost to growing unionization among white-collar workers. In France, 1968 is well known as a key turning point. What is much less well known is that it was followed by a major eruption of local private-sector strikes. French strikes are notoriously difficult to count, and until the 1980s they entirely excluded public-sector stoppages. However, it is possible to see their numbers and the estimated numbers of workers they involved in the private sector, as shown in Figure 3.[24]

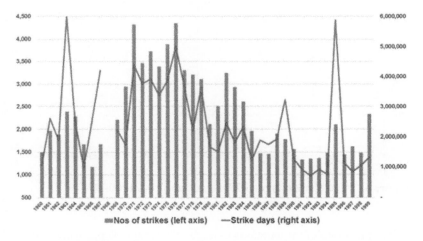

Figure 3: Numbers of private-sector strikes and numbers of striker days recorded in France, 1960–99[25]

One result of this more generalized level of strike activity and the growth in union membership and organization was an increase in the average share of

23 J.-P. Jacquier, *Les Clés du Social en France* (Editions Liaisons, Paris: 1998).

24 In 1968 those responsible for collecting strike data were also on strike.

25 J. Simon, 'Les conflits du travail en 1981', *Bulletin mensuel des statistiques du travail*, Supplement 95 (1981), pp. 121–33; S. Jefferys, 'France 1995: The Backward March of Labour Halted?', *Capital and Class* 59 (1996), pp. 7–21; R. Merlier, 'Les conflits en 2000: le Regain se confirme', *Premières syntheses* 09.1 (2002), pp. 1–8.

the total economy going to wages: up above 1960s levels by 0.5% in France and by as much as 2% in the UK.[26] In the UK the peak year for wage-share of gross domestic product (GDP) was 1975; in France there was one peak in 1976 and then another in 1982, the year after François Mitterrand was elected and raised the national minimum wage. The details in Figure 4 show how year-to-year changes were volatile but that the gains of the 1970s had been eroded in both countries by 1986 – with French workers' wage-share continuing a decline through to 1997, and after another upward turn, the wage-share of British workers falling to below its 1960 level in 1996 and 1997.

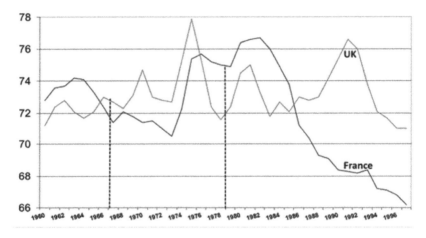

Figure 4: Wage-share (%) of GDP, France and UK, 1960–97[27]

The implications of the increases in wage-share that took place in the 1970s in France and the UK for employers were lower levels of profitability. Figure 5, covering the period 1960–95, shows how the share of gross profit in manufacturing fell dramatically in both countries with the onset of the 1973–75 crisis and the higher levels of union density and worker resistance described above.

Driven by falling profits and intensifying international competition, while faced with strengthening workers' voice, employers in both countries

---

26 The gains were concentrated in the early 1970s after the two successful miners' strikes of 1972 and 1974.

27 Table 32, pp. 254–5: 'Adjusted wage-share; total economy – Percentage of gross domestic product at factor cost'. European Commission (1997), *European Economy 1997*, No. 63 (Annual Economic Report for 1997).

were on the defensive. In the UK where the Wilson–Callaghan Labour Party was in office from 1974, a 'social contract' was negotiated to reduce levels of wage demands. Margaret Thatcher became Prime Minister in 1979; five years later the Conservatives engineered the full-scale defeat of the miners, 1984–85.[28]

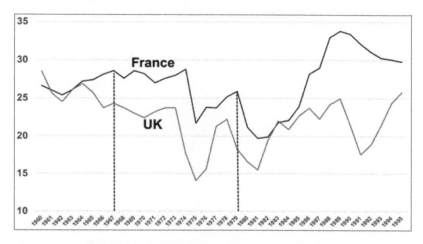

Figure 5: Gross profit share (%) in manufacturing in the UK and France (adjusted for self-employed income), 1960–95[29]

In France, the political right represented by the Presidents Georges Pompidou–Giscard D'Estaing was in power following Charles de Gaulle's 1969 resignation, right up to 1981. Attempting to placate its mobilizing working class, it introduced several reforms to the welfare state and to employment rights, as shown in Table 2.

---

28 J. Phillips, 'Containing, Isolating, and Defeating the Miners: The UK Cabinet Ministerial Group on Coal and the Three Phases of the 1984–85 Strike', *HSIR* 35 (2014), pp. 117–41.
29 A. Glyn, 'Does Aggregate Profitability Really Matter?', *Cambridge Journal of Economics* 21 (1997), pp. 593–619.

Table 2: French 'acquis sociaux' – Welfare and Employment Rights,
1966–80[30]

	Welfare Rights	*Employment Rights*
1966		Recognition of five nationally 'representative' union confederations
1967	Redundancy payments scheme National Employment Agency (*ANPE*)	Minimum working age raised from 14 to 16
1968		Legalization of workplace union organization Union workplace delegates introduced
1969		Four weeks' paid annual holiday
1970		National Minimum Wage SMIC (partly indexed to wages) replaces SMIG
1971		Monthly Pay law Continuing Skill Training law with 0.5% apprenticeship tax
1972		Equal Pay law
1973		Bankruptcy wages guaranteed Dismissals only for real and serious fault
1974	Start of school-year allowance paid to parents	
1975	Realistic guaranteed minimum old age pension Disability benefit	Labour inspector authorization necessary for redundancies
1976	Single parent benefit	
1977	Housing benefits	Law requiring large firms to include social audit in their annual reports
1980	Minimum family income (for 3-child families)	

In 1981 the Socialist Party's François Mitterrand was elected President on a strong social-democratic reform programme which included nationalizing most of France's remaining privately owned banks. Two years later, however, he presided over a major political and economic U-turn. The

30   Source: Jefferys, *Liberté, Egalité and Fraternité at Work*, Table 3.4.

Communist Party left the government and Mitterrand adopted many of the tenets of neoliberalism.

From 1985, in both countries a long process of working-class retreat set in.[31] There was a renewed ascendancy of widespread inequality – both of income and of control at work. Capitalists and their neoliberal political allies initiated privatization policies. In the institutionalized employment relations systems in both countries, industrial relations and personnel officers began to be phased out, and direct negotiating between worker representatives and line managers increasingly gave way to the newly dominant rhetoric of 'human resource management'.

Eric Batstone's capture of French workplace dynamics in the late 1970s is original and valuable for an understanding of both the French and the British contexts at the time. But I would suggest, finally, that the term he used to describe the conflictual interface between French workers and employers and its resulting outcomes as *arm's-length bargaining* is only partly accurate. The image, for me at least, of *arms'-length bargaining* – wherever the apostrophe goes – is of bargaining that is taking place *somewhere else* – removed from the workplace. Or of bargaining being conducted by *people other* than the workers themselves. What Batstone describes so brilliantly here is not that. Instead it is what I would prefer to call 'nose to nose' bargaining. It is bargaining that has not been institutionalized or entirely ritualized. It is conflict and conflict resolution in the raw. Conflict where it is not at all certain in advance that one side or the other will move towards the other's position. Conflict that was – and in many areas of France remains today – a form of struggle and mobilization that can still take a much wider range of forms, including direct action.[32]

London Metropolitan University
Holloway Road
London N7 8DB

31 There was one major difference between the subsequent retreats in the two countries. The absence of a single major defeat for French workers on a similar scale, and with similar repercussions to that of the British miners, enabled working-class and union resistance to survive and even to generate a new French strike wave between 1995 and 2004. See S. Jefferys, 'A "Copernican Revolution" in French Industrial Relations: Are the Times a' Changing?', *British Journal of Industrial Relations* 38:2 (2000), pp. 241–60; *idem*, 'Rebel France: Defending Republican Values', *French Politics* 1:3 (2003), pp. 355–68; *idem*, 'The Next French Upsurge?', *Labor History* 45:3 (2004), pp. 333–41.
32 S. Contrepois, 'Labour Struggles against Mass Redundancies in France: Understanding Direct Action', *Employee Relations* 33:6 (2012), pp. 642–53.

HSIR 36 (2015) 73–136

doi:10.3828/hsir.2015.36.4

Arms'-Length Bargaining: Industrial Relations in a French Company

Eric Batstone

A review of the French literature on industrial relations demonstrates marked contrasts to the English literature.[1] In addition to a variety of studies of specific and substantive issues such as redundancy or job classification, two types of study are particularly common. The first is the study of strikes, and the second concerns the motivation of militants or trade-union activists. The discussion of collective bargaining tends therefore to be seen as a subsidiary feature of strike action or merely one element of the activity of militants.

In one sense the concentration of work is a fairly accurate reflection of the actual situation in France, where collective bargaining as understood by the Anglo-Saxons is indeed rare, particularly at plant level. On the other hand, this concentration of work upon the key distinguishing features of French industrial relations makes it somewhat difficult to understand French industrial relations at plant level in more conventional and less dramatic situations. For, despite the emphasis upon strike action, it has to be remembered that the frequency and scale of strikes in France are significantly lower than in Britain during this decade. The focus upon the

---

The paper, dated May 1978, was left unrevised by Eric Batstone (1944–87). Thanks to the copyright holder, Duncan Ledger, for permission to publish it. It has been copy-edited to clarify the argument and to conform to the house style. Thanks to Steve Jefferys for help with the footnotes.

1 For discussion in English of the French unions and system of industrial relations see Commission on Industrial Relations, *Worker Participation and Collective Bargaining in Europe* (HMSO: 1974); W. Kendall, *The Labour Movement in Europe* (Allen Lane: 1975); J.-D. Reynaud, 'France: Elitist Society Inhibits Articulated Bargaining', in S. Barkin (ed.), *Worker Militancy and its Consequences* (Praeger, New York: 1975); Y. Delamotte, 'France', in International Labour Organisation, *Collective Bargaining in Industrialised Market Economies* (ILO, Geneva: 1974).

mobilization aspects of French industrial relations would therefore appear to miss the crucial features of the situation, even though such work may accurately reflect the key driving force behind developments in France.

Moreover, it can be argued that it is only by investigating the broad pattern of industrial relations in France that the impact of worker and union mobilization can be fully understood. Certainly many strike studies, notably those undertaken at the *Groupe de sociologie du travail*, do touch upon this issue. But it might be suggested that much of this work, given its primary focus, provides only a limited picture of day-to-day industrial relations.

This paper seeks to understand the broader pattern of industrial relations in two French plants and, where possible, to assess the typicality of the findings. It focuses upon what will be termed "arms'-length bargaining", by which is meant that at plant level, bargaining in terms of negotiations around a table, in other words, of an institutionalized form, is of limited significance. Nevertheless, the two parties have a considerable impact upon each other; that is pressures are imposed at the workplace rather than at the bargaining table. In such a situation, the crucial factor from the union point of view is to prove to management that the demands put forward are strongly felt by the workforce. It is in this respect that the strike and other forms of collective action assume particular importance. Arms'-length bargaining therefore involves two crucial types of strategy for both employers and the unions: the first is issue-specific, while the second seeks to influence the broader background conditions in one's own favour.

The concept of arms'-length bargaining therefore seeks to integrate the traditional emphasis upon strike mobilization into a more general plant context. At the same time it permits recognition of the role of other features of French industrial relations, notably the *comité d'entreprise* and the *délégués du personnel*. Similarly, it raises the question of why bargaining should assume an arms'-length nature. It will be argued that this is primarily a reflection of employers' attempts to minimize the role of the union and to defend a more autonomous if not paternalist relationship with the workforce.

The empirical research on which this paper is based was undertaken in 1977 and 1978 in two plants belonging to a foreign multi-national engineering company. Both employed between 2,500 and 3,000 workers; one – plant A – was located in a traditional industrial area, and was, in French terms, heavily unionized. The second, plant B, in which rather less research was undertaken, was located in a predominantly rural rea and was less strongly organized. Data was obtained through interviews with militants and the study of documentary sources, although in addition the personnel director was interviewed. The final refusal of the company to co-operate in the research – on the grounds that the unions would 'exploit' the findings – prevented observation in the plant and any further interviews with management. The study focused upon the *Confédération générale du travail* (*CGT*) and the *Confédération française démocratique du travail* (*CFDT*) as these were the dominant unions, and were of particular interest given their commitment to 'the class struggle'.

Before proceeding to the main argument of this paper, one other point should be made. The data obtained had to be treated with a good deal of caution because of the perspectives employed by the militants. As someone who had undertaken similar research in England, it was inevitable that the English situation became a point of comparison. But comparisons based on interview data were particularly difficult given the very different orientations of French militants and British shop stewards, and the very considerable distinction between institutional and real influence on the part of the unions. In an attempt to reduce these problems, I have only used interview data for this paper which is supported by two or more separate sources, preferably of a documentary kind (that is, in the terms beloved by methodologists, I have sought to use the technique of triangulation).

The structure of this paper is as follows. A first section looks at the formal sources of conditions within the workplace and the role of union–management meetings, the *comité d'entreprise* and the *délégués du personnel*. In institutional terms the various types of contact between management and worker representatives appear to be of limited significance, and yet militants claim that they have considerable influence over the situation of the worker in the plant. Such influence is derived primarily from strike action and the informal relations of *délégués,* which derive from the ever-present possibility of strike action. This, then, is the situation where arms'-length bargaining exists.

A second section looks at the strategies of management, both in terms of their issue-specific endeavours and in terms of their attempts to influence the attitudes and behaviour of the workforce. This leads to a discussion of the reasons underlying managements' attempts to minimize the apparent impact of the union. In the third section, attention is turned to unions' strategies and the extent to which they are able to mobilize the workforce.

While arms'-length bargaining is the dominant pattern in the plant, in certain situations informal bargaining and direct mutual accommodation occurs. This is most clearly the case with certain foremen, and in the fourth section a consideration of the role of first-line supervision seeks to trace this process of accommodation. The final section of the paper looks more generally at the nature of arms'-length bargaining and compares it to the pattern of collective bargaining typical of Britain.

The formal structure of management–worker relations and its significance

A convenient starting point for a consideration of the nature of arms'-length bargaining is to look at the formal sources of the major terms and conditions of employment in the plant. As far as the author is aware, no complete list of these is available but in plant A the *CFDT* produces annually a list of the major terms and conditions of employment. From this document it is possible to learn the formal source of rules and decisions relating to forty-three key areas. 49% of these derive from formally unilateral decisions by management, 30% from national or regional agreements, and the remainder (21%) from the law. None of those listed originate from formal plant or company agreements. This somewhat exaggerates the picture for there have been one or two enterprise agreements, by far the most important of which concerns the guaranteed week in the event of lay-off. Nevertheless, the dominant picture is one of an extremely limited role for plant or company bargaining.

This pattern seems to be fairly typical of France more generally. Since 1968 the state and revamped employers' associations have attempted to bring new life to industrial relations and collective bargaining. As a consequence, while between 1958 and 1968 there were only about twenty laws and national agreements, there were almost five times as many in the next decade.[2] But below this level such initiatives have met with opposition from employers, particularly in metalworking.[3] As a consequence, company- and plant-level agreements are still of limited significance. Hence, in a study of fifty companies published in 1974, Bachy, Dupuy and Martin found that only about a quarter of them had agreements covering a wide range of issues, although over half had, like the company studied here, some form of agreement on some issues.[4] A more recent study of a larger sample in the Rhône-Alpes region concluded that 'negotiation in the companies is not more lively or frequent. From 1973 to 1975, only 30% of the companies and establishment in our sample had concluded at least one agreement with the workers' representatives.'[5]

Unilateral decisions by management are therefore the general rule rather than the exception in France. Bachy *et al.*'s study investigated how decisions were made in a large number of areas covering the general

2 P. Dubois, *Travail et conflit dans l'industrie*, Thése de doctorat d'état es-lettres Université Paris VII, Sociologie (1978).
3 J. Bunel and J. Saglio, 'La Faiblesse de la négociation collective et le Pouvoir patronal', *Sociologie du Travail (SdT)* 4/77 (1977), pp. 383–401, p. 385.
4 J.-P. Bachy, F. Dupuy and D. Martin, *Représentation et Négociation dans l'Entreprise* (CRESST, Université de Paris-Sud: 1974).
5 Bunel and Saglio, 'La Faiblesse de la négociation collective', *SdT*, p. 389.

management of the company, the organization, and conditions of work and personnel management. Overall, they found that only 14% of issues involved negotiation, whether or not there was any formal agreement. Unilateral decisions by management were therefore typical, and in half of these there was no consultation with, or information given to, workers' representatives. No negotiation at all occurred in the area of the general running of the company; it occurred overall in only 16% of issues relating to personnel management and in only 12% of those relating to the organization and conditions of work.[6]

Nevertheless while agreements at plant level may be rare, there are meetings between management and the unions, or other workers' representatives. Hence, in nearly two-thirds of the cases where no formal agreements had been signed, Bachy *et al.* found that informal negotiations occurred and the same was true in about half the companies where agreements relating only to one or a few specific topics had been signed.[7] The outcomes of such meetings may sometimes lead to informal agreements,[8] but more often to unilateral management decisions.[9]

In the company studied, meetings do occur between management and the unions. Perhaps the most significant of these is an annual meeting at company level concerned with general wages and conditions. Prior to this meeting the unions present a set of demands. The main elements of this in the last year concerned an increase in wages to keep pace with the standard of living; a common status for all workers; shorter working hours in terms of a reduced working week of forty hours, a fifth week's holiday, and retirement at sixty; and a guarantee of income and employment. Prior to the meeting, management has also established its policy. The nature of the meetings can be illustrated from the statements of the personnel director, a full-time official, and a key militant, all of whom attended these meetings for a number of years.

Personnel director:

> National negotiations are brief: it is simply a case of the unions presenting their demands and then I have to try to work out which are the most important. Then I just tell them what the company is prepared to do, and that's that.

---

6 Bachy *et al.*, *Représentation et Négociation dans l'Entreprise*, pp. 307, 315.

7 *Ibid.*, pp. 201ff.

8 J.-D. Reynaud, *Les Syndicats en France, Vol. 1* (Editions du Seuil Reynaud, Paris: 1975), p. 195.

9 Bachy *et al.*, *Représentation et Négociation dans l'Entreprise*, p. 179.

Full-time official:

> It's simply a case of the unions tabling their demands and management reacting.
> There is no negotiation. Management simply say 'yes' or 'no', and the only other
> thing is the possibility of a strike. The whole thing generally takes less than
> three hours.

Militant:

> In the meeting we in the union will face the general management and they will
> put to us their wage policy for the next year … management reveals its plans for
> wages and afterwards we talk for a few hours, they do not move and that's it. It
> is what goes by the grand name of *concertation*[10] because they have indicated
> their intentions and they have discussed them. But even if they did not hold the
> discussion, things would have been exactly the same … They are not negoti-
> ations because often they don't take any notice of us at all … in the discussions
> management never deals immediately with things raised by the unions … they
> have never given satisfaction even if there's a strike.

At plant level, other meetings are held between management and the
unions. For example, there is an agreement that a meeting will be held each
quarter to discuss the wages of skilled workers in the context of the industry
agreement on grading. But, according to the union tracts, management
not only appear to refuse almost systematically to concede points relating
to relatively minor aspects of the grading structure, but even to meet the
unions in accordance with the agreement.

Regular meetings between management and worker representatives (all
of whom are trade-unionists in the plants studied) are more common in the
legally backed *comité d'entreprise* and the role of *délégués du personnel*.
Each of these will be considered briefly.

It is not the intention here to discuss in detail the legal requirements
relating to the *comité d'entreprise*; this information is easily available
elsewhere.[11] In broad terms, the *comité* operates at two levels in a
multi-plant company – the plant and the company level – and its role can
also be divided into two areas. In the 'social' area, such as canteens, sport,
and leisure pursuits, the *comité*, and hence in effect the workers' representatives, can run affairs themselves subject to the limits of the financial

---

10 Ed.'s note: *Concertation* may be understood as a process of debate that does not
   end in an agreement or opinion, which gives an opportunity for an exchange of
   views.
11 Ed.'s. note: For a contemporary view see http://www.eurofound.europa.eu/
   observatories/eurwork/comparative-information/national-contributions/
   france/france-industrial-relations-profile.

contributions of the company. In the social area in plant A, a large number of workers (not necessarily trade-union members) were engaged – mainly in their own time – in a variety of sub-committees concerned with a wide range of activities. The main issues arising from the social area which led to discussions with management within the *comité d'entreprise* concerned attempts to persuade management to increase its financial contribution. Management systematically refused to do so but did on occasion agree to provide some additional finance for specific tasks.

Of greater relevance to the present discussion was the *comité*'s role in the 'economic' area, this including matters such as training, and health and safety, for which a variety of sub-committees existed. The *comité* has only a consultative role in respect of these economic issues and, with the exception of health and safety where the worker representatives could resort to relatively specific legal regulations, the militants thought that the *comité*'s role was of very limited significance. In answer to a question asking how workers and the unions were able to achieve influence over five areas – wages, the pace and organization of work, job grading, discipline, and working conditions – only 12% of militants' references were to the *comité*.

According to the law, management is required to consult workers' representatives and provide them with a range of data concerning the enterprise. In practice, management limits this to the legal minimum, and, despite repeated requests, has consistently refused, for example, to inform the workers' representatives of the state of the order book. The typical meeting therefore involved management listing data on levels of employment, turnover, absenteeism, and monthly production programmes, and providing scarcely any information on longer-term plans and problems. For example, on one occasion the unions sought information concerning company proposals to shift production of one product to another country on the grounds that this could have serious implications for employment, but the company refused. One militant summed up the economic role of the *comité* in the following terms:

> The information we get is defined by the law, and the company keeps strictly to this. For example, they refuse to provide data on the breakdown of wages by different groups ... they refused to give information on the shift of production ... Management follows the letter (and not the spirit of the law), but as it is interpreted by the employers' association – and so it is a very restricted interpretation.

As a consequence, 'the real situation remains unknown to us' and, in their view, the requirement of consultation 'is seen by management simply as a formality to be fulfilled'. Another militant stated:

> nothing changes and co-operation is a one-way thing despite management's grand statements ... there are two languages: at the board of directors there are

no anxieties, investment continues and so on ... but at the *comité d'entreprise* management regularly pick up the violin to play us the same music [about a lack of profits;] they have been for years!

The limited economic role of the *comité d'entreprise* appears to be common in France. A recent study by Beauviala argues on the basis of interviews with militants that, 'In effect the impression which comes from their statements is a very nearly general opposition of managers in the company to the very idea of consultation.'[12] Weiss similarly argues that the information received is fairly limited and is confined generally to that required by law.[13] In plant A the militant's view of the significance of the *comité*'s economic role can be seen from three indicators. First, less than two-thirds of those eligible to attend on average do so. Second, it has only recently been the case that the unions have decided to demand the establishment of an economic sub-committee, and this has been done only because of the insistence of one militant.

The third indication of the worker representatives' disillusion with the *comité d'enterprise* is the sort of issue they raise outside the social area. Only about 10% of their questions and statements relate to the economic position and policy of the company, and a similar number concern queries relating to the employment position. Matters relating to training, safety, and the social area assume far greater significance.

Beyond largely parochial issues or matters which have only an indirect relevance to the mainstream of production and the work situation, the main role of the *comité d'entreprise* is the provision of a platform where management and unions can declare their broader philosophies and positions with minimal impact upon the actual course of events within the company. In general terms the company seeks every opportunity to prove its sense of responsibility and concern for the welfare of workers by directing investment into the plant in order to maintain employment. The unions reply that the sole reason for investment is profit and that, if management were really so concerned with worker welfare, it would be investing money in order to improve amenities and conditions in the plant. Similarly, in a discussion of training, the unions criticized management for

> devoting nearly the whole of the training budget to training proposed by the employer, while from the beginning the agreements and the law on continuous training envisaged as much, if not more, the opportunity for everyone to choose some courses from outside the framework of the company and the employer ...

12 C. Beauviala, *L'Opinion des délégués sur l'Information et l'Intervention des comités d'entreprise* (Université des Sciences sociales de Grenoble: 1975), p. 33.

13 D. Weiss, *Les Relations du travail* (Dunod, Paris: 1975), pp. 125ff.

the major part of the courses are in the interests of the company while, on the other hand, the training provides no improvement in the skill level for already some qualified workers are and remain under-qualified in the company ... 50% of managers, over half of whom are of a senior level, have received training compared to only 11.5% of unskilled workers, 9.3% of skilled workers and 13.4% of technicians and supervisors.

Denying any bias in the training programme, management emphasized the importance of improving its skills in order to improve the situation of everyone in the context of fierce competition. The debate had no impact upon the actual training programme, but once more management and unions had put forward their conflicting orientations.

The second legally backed form of contact between management and worker representatives is the *délégués du personnel*. Their role, according to the law, is to present to the employer all individual or collective grievances which have not been directly satisfied in relation to applying rates of pay and job gradings of the Labour Code and other laws and regulations, relating to the protection of the worker, health, safety, and social provisions! They may also have to resort to the Labour Inspector. The role of the *délégué*, then, relates primarily to relatively parochial grievances and problems. One militant compared the role of *délégués du personnel* and the *comité d'enterprise*:

> Management try to get the *délégués* tied up in little questions. One may sometimes tend to get caught in that trap. A few workers have a little problem, you try to sort it out and the manager rejects the grievance. But on the big questions on the *comité d'entreprise* the committee has no power and one can only put forward views ... The *délégués du personnel* are occupied in trifles where management can say yes when things don't cost them much; and on other thing, the big questions of the future ... which apply to the whole works ... one does talk to them at the *comité d'entreprise*, but one needs to talk to them in a less abstract way. The management says, 'yes, there is a possibility of this or that', and so on, but never anything specific.

Certainly a major part of the time of the *comité d'entreprise* appears to be taken up with minor issues such as errors in pay, and rather more significantly, matters relating to safety and conditions. If these cannot be resolved at lower levels of the management hierarchy, then they are raised at a monthly meeting with management as laid down in the law. From the minutes of these meetings over a year, it is possible to gain an idea of the sorts of issues which *délégués* raise with management and the way in which they are dealt with. Over a third of issues concern safety and conditions, while wage issues (generally relating to individuals or small groups), work organization, and social facilities each account for about one-fifth of issues raised. In the main, then, the activities of the *délégués* largely conform – at least in terms of grievances raised at the monthly meeting – to their role as envisaged in law. Their role, while possibly important in terms of the day-to-day lives of workers, cannot be seen as one which involves the negotiation of major issues and problems.

Nevertheless, the minutes of these meetings between management and *délégués* indicate that the former still adopt the strategy of arms'-length bargaining. An analysis of about three hundred issues indicates the management clearly accepted the demands of the *délégués* in only a minority of the cases. The two most common management replies to grievances were to question the accuracy of the claim or to argue that the proposed solution was technically impossible (30% of issues). In 22% of cases, grievances received an outright rejection, whereas in only 12% of cases did management accept the legitimacy of the grievance and agree to act upon it. In overall terms, it might be said that management acted upon almost half of the grievances raised. Whether this is seen as a reasonable rate of action is a matter of debate; it certainly does not seem especially high given the minor and moderate nature of the great majority of the demands. What is far more significant is the way in which, in three-quarters of the grievances that the management accept as inherently legitimate, it appears to seek to deny the role of the *délégué* by saying that the matter is already being dealt with. This is particularly significant in view of the fact that first, prior to being presented at the monthly meeting, the grievance will have been pursued by the *délégué* at a variety of levels of management where the issue might have been resolved; and, second, that the law requires that answers to *délégués*' grievances at the meeting should be in written form and hence publically available to the workforce. The procedure of the monthly meeting of *délégués* can be seen as facilitating this managerial strategy, for the *délégués* have to present their grievances in writing prior to the meeting. It is therefore possible for management to instigate studies or some other course of action prior to the meeting and then at the meeting imply that many of the grievances raised by the *délégués* are superfluous.

This review of the unions' institutions within the workplace suggests that negotiation with the unions is of very limited significance, at least in terms of leading to agreement on specific issues. Management seeks formally to maintain its autonomy and freedom to manoeuvre. Moreover, within the 'economic' area, it seems that management strictly limits the role of the *comité d'entreprise* despite its formally consultative nature. Finally, while the *délégués* appear to play a significant role on minor issues, it appears that even here management is loathe to recognize publicly its influence and importance. It is not surprising, therefore, that – in formal terms – the role of plant- or company-level negotiations and discussions appears to be minimal in terms of establishing the pattern of rules and rewards within the workplace, as was shown at the beginning of this section.

Similarly, the militants are very critical of the role that they are formally permitted to play by management, and evidence to this effect has been cited in this section.[14] Nevertheless, the same militants believe that in practice they do have a significant degree of influence. Nearly two-thirds of those questioned thought they had 'a great deal' of influence over wages and over the organization and speed of work, and even more thought they had a 'great deal' of influence over the conditions of work. In relation to the question of job grading, militants were less confident of their influence but, even so, over half of them thought they had 'a fair amount' of influence. Just under half thought they had a great deal of influence over disciplinary matters. Tracts which are sometimes distributed – for example, at the end of the year or just before the summer holidays – and which seek to assess the state of play to date, similarly claim a significant, although insufficient, degree of influence and success over such matters as safety and wages.

The contrast between the limited gains formally won from the institutions in which management and workers meet, and the claimed success of the unions, suggests that the most effective means of pursuing grievances lie outside the formal institutions. This certainly appears to be the view of the militants. When asked how they achieved their influence in the five areas above no reference was made to formal management–union meetings, and, as has already been noted, only 12% of references were to the *comité d'entreprise* (a figure almost as low as for individual action on the part of workers). 40% of references were to strike action and other forms of collective sanction, and 38% to the role of the *délégués du personnel*. However, it seems probable that the perceived influence of the *délégué* derives less from his formal position than from his close involvement with shop-floor problems, where threats of possible sanctions can often be effectively imposed upon lower levels of management. Certainly in discussing specific problems, militants made frequent reference to their use of this threat with foremen. It would therefore appear that the militants are firmly convinced of the efficacy of *rapports de force*. It is this situation of the limited significance of formal institutions and the determining role of unmuted power relationships that is the essence of what I have termed arms'-length bargaining. In order to understand this method of conducting industrial relations, consideration is now turned to management strategy.

---

14 For similar findings, see D. Gallie, *In Search of the New Working Class* (Cambridge University Press: 1977).

Management strategy

A distinction was previously made between the issue-specific strategies of management and its strategies oriented towards influencing the position of the union more generally. Each of these will be considered in turn.

Issue-specific strategies

Management in the company studied was clearly aware of the importance of the *rapports de force*. In order to assess whether, and, if so, how far, concessions should be made to union demands, consideration had to be paid to the economic position of the enterprise on the one hand, and the extent to which workers backed union demands on the other. Management's position was also facilitated if it was possible to predict the demands which the unions were likely to make. As the personnel director explained:

> I have to look beyond the interlocutors to what the workers really think and feel, and it is their wishes that I to try to accommodate. At the same time, it's extremely important for me to understand the political situation and so be able to predict the sorts of demands which the unions are likely to put up. Then I have to assess whether the workers are ready to back the unions' demands.

The assessment of union demands and workers' support for them requires that the personnel director has a relatively sophisticated network of contacts and sources of information. Such contacts are of a variety of kinds: political, with other employers, with union officials, and within the plants themselves. Through its board of directors the company has close links with key members of the government and with a variety of employers' bodies in the industry. In particular, the personnel director is an important member of the *Union des industries métallurgiques et minières (UIMM)*, the employers' association in the 'metalworking' industry. Not only does this mean that his position requires him to recognize the various agreements reached above company level between the employers and the unions, but also that he is in a position to see and better comprehend the pattern of union pressures within the industry.

In addition, through his active involvement in the employers' association, the personnel director sits on a variety of joint management–union committees, such as those concerned with the payment of various social benefits. Through these meetings he has built up relatively close contacts with a number of union officials. These contacts appear to have a double significance. First, in discussions before and after them he gains a greater understanding of the thinking of the unions. Hence when discussion turns to political issues, he is able to identify possible changes in the strategies of the unions. Second, it seems that, particularly due to the divisions between the unions, some officials – those belonging to the 'reformist' unions – are prepared to give him 'tips' and discuss the situation within the plants. For example, during a lengthy strike one official informed the personnel director of his opposition to the strike and his assessment of workers' attitudes. This information had been a significant consideration in the strategy subsequently employed to defeat the strike.

In the main, the patterns of contacts outside the company assume significance primarily by adding to more readily available information concerning the general strategy of the unions. The personnel director's network of contacts within the plant are oriented much more towards understanding – and forewarning about – the workers' strength of feeling and the activities of militants. To this end he maintained a close liaison with management in the plants; hence, for example, militants frequently referred to the plant personnel manager as simply 'a listening post' or a 'post-box', transmitting information from the militants to company level. The personnel director's contacts are not, however, confined to the personnel function. As he explained, 'I have to maintain a close liaison with the foremen in the plants who can keep me up to date on workers' feelings'. In addition, in plant B the militants claim that security personnel are used to keep a close check upon the activities and contacts of the militants.[15]

The foremen are not merely used as a warning device, but are also encouraged to adopt a more active role. Attempts to individualize their relations with workers will be discussed below. But in addition to this ongoing endeavour, during a lengthy strike in plant B the foremen were sent to workers' homes to persuade them individually to return to work, pointing out that the strike was politically motivated and that, despite the fact that no work could be done, non-strikers would be paid at their normal rates.[16]

In strikes the company has adopted a number of strategies. For example, in a recent strike in plant B the workers occupied the factory. The company went to the law and had the riot police expel the strikers. After the strike, a number of militants were sacked and the legitimacy of this action was finally accepted by the authorities. After a particularly lengthy strike in plant A the company tried to persuade workers to sign a petition stating that they no longer wanted *délégués* in the plant. More generally, given that rarely do all workers engage in a strike, the company seeks to divide the workforce. As a militant explained, this has led the unions to drop the use of pickets:

---

15 Such a practice appears to be quite common in France; see, for example, H. Rollin, *Militant chez Simca-Chrysler* (Éditions Sociales, Paris: 1977).

16 C. Durand and P. Dubois, *La Grève* (Armand-Colin, Paris: 1975), p. 21.

> We used to have strike pickets for years and years who stopped workers entering the plant ... But now where there is a strike the *délégués* come to the plant gates but do not prevent people from entering; they explain to their comrades that it is in their interests to show solidarity and not go in. This is because we have learnt that management, as soon as there is a strike, exploit the situation and turn the men inside the plant against those who are outside.

Such strategies are commonly employed in France. In their study of 123 strikes, Durand and Dubois found that aid to the non-strikers and mobilization of the forces of law were common. In 14% of cases, strikers were physically expelled from the plant, in 16% of cases some of the strikers were sacked, and in 11% physical force was used against them.[17] More generally, a study of medium-sized firms commissioned by a management journal found that a third of them had sacked at least one worker representative protected by the law in the last three years.[18]

Whether or not strikes occur, management in the company has rarely made any clear concessions to the unions in a manner that might be expected in a bargaining situation. Often, prior to meetings with the unions, management has determined its position (partly on the basis of assessments of workers' attitudes derived from its networks) and does not move from this position. If management does decide to make some concessions it does so only after some delay. The refusal to concede immediately can be seen as a further means of seeking to reduce the apparent influence of the unions. As a militant explained: 'In the discussions, management never deals immediately with matters raised by the unions. They have never given satisfaction immediately if there's a strike. But we have the fruits of our movement a few months later.' Again, it seems that such managerial strategies are common. Durand and Dubois found that few employers were ready to negotiate given a strike, and that such a tendency became stronger as the duration of the strike increased.[19]

While management may adopt a variety of strategies in relation to specific sets of demands, these are only likely to achieve their ends if they are based upon a more general pattern of managerial behaviour in the company. This is the subject to which the discussion now turns.

Management attempts to mobilize bias

Much of managerial strategy can be seen as being oriented towards discouraging the role of the union and fostering the individual commitment of workers. In these respects it would appear that the room for manoeuvre

---

17 *Ibid.*
18 *L'Expansion* (1976), p. 120.
19 Durand and Dubois, *La Grève*, p. 204.

of the case-study company was rather less than that found in many others, if only because of the relative strength of the unions. Hence, the company had to accept some role for the unions whereas, according to Bachy *et al.*, employers have sought, where weak unions permit, to foster the role of the *comité d'entreprise* and the *délégués du personnel* since the trade-union section gained legal recognition in the plant in 1968.[20] Similarly, while some French companies have keenly pursued ideas of autonomous work groups and participative styles of management, the company has not done so. This approach, which has been termed by some French authors 'neo-paternalist', is to be found primarily in the professional services sector and those industries where technical knowledge is important. But two points are worthy of note in relation to this management style. First, it is associated with a greater tendency to sack workers and to make the position of the unions and militants difficult. Second, it seems that such approaches tend to disappear in the face of industrial conflicts, particularly under conditions of economic crisis. Accordingly, the role of various 'left' employer groups has tended to decline in recent years.[21]

Within the case-study company the broad strategies adopted to limit the role of the unions, particularly the *CGT* and the *CFDT*, can be seen as focusing upon their institutional position, the role of their militants, and a fostering of individualism among workers. Each of these three strategies will be considered in turn.

In the past the company has on occasion attempted to change the pattern of representation on the *comité d'entreprise* at plant A. Representation is stratified by occupational level, and the company has – unsuccessfully, thanks to the intervention of the Labour Inspector – sought to increase the number of seats held by management representatives belonging to moderate or reformist unions. In plant B such a problem does not arise, for managers themselves hold control of the *comité* between a balance of the *CGT* on the one side and the *Confédération française des travailleurs chrétiens* (*CFTC*) and *Confédération générale des cadres* (*CGC*) on the other. This means that they can ensure that the *CGT* does not control the secretaryship of the committee. This post is of importance because it frequently requires a good deal of time off and can be an important forum in terms of relations with workers through the various social activities of the *comité*. In addition, because of this balance of power the company has been able to prevent

20 See also G. Adam and M. Lucas, 'Les Institutions de représentation du personnel en France: Bilan et Perspectives', *Droit Social* 3 (1976), p. 82; and D. Martin, 'Les Systèmes de négociation et de représentation dans l'entreprise', *Droit Social* 3 (1976), p. 93.
21 For a fuller discussion of these themes, see P. Bourdieu and M. de Saint-Martin, 'Le Patronat', *Actes de la recherche en sciences sociales* 20/21 (1978), esp. pp. 66ff.

workers' representatives taking over the social affairs of the company in plant B.

The company has a variety of smaller, largely servicing, plants throughout France and also a large head office separate from the major production sites studied. As a consequence, there is a fairly high proportion of white-collar and managerial staff in the company. This, and the importance of *CFTC* at plant B, means that the 'unions of class struggle' are unable to obtain a majority on the central *comité d'entreprise*, and accordingly the personnel director's casting vote is the determining factor.

Crucial to this power of management in the *comités* is the ability of the *CFTC* in plant B to win a number of seats in the elections for shop-floor and clerical representatives. Formerly *Force ouvrière* (*FO*) had been involved in the plant but appears to have disappeared due to lack of workers' support, only to be replaced by the *CFTC*. According to the *CGT*, the company actively supports the *CFTC*, not only by ensuring that it has the key post of the secretary of the *comité d'entreprise*, but also permitting its militants greater freedom in terms of taking time off and by conceding more readily to its demands, even when these are identical to those of the *CGT*. Clearly, however, the *CFTC* is still a union and has on a number of occasions sponsored strike action or demands jointly with the *CGT*. Nevertheless from the company's viewpoint it is an easier organization with which to deal, because it adopts a more moderate political approach and because management can often expect its support in a number of issues. So, for example, when, in accordance with the law, the company brings to the *comité d'entreprise* its intention to sack *CGT* militants in legally protected positions, members of the *CFTC* have voted in support of the company's proposal. Again, management encouragement of reformist, if not 'house', unions appears quite common in France. According to the *CGT*, a number of companies have been actively involved in setting up and running the *Confédération des syndicats libres* (*CSL*) (formerly the *Confédération française du travail* – *CFT*), which has been used to check militancy in an aggressive manner.[22]

It has already been noted that the company treats *CFTC* militants somewhat less formally than those of the *CGT* in plant B. In plant A the situation is somewhat different on the shop floor, largely, in the words of a *CGT* militant, 'because we are a force to be reckoned with'. Nevertheless, on occasion, for example after strikes, and particularly in relation to more '*gauchiste*' representatives, management does keep a strict control to ensure that it does not pay them for more than the legally specified amount

---

22 M. Caille, *Les Truands du Patronat* (Éditions Sociales, Paris: 1977); *idem, L'Assassin était chez Citroen* (Éditions Sociales, Paris: 1978); Rollin, *Militant chez Simca-Chrysler*.

of time off. Hence, one *CGT* tract argued that with the arrival of a new works manager the company was adopting a new, 'tough' line. Among many others, one example was that, 'Suddenly one morning [a manager] called in a *délégué*, and in the afternoon [three other] *délégués*, and told them to keep within their permitted time off in future. There was also to be a limitation of their time off for training. For fifteen years this has not been limited.' Nor, as the law permits, has the company formally agreed to permit a greater number of hours off than the minimum laid down in the legislation. The representatives therefore accept as a matter of course that, despite the *CGT* partly making up lost earnings, they will lose money through their activities.

In plant B the control over *CGT* representatives with time off is even stricter. It has already been noted that their activities are noted by security personnel and that their time off is more systematically controlled and checked. In addition, they are required to obtain passes to move from the area in which they work to other parts of the plant. This can be seen as particularly obstructive since such representatives are elected not to represent particular departments but the whole of the workforce within a particular grade. Further, since until recently a few militants at plant B tended to hold between them the great bulk of representative positions, such constraints on their freedom of movement were especially effective. In the same plant a final constraint upon the activity of militants is a work's rule which states that, during working hours, no more than three people are allowed to talk together.

More generally, militants claim that management discriminates against them in a variety of ways in relation to their work. It is frequently argued that 'to be a militant is to ruin your chances of promotion'. Management is also accused of discriminating against militants and those who display union sympathy or engage in strike action in terms of a whole range of issues, including the payment of various bonuses and the allocation of work. Even in the more strongly organized plant it is not uncommon to find tracts condemning the action of management in shifting a militant from one job to another. For example, a *CGT délégué* 'was off ill and when he returned to work after he had recovered, he was immediately shifted to another area'; and, 'a *délégué* … elected in May who had for years been working on days is suddenly told that he will be working shifts in another department'.

The activities of the militants are also obstructed in a variety of physical ways. Tracts and meetings of the *délégués du personnel* often record cases of union noticeboards being obstructed by stacks of components. Similarly, the company recently intended to move the union offices (which they are required to provide by law) to a more remote part of the plant. As a tract argued:

Management has decided to transfer the union offices ... despite our protests and alternative proposals. We say quite simply that this is with the sole aim of obstructing the union organizations, for with a little bit of common sense on the part of management, we would have been able to reach agreement on a suitable alternative location.

Finally, the way in which management itself is organized, and the way in which it arranges work and payment may also be seen – at least in part – as a means of influencing the position of the union.

In France, personnel specialists have traditionally been a somewhat rare breed and, where they did exist, they tended to be former military officers rather than persons trained in aspects of personnel or industrial relations. More recently this pattern has changed, with such posts becoming filled by technically trained people and, as indicated by their salaries, becoming more important.[23] However, it seems possible that this trend towards the increasing use of personnel specialists has ceased. A study of adverts for such posts indicates that the demand for personnel managers in France declined almost three times as rapidly as for management generally.[24]

The role of personnel management in the company studied is also of interest. The task of personnel director is to 'co-ordinate the management of the workforce and social relations' in the various establishments. The head office personnel staff, in addition to a section specifically concerned with head office staff, is divided into two functions. The first is concerned solely with management selection and training. The second is concerned with the administration of retirement and security funds. In other words, there is no specialization in an area comparable to industrial relations managers in Britain. The personnel director explained that, 'industrial relations as such, in terms of negotiations, take up virtually none of my time ... in France there is no overall framework ... so industrial relations are conducted very much on a day-to-day pattern with no overall direction'.

Moreover, the company has engaged in two broad types of strategy which also appear to be common in France. The first of these is the location of new plants in traditionally rural areas; this was the case with plant B. The attraction of this strategy is largely the availability of unskilled labour at lower rates of pay; but in addition, at least initially, the lack of strong union organization and strike action has a strong appeal.[25] The second strategy is one of strong centralization of the personnel function, even more so than

23 *Le Matin*, 18 avril 1978, 'Les Salaires des états-majors'; see also G. Benguigui, A. Griset, A. Jacob and D. Monjardet, *Recherche sur la Fonction d'encadrement*, Groupe de Sociologie du travail (CNRS, Paris: 1975), pp. 404ff.
24 *Le Matin*, 20 avril 1978, 'Les Cadres les plus recherchés en Europe'.
25 See S. Bosc, P. Dubois and C. Durand, *Décentralisation industrielle et Relations de travail* (La Documentation française, Paris: 1975).

with many other management functions. Indications of this have already been given, but it seems that, as in Britain, such a policy is adopted in the face of relatively strong union organization in an attempt to reduce the impact of fractional bargaining.[26] The success of such a strategy is, however, open to doubt both in Britain and in France (see below).

Centralization in France, however, appears to go considerably further than in Britain, with very clear status gaps between the various levels of the company, reflected often in academic background,[27] and in wage levels. For example, the ratio of median managers' salary and the median workers' wage (males) was, in 1972, 63% higher in France than in Britain.[28] As a comparative study of France and Germany showed, French firms are more stratified, hierarchical and centralized. Further, the administrative workforce is larger in France, and it appears that levels of supervision tend also to be higher.[29]

The organization of work and the system of payment can also be seen as oriented towards denying union influence and informed by a desire for an individualistic relationship with workers. The most obvious aspect of this is the unilateral nature of decisions. This is true not merely of wage increases but also of changes in work organization and required rates of output. Management implements its plans, and discussion only occurs if workers react against them, notably by striking. Moreover, if workers do have grievances they are encouraged to take them to their foremen rather than to the *délégués du personnel*, and conversely, foremen are encouraged to deal with these problems. The works' rules outline the formal procedure for pursuing grievances but the only reference to the *délégués* is that 'if the worker is unable to resolve the problem with management' he may go to the *délégué*.

Within the constraints laid down by the wider management structure, the foremen have a degree of discretion oriented towards encouraging workers' compliance. While piecework exists only in particular production areas in plant B, the ability of the foreman to pay make-up for such workers constitutes a significant form of control. In discussing the use of make-up, the payment of special bonuses and the reclassification of jobs, one militant

---

26 C. Morel, 'Physionomie statistique de grèves', *Révue française des Affaires sociales* 29:4 (1975), pp. 183–95.

27 See Bourdieu and Saint-Martin, 'Le Patronat', *Actes de la recherche en sciences sociales*.

28 Documents du Centre d'Étude des revenus et des coûts, *Dispersion et Disparitiés de salaires à l'Etranger*, 2930 (1976), p. 119.

29 See M. Maurice, 'L'Encadrement en France et en Allemagne', in C. Durand (ed.), *La Division du travail* (Éditions Galilée, Paris: 1978); E. W. Burgess, 'Management in France', in F. Harbison and C. A. Myers (eds), *Management in the Industrial World* (McGraw-Hill, New York: 1959); and Bachy *et al.*, *Représentation et Négociation dans l'Entreprise*, pp. 158ff.

explained that these could be less easily obtained if the workers were 'a good element workwise but are, unfortunately unionized, or are involved in a political party outside, or who often strike. Then one does not succeed [in claims], that's even if they're important workwise and are good workers.' Another militant explained, with reference to piecework areas:

> At the end of the day, the worker goes to his boss and says 'I've had bad jobs today, you must give me make-up'. If supervision is well satisfied, if he hasn't had to reprimand the worker, if the worker hasn't been running around ... if it is a question of a worker who does not strike too often, doesn't muck about, who is docile and works well, supervision will generally give him what he asks ... so there is a control which forces one to go begging to supervision. But this does stop work-study from trying to reduce the good bonus jobs down to the norm.

More generally, the system of payment consists of a wide range of bonuses which, in addition to those relating to shifts etc., contain an important element of individualism and paternalism. The level of wages is related to the number of years' service in the company, and this bonus can add up to 17% of workers' wage as defined by minimum regional rates. The paternalistic element can be seen in the continued existence, even at somewhat lower rates, of allowances for accommodation and travel, and holiday and Christmas bonuses. But the most significant element is the bonus for regular attendance, which can amount to about 5% of a worker's wage. This bonus was introduced after a lengthy strike and occupation of a plant in 1968 and has been the element of the pay packet which has increased most rapidly in the last decade. The condition of its payment is that workers, during a quarter, should be absent on less than three occasions. This bonus is seen by all the militants interviewed to be an anti-strike bonus, and as such it certainly appears to have been quite effective. Such payments appear to be relatively common in France, along with a variety of other 'merit' bonuses determined unilaterally by management.[30]

Finally, the very fact of giving unilateral concessions in such a way as to forestall union criticism and to provide wages and conditions at least comparable to the average in the area may be seen as a means of limiting workers' dissatisfaction. This, of course, is a basic strategy of the great majority of employers in all countries. And, in the case of plant A in particular, the company pays rates above the average.[31]

In this section a number of managerial strategies have been outlined which are oriented towards limiting the role of the unions, and in particular of those which are class-oriented. As Martin has pointed out, where employers do not engage in formal bargaining there is almost invariably a pattern

---

30 See Gallie, *In Search of the New Working Class*, pp. 64–6.
31 *Ibid.*, pp. 55ff.

of relationships defined by company paternalism and seeking to integrate workers. This involves an acceptance of trade-unionism only if it remains 'inoffensive'. The basis of employer power lies in the ability to impose a tacit contract of loyalty: in exchange for job security and a reasonable level of wages, workers do not pursue grievances through collective means. This system operates informally in small companies. But:

> The large companies which pursue a policy of selection on the basis of indicators of 'good spirit' pursue the same logic; to varying degrees, the refusal of dialogue, the climate of fear and the blackmail of dismissal aid the atmosphere of 'good co-operation'; the elected institutions reflect the same concept of the loyalty contract, the combination paternalism – authoritarianism varying to only a limited degree.[32]

The philosophy of management

> The employer, by his policy of equal negotiation, which he has undertaken for some years, and by the content of that policy, has proved that he recognizes the union as a partner not only outside, but also inside the plant.

This statement is taken from *Patronat*, the journal of the *Conseil national du patronat français* (*CNPF*),[33] and can be seen as part of the philosophy of the *CNPF*. More generally in recent years the *CNPF*, or least a number of its national officials, has sought to develop and promote an enlightened social philosophy. Its main themes, as reflected for example in its congresses and its journal, concern the importance of the enterprise and its technically competent management for the pursuit of the good of all by means of the creation of wealth and economic growth.

However, even this philosophy gives in practice only a very limited degree of access for the unions. Three pieces of evidence for this view can be taken from recent articles in *Patronat*. The first is that the quote at the head of this section comes from an article on the *comité d'entreprise* in which the author argues that the unions should cease to have a monopoly over nominations for the first round of elections (the aim being to make a clear division between co-operation and collective bargaining). Given that the *comité* is one of the most important bases of union activity in the plant, the employers' proposals might well endanger union influence (support for this view is widespread among employers[34]). Further, many French employers not only were strongly opposed to the law permitting trade-union sections

---

32 Martin, 'Les Systèmes de négociation et de représentation dans l'entreprise', *Droit Social*, p. 99.
33 *CNPF*, 'Le Comité d'entreprise', *Patronat No. 362* (1975), p. 24.
34 *CNPF*, 'Quelles réformes?', *Patronat No. 354* (1974).

in the plant,[35] but, since their introduction, have sought to develop the role of the formally less conflict-oriented *comité d'entreprise*.[36]

The second piece of evidence derives from an article in the same journal concerning the 'problem' of politics in the workplace; it condemns any political activity in companies on the grounds that 'the enterprise must be a politically neutral place, devoted to work'.[37] It insists that employers fully recognize the exercise of union rights in the plant, but given the orientation of the major unions which seek to raise larger and more basic issues, that are necessarily of a political kind, it would seem that employers do not fully accept the activities of the unions. A similar point is reflected in an article which seeks to argue that, despite the claims of many trade unions and commentators, collective bargaining has not declined in recent years. In discussing the future course of negotiations no reference is made to the two main unions, but only to *FO*, *CGC* and *CFTC*.[38]

What the *CNPF* really seeks is made more clear in an article concerning strikes, in which it is argued that the right to strike must be limited so that it respects other rights – the individual right to work, personal freedom of movement, and freedom to run the means of production. More generally it argues that:

> The method of bargaining has proved itself. It allows the social partners – employers and unions – to study problems at the level that they arise – the industry, the region, the company – and to bring to these the best solutions. Instead of the trial of strength, equal negotiation substitutes an effective method to resolve collective conflicts of work, in confronting the divergent interests, and at the same time maintaining the running of the institutions of social progress – the company, industry and the economy in its totality.[39]

This statement might well be agreed by many, and would certainly be accepted by many British employers. The difference between Britain and France, however, is that such a view is carried out in practice far less than in the latter, as has been seen above. In other words, even the 'moderate' philosophy of the *CNPF* is scarcely pursued by the bulk of French employers. Hence, for example, Bunel and Saglio found that only 21% of the employers

---

35 Reynaud, *Les Syndicats en France, Vol. 1*, p. 247.
36 Adam and Lucas, 'Les Institutions de représentation du personnel en France', *Droit Social*, p. 82; Martin, 'Les Systèmes de négociation et de représentation dans l'entreprise', *Droit Social*, p. 93.
37 *CNPF*, 'La Politique dans l'Entreprise', *Patronat No. 373* (1976), p. 13.
38 *CNPF*, 'Politique contractuelle: Où en est-on?', *Patronat No. 379* (1977), p. 11.
39 *CNPF*, 'La Grève', *Patronat No. 368* (1976), p. 28.

they interviewed had actually signed company agreements and planned to do so again in the future.[40]

The reasons for this practical dislike of company agreements relate, according to employers, to the political orientation of the major unions and their refusal to guarantee 'social peace' upon signing an agreement. As the personnel director of the company stated: 'It is impossible to negotiate with the *CGT* or the *CFDT*: they are both committed to the removal of the existing order and will not sign agreements even when they think they are acceptable ... the *CGT* and the *CFDT* are mainly concerned with political matters.'

Such a view is reflected in statements of the *UIMM*, the employers' association in metalworking: 'The *CFDT* rejects any solution which is favourable to the workers but which is not consistent with its line of disorganizing production and the economy';[41] while the *CGT* is 'a prisoner of analyses and slogans which no longer often take account of the reality of things'.[42] The state is also criticized for reducing the freedom for negotiation. Bunel and Saglio add that, according to the employers:

> Any development of negotiations must be ... subordinated to the economic situation on the grounds social progress is always the consequence of economic progress. Thus when the economic euphoria of the five years which followed 1968 gave place to crisis, negotiation appeared less useful. The employer could no longer distribute anything to workers.[43]

They quote the president of *UIMM*, who stated in 1974: 'After the intense development of bargaining that we have experienced, a change of pace in the social area is now imperative. Moderation is the condition of survival of our companies.'[44]

It should also be remembered that the statement of the *UIMM* refers to bargaining at all levels and not merely within the company. Bargaining at regional level, however, has generally concerned minimum wages, so that employers are able to make unilateral decisions concerning real rates of pay; in metalworking in 1975 only fifteen out of more than ninety regional agreements dealt with anything other than minimum wage rates.[45] Moreover, agreements need not involve the major unions, for under French law if any one recognized union signs an agreement then it applies to all

---

40 Bunel and Saglio, 'La Faiblesse de la négociation collective', *SdT*, p. 390.
41 *UIMM, L'Année métallurgique* (Paris: 1974), p. 40.
42 *Ibid.*, p. 45.
43 Bunel and Saglio, 'La Faiblesse de la négociation collective', *SdT*, pp. 385–6.
44 *UIMM, L'Année métallurgique*, p. 3.
45 Bunel and Saglio, 'La Faiblesse de la négociation collective', *SdT*, p. 389.

workers in the sector concerned. Hence it is common for unions such as *FO* to sign an agreement which is opposed by the *CGT* and *CFDT*.

The reason for the opposition of employers to bargaining at plant and company level may in part be attributed to their fears of the political orientation of the major trade unions. But, in reality, it seems that employers are prepared to accept bargaining if it does not endanger their position and their freedom of manoeuvre; in other words if bargaining is ineffective: 'They are quite happy with collective bargaining, but to the extent that it does not impose any check upon the autonomy of their decisions and that it does not deal with conflicts and demands which are expressed in their company.'[46] In other words, employers in France hold dearly to their independence and autonomy. Meaningful collective bargaining might be seen as encouraging trade-unionism and hence further challenging the freedom of the employer. Accordingly, there is little incentive for the employer to engage in meaningful bargaining (unless the unions impose sufficient pressure) precisely because it is in an essentially defensive position – bargaining on the demand of the union can only lead to a worsening of its position.[47] Moreover, while plant bargaining may on occasion be useful as a means of taking a more general pressure off employers, it serves to weaken their unity and thereby further endanger plant autonomy.

It could be suggested that a concern with plant autonomy might foster plant bargaining. But this is not possible because of the desire to neutralize the unions in the interests of employer autonomy.[48] Such an attitude may in part be seen as a reflection of the nature of traditional French industry – small, privately owned companies. But while this may help to explain the origin of a tradition, it seems that many public companies, including those of foreign origin, are quite ready to adopt a similar approach.[49] Indeed, this concern with the freedom of the employer is to be seen not only in the traditional attitude of numerous companies, but also in the 'new' orientation displayed by many. Hence, the *CNPF* not only sees the company as the mainspring of greater well-being for all, but argues that this requires the freedom for managers to exercise their skills – managers are realists in a world of absolute ideologies.[50] Accordingly, 'One of the essential roles of the managing director is ... at every moment to arbitrate between the different interests for which he is responsible ... interests which are nearly

46 *Ibid.*, p. 400.
47 F. Sellier, *Stratégie de la lutte sociale* (Éditions Ouvrières, Paris: 1961), pp. 173–4.
48 *Ibid.*, p. 163; Bachy *et al.*, *Représentation et Négociation dans l'Entreprise*, p. 171.
49 See Bunel and Saglio, 'La Faiblesse de la négociation collective', *SdT.*
50 *CNPF*, 'L'Esprit d'entreprise et ... L'Entreprise de demain', *Patronat No. 385* (1977), p. 45.

always contradictory – at least in the short-run – without forgetting the primary interest which dominates everything, that of the enterprise.' This role, for example, would be reduced if any form of codetermination were to be introduced; for this would lead to a paralysis of the company, or deals between shareholders and workers such that the company itself would be endangered.

French employers, it might be argued, are simply stating views that are common in many other countries. Certainly their arguments bear a good deal of similarity to many of those put forward by the Confederation of British Industry and other employers' bodies, particularly with reference to the Bullock proposals.[51] Two factors, however, appear to distinguish the French attitude. The first of these is that very often French employers place their independence above any other consideration. Hence, Bunel and Saglio found that 55% of the employers 'accord priority to independence over expansion, and only 38% made the opposite choice. 18% of the former are inclined to negotiate within their company, compared to 50% of the latter.'[52] Those more prepared to negotiate define themselves much more as part of a 'technostructure' – 'they are agents of growth and not the defenders of property and the freedom of enterprise'.[53] The emphasis upon employers' freedom means that preference is given to 'training' as a means of resolving conflicts rather than negotiation. The second difference is that, given the level of union organization in France, there has been insufficient pressure in France – unlike Britain – for the employers to adopt a more 'pluralist' or pragmatic approach. Given this lack of pressure, their lack of inclination to bargain follows logically from the philosophy.[54] The strategy of the employer cannot, therefore, be divorced from the strategies of the union and the extent to which they are able to impose pressure upon employers.

Union strategy

The previous section has indicated that employers in practice demonstrate little readiness to engage in collective bargaining, particularly at company and plant levels. In general, bargaining exists where employers do not conform to the dominant attitudes of their peers or where unions have

---

51 Department of Trade and Industry, Committee of Inquiry on Industrial Democracy (Bullock), *Report*, Cmnd 6706 (1977). Ed.'s note: See J. Phillips, 'UK Business Power and Opposition to the Bullock Committee's 1977 Proposals on Workers Directors', *Historical Studies in Industrial Relations* 31/32 (2011), pp. 1–30.
52 Bunel and Saglio, 'La Faiblesse de la négociation collective', *SdT*, p. 400.
53 *Ibid.*, p. 393.
54 Gallie, *In Search of the New Working Class*, pp. 309ff.

sufficient power to make employers believe that negotiation is a logical course of action. Accordingly, trade-union strategy has to focus upon developing sufficient strength to impose pressure upon employers.

However, it might be inferred from the preceding discussion that trade unions are seeking to develop collective bargaining. However, employers argue that this is not the case; the unions, or at least the two major confederations, are primarily politically oriented and accordingly have no real interest in bargaining. Before analysing particular union strategies, therefore, it is advisable to focus on union attitudes towards negotiation.

Negotiation and the philosophies of the CGT and CFDT

Both the *CGT* and the *CFDT* claim to be class-oriented trade unions. This term refers to their commitment to socialism, and their conception of society as riven by class conflict. Accordingly, the notion of 'class struggle' is central to their conception of a trade union's role. Given the centrality of their views, fostered in part by employer intransigence,[55] the unions have traditionally demonstrated a degree of ambivalence over engaging in negotiations. As Adam *et al.* state, the union position basically centres around three tendencies: a total refusal of any compromise, workers' control (seeking to conquer the ability to negotiate while rejecting any form of integration), and co-management in particular substantive areas.[56] At the extreme, negotiation may be seen as inevitably incorporating the unions and hence compromising their commitment to socialism.[57] Certainly, negotiation is not seen as in itself important. The unions conceive of it as part of the total pattern of struggle; for example, in the various statements of the union confederations the terms 'demands' and 'struggles' are to be found far more frequently than 'negotiation'. The latter is merely one means to pursue goals; negotiation therefore has a tactical rather than a strategic significance,[58] and union attitudes towards engaging in such activity are therefore influenced as much by short-term as by long-term considerations.[59]

Nevertheless, the unions have engaged in a great deal of negotiation and have frequently criticized the employers for refusing to engage in any meaningful debate. Hence, after the recent election defeat of the Left, Georges Séguy declared, 'We are ready to negotiate no matter what the

55 Sellier, *Stratégie de la lutte sociale*, p. 162.
56 G. Adam, J.-D. Reynaud and J.-M. Verdier, *La Négociation collective en France* (Editions Ouvrières, Paris: 1972), p. 79.
57 S. Erbés-Seguin, 'Les Deux Champs de l'affrontement professionel', *SdT* 2/76 (1976).
58 Bachy *et al.*, *Représentation et Négociation dans l'Entreprise*, p. 180.
59 *Ibid.*, p. 168.

political colour or the ideological nature of our interlocutor. We are trade-unionists who are realists, responsible and exacting.' The *CGT* therefore had a strong desire for negotiations, particularly at national level, although 'we do not make a fetish or a religion of negotiations at the summit'.[60] More generally, in a discussion of negotiation in a *CFDT* journal, Albert Mercier declares that 'the risk is less in the dangers of negotiation than its too great absence' for 'negotiation is an integral part of trade-union action … struggle and negotiation are inseparable. It is negotiation which permits the crystallization and concretization of the gains of struggle at any given moment, of confirming a state of the balance of power.'[61]

It would seem, then, that despite any theoretical hesitations concerning negotiation, the main trade unions in France are committed in practice to this method as part of a more general pattern of activity. Nevertheless, this does not mean that they are quite ready to sign agreements. In particular, the *CGT* and *CFDT* have frequently refused to endorse agreements that other unions have signed. The agreements have some real value in themselves; in addition – unlike the employers – the unions do not accept that the signing of an agreement on a specific issue involves a commitment not to strike or take other forms of action over other issues:

> It is this ambiguity between the idea of negotiation and that of co-operation that the employer and the government use to refuse firmly negotiation of demands under the pretext that the unions do not subscribe to a logic of co-operation. For the *CFDT*, on the other hand, the wish to negotiate demands does not signify an abandoning of class struggle, for its perspective is both to negotiate immediate demands to improve living and working conditions of workers and at the same time to work for radical transformation of society.[62]

In some respects it seems that the problem of integrating the two aims is more difficult for the *CGT* because it is more closely attached to a political party, the *Parti communiste français* (*PCF*), and hence it is through this that political transformation is often seen to be achieved. For the *CFDT* there is a greater quest to link the two and ensure that immediate demands and negotiations do not in any way compromise the longer-term goal.[63] Other differences in the strategies of the two main union confederations relate to their differing conceptions of socialism, the *CFDT* seeking a broader view which relates not merely to the economic structure, but also

---

60 J. Lambert, 'Travailleurs: "L'Ouverture", c'est vous!', *Vie Ouvrière*, No. 1754, 1978.
61 A. Mercier, 'La Négociation', *CFDT Aujourd'hui*, mai–juin 1976, pp. 16–17.
62 *Ibid.*, p. 17.
63 E. Maire, 'Dix Questions franches à Edmond Maire', *CFDT Aujourd'hui*, jan.–fev. 1976, p. 36.

to hierarchical, bureaucratic, technological, and cultural elements best summed up in the concept of *'autogestion'*.[64] While, therefore, the two unions have often co-operated and have developed a common platform at a variety of levels, that co-operation is often uneasy.

For example, while both unions largely accept negotiation, there are differences concerning the level at which demands should be pursued. The *CGT*, consistent with its emphasis upon representing a class, shows a marked preference for national bargaining. The *CFDT* frequently argues that, notwithstanding the importance of this level, certain issues can only be dealt with at company level (this is, of course, also consistent with its emphasis on *autogestion*).

Despite this difference of emphasis, however, both unions have demonstrated some hesitancy over making agreements at company level. In broad terms, these hesitancies concern the incorporation of militants and the development of a parochial attitude that would militate against class action.[65] Hence, for example, both the *CGT* and the *CFDT* place great emphasis upon trade-union sections within companies being closely integrated with the union more generally.[66] Hence, particularly in the *CGT*, stress is placed upon recruitment and mobilization at shop-floor level in support of demands at national and regional level.

Beyond this, however, there does appear to be a considerable acceptance of company bargaining, even though this may not be seen as the primary or most desirable level of action. In part, company agreements are seen as part of a broader strategy, insofar as they may serve to make some inroads into employer resistance which might then be generalized. This, for example, appears to have been one effect of the earliest company agreements.[67] More generally, Martin states that

the wish to achieve some 'holes' in the employers' front has led for some years to flexible practices, depending on the refusal or acceptance of negotiation at the branch level by the employer. The primary aim remains the negotiation or improvement of national agreements; if these are not achieved, the federations encourage the best-placed enterprises to negotiate agreements often through

64 P. Rosanvallon, 'L'Analyse de la CFDT et son identité', *CFDT Aujourd'hui*, sept.–oct. 1976, pp. 18–29.
65 Bachy *et al.*, *Représentation et Négociation dans l'Entreprise*, p. 173.
66 See G. Declercq, 'Le Délégué syndical', *CFDT Aujourd'hui*, juill.– août 1977, p. 7; *Le Peuple*, '1000/6', No. 1022 (1977), pp. 8ff.; *Le Peuple*, 'Pour une Formation syndicale de départ', No. 995, 1976, pp. 10ff.
67 Reynaud, *Les Syndicats en France, Vol. 1*, p. 194.

union officials working in them. A company agreement is simply a springboard to foster a change at a higher level in the branch agreements.[68]

In this sense, the unions seek to develop a form of articulated bargaining in which there is a clear relationship between the sets of demands put forward at a variety of levels. Indeed, at least when it comes to a consideration of union activity within the plant, the unions accept that the militants should seek to put up demands at this level and to negotiate them. The *CFDT*, for example, emphasizes the importance of the plant level in obtaining demands because 'it is there, where the balance of power manifests itself in the most concrete form, that it is easiest to advance and to mobilize'.[69] Such an approach is recognized to a degree by the *CGT*, particularly in relation to large companies, since these are 'the bastions of capitalism'; the grand demands must find a concrete expression at local level.[70] Such demands will inevitably require some amendment to take account of the particular nature of specific situations. As will be seen below, this approach was important in the plant studied.

A further reason for the importance of company negotiations, according to both the *CGT* and the *CFDT*, is that a major feature of the union's role is to defend the interests of the workers: 'the company is ... the location of vital trade-union activity for the defence of workers' interests, and also the place where those workers can naturally unite to fight'.[71] Moreover, it has to be recognized that the general platform of demands does not encompass all problems or grievances experienced by workers. It is essential that the union deals with these issues – 'none of these questions can be considered as minor, none can be left on one side ... it is certainly the primary mission of the union to take charge of the defence of the material and moral interests of all workers, including those which appear to be the most minor'.[72]

Before moving from a consideration of the position of the unions as organizations, in relation to negotiations, to the views of the militants themselves, one further point should be noted. The unions, and in particular the *CGT*, place considerable emphasis upon their responsible and realistic behaviour. By responsible is meant that, if they do sign an agreement, they will abide by it. By realism is meant that the sorts of demands which they put forward in negotiations do not embody a basic challenge to the very foundations of capitalism. This can be seen, for example, in their broad

---

68 Martin, 'Les Systèmes de négociation et de représentation dans l'entreprise', *Droit Social*, p. 96.
69 Mercier, La Négociation', *CFDT Aujourd'hui*, p. 26.
70 *Le Peuple*, 'Renforcer la CGT et accroître notre Capacité d'action dans les Grandes Entreprises', No. 1008, 1977, p. 16.
71 *Le Peuple*, 'Pour une Formation syndicale de départ', p. 20.
72 *Ibid.*, p. 22.

pattern of demands which is broadly comparable to that put forward by many other trade-union movements with less radical claims. Hence, in 1977 the main demands include an increase in minimum wages, the maintenance of real wages, a satisfactory job grading and wage structure and career structure, and a fairer wage distribution.[73]

This discussion has so far focused upon the official positions of the *CGT* and *CFDT*. However, it is not necessarily the case that militants at plant level accept these views, or place the emphasis on the same points. Attention is now turned, therefore, to the views of the militants and the strategies which they pursue.

Militants and negotiation

A good deal has been written in France on the nature of militants.[74] Much of this work has focused on why those who become trade-union activists have 'a need to struggle'. From the work of Andrieux and Lignon[75] it would seem that activism stems mainly from the experience of work and that this later leads to some form of ideological commitment. The nature of trade-unionism in France fosters the expectation that militants will be politically radical, and this seems generally to be true. Moreover, there are clearly considerable variations in attitude, even within the *CGT* and the *CFDT*. The work of Durand, for example, indicates that only a quarter of militants have a fully developed class orientation, in terms of identity, opposition and totality.[76] Moreover, as the unions have achieved some sort of position within the companies, union activism requires rather less commitment than might once have been the case; 'the era of the militant "martyr" or "hero" is over'.[77]

Nevertheless, the role of the militant is still problematical, in terms of both day-to-day activity and ideological position. Balancing the need to remain part of the shop floor and at the same time play a role of mobilizer, and, more recently, a holder of various institutional positions, remains a continuing problem.[78] Indeed, a variety of movements – both within and

73 *Le Peuple*, 'Positions et Revendications de La CGT', No. 1009, 1977, pp. 20–6.
74 See P. Rosanvallon, 'Militantisme! L'Envers du décor', *CFDT Aujourd'hui*, juill.–août 1976, pp. 4–12; Y. Bourdet, *Décentralisation industrielle et Relations de travail* (La Documentation française, Paris: 1976).
75 A. Andrieux and J. Lignon, *Le Militant syndicaliste d'aujourd'hui* (Denoël, Paris: 1973), p. 59.
76 C. Durand, *Conscience ouvrière et Action syndicale* (Mouton, Paris: 1971).
77 Rosanvallon, 'Militantisme!', *CFDT Aujourd'hui*, p. 7.
78 Mercier, 'La Négociation', *CFDT Aujourd'hui*; Adam *et al.*, *La Négociation collective en France*, pp. 75–7; D. Mothé, *Militant chez Renault* (Editions du Seuil, Paris: 1965).

outside the unions – have attempted to provide a range of solutions to these problems.[79]

In what is perhaps the most insightful discussion of the nature and the role of the militant, Mothé distinguishes three broad types of orientation. The first, the tribune, is primarily oriented towards the workers he represents and seeks to mobilize them. The second is primarily oriented towards other militants and is above all a defender and a promoter of a particular ideology. The third type is much more a technician, using his skills to negotiate, and is therefore oriented more towards the established structure of power.[80] These are, of course, ideal-types, but an attempt was made to assess how militants in the company studied defined their roles in accordance with Mothé's categories. Only one in eight of the militants defined their role as anything other than a negotiator. The role of the union, according to a *CGT* militant, was 'to negotiate everything and anything which affects the worker and to seek to improve his conditions, both financial and moral'. Furthermore, at least on most day-to-day grievances, there is a preference for negotiation and discussion prior to the imposition of any form of sanctions, although this is not necessarily so on larger issues.[81]

Moreover, particularly for the *CGT*, there is an acceptance of the linking of their main platform of demands to those laid down by the unions nationally, and key militants from the plant are active at a variety of levels of the union:

> the platform we have presented for the plant has already been presented at national level. But the platform cannot be applied everywhere because there are some things, like the fifth week's paid holiday, which some workers already have. But the grand lines of the platform are followed ... what has happened is that in the *CGT* we have *délégués*, such as myself, who represent my union at the union local; there is another meeting at department level and another for the industry. And at each level their questions are discussed and an agreed platform established ... At department level we have a co-ordination committee where there are fellows from our plant and from others ... and that committee discussed demands.

For the *CFDT* there are similar links between national and local demands, although the extent to which the militants are active outside the plant is considerably less. An analysis of tracts shows that there are considerable variations in the extent to which the unions emphasize demands and issues above the level of the company. In plant A both the *CGT* and the *CFDT*

---

79 Rosanvallon, 'Militantisme!', *CFDT Aujourd'hui*, p. 5; see also R. Linhart, *L'Établi* (Editions de Minuit, Paris: 1978).
80 D. Mothé, *Le Métier de militant* (Seuil, Paris: 1973), pp. 109–56.
81 See Durand and Dubois, *La Grève*, p. 184, for comparable findings.

devote much space in their tracts to national issues, whereas in plant B, where the position of the *CGT* is much less strong, the tracts devoted to national issues are much more rare.

Despite this integration with the larger union, the militants tend to place greater emphasis upon the level of the company than do the unions themselves: 'The most important level of bargaining is the enterprise. All negotiations are important, but at plant level we are able to gain more ... We have made our priority the fact that we are in the enterprise before trade-unionism.' Similarly, the great majority of militants believed that concrete demands should be given priority over general objectives, and saw the union primarily in terms of the militants and members in the plant. The systems of argument which militants claim they use most frequently similarly reflect a concentration on the plant level: almost two-thirds of the arguments relate specifically to workers in the plant while less than one-fifth relate to class or to general trade-union aims. It would appear, then, that at plant level the focus of the militants is somewhat different from that found in union statements. Nevertheless, the integration of the militants within the larger union appears to be higher than for shop stewards in England: four-fifths of them, for example, claim that they attend meetings of the union at local level 'very often' or 'often'.

The fact that the militants accept a role primarily as negotiators and focus on the plant does not mean that they wholeheartedly accept the idea of negotiation or that they reject a conflict notion of industry. It is true that they placed greater emphasis upon negotiation and strikes, rather than political action, as the most effective means of pursuing workers' interests. Similarly all but one-fifth of them thought that 'the defence of workers' rights and the promotion of their solidarity' was a more important reason for union membership than 'to struggle for socialism and a new society'. But there was a clear awareness of the political nature of their activity; they did not accept a distinction between 'industrial' and 'political' matters. As a militant explained: 'Among the workers the view is very clear that the union is more important than politics. But all the militants say that when we protest about the increase in prices and we demand an increase in wages, we're making a political demand. All the militants here are aware of that.'

However, the way in which concrete demands and socialist aspirations are integrated varies between the *CGT* and the *CFDT* in plant A. The key *CGT* militant explained the position:

> We negotiate because the union is a union of class struggle. Because of that we could say small things are not important, we won't negotiate them. But we say 'no' to that: we defend the immediate interests of workers as well. We fight against poor working conditions but at the same time we have a very distant orientation; we have a struggle for money in the present, for workers' immediate

interests; then we have a more or less distant perspective such as the platform of demands; and then, finally socialism.

The *CFDT* is rather more concerned to integrate its broader orientations into concrete demands; in comparison, the *CGT* is 'more realist'. In the *CFDT*, according to one of its most active militants,

> We talk a lot more and struggle less ... We have a lot of intellectuals even among the workers. They want the revolution and reject any compromise. We debate ... and as we discuss, the issue is past. [On a particular issue in the plant] we discuss and the issue is past ... we have not fixed our position because everyone says immediately, 'yes, it's capitalism'. Certainly, but then what concrete demands are we to make? ... There are grand ideas and projects for the future, the directions in which we must go. But for life from day to day, how are we to know what to do?

Moreover, the link between parochial issues and class action takes on particular significance in the case-study company, in part because of the *CGT* policy of focusing on large companies. For the militants and the unions, the company is a 'target' plant, in part because it is large and foreign-owned. But in addition it is a 'true field of class conflict' because some of the local *CGT* militants play a key role in their union while the company is closely involved with the employers' association.

The notion of conflict is also clear in the attitudes of both *CGT* and *CFDT* militants in the plant concerning agreements on major issues, or becoming involved in particular aspects of workers' problems. Several years ago the company offered an agreement but this included a no-strike clause and was accordingly rejected. More generally, some in the *CFDT* have even shown hesitancy over managing the social areas under the control of the *comité d'entreprise* because activities such as the canteens are an aid to management. On the question of company agreements, all the militants appear to have some hesitations. A key *CGT* militant explained:

> It is necessary to say that we rarely sign company agreements because they are rarely valuable. If we commit ourselves for a few years, there is no way of knowing whether the agreement we sign is good. It might be good for this year but not for two years' time, and we wish that, if we sign an agreement, we are going to respect it ... Many matters are like an iceberg; there's a part you see and a part you don't see, and one cannot get involved in things like that. On the other hand, one accepts a commitment, so we have an agreement on the guaranteed week ... There are problems because we are always 'the butt of the joke' ... We do not get involved thoughtlessly in agreements.

A similar caution is reflected in the position of the militants in relation to the organization of work and discipline. For example, the militants do not negotiate piecework times (although they may advise individual workers):

> The *CGT* thinks it is dangerous to say, with a stop watch in your hand, 'yes, you have too much or enough', and for the *CFDT* it has been decided that we will not discuss piecework – the principle is rejected. Even if the time is fair, we do not wish to enter into the timing game … We negotiate wages, but we don't want to take the responsibility for the organization of work. If it is not a question of safety, one simply contests; we do not wish to manage. One contests, contests, contests.

The same hesitancy is found in relation to disciplinary matters; the union seeks to defend workers but is also very careful not to become involved in a policing role.

In overall terms, then, the militants in the plant can be seen as favouring negotiations but having some hesitations over signing agreements in all areas.[82] Moreover, they place greater emphasis upon the company level than do the unions nationally. But there is a common acceptance, despite a somewhat limited emphasis upon the party political sphere (see below), of the need to question and struggle. Hence, negotiation is seen as only part of the larger strategy. On big issues, such as the annual wage discussions, the militants accept that: 'the crucial thing is to have strikes before the meeting to show management that the men are serious about their demands'.

Given this awareness of conflict and the emphasis upon struggle, particularly in the context of management opposition to the union, it is clearly necessary for the unions to employ a number of strategies oriented towards mobilizing the workforce. The next section turns to these strategies.

Union strategy

The orientation of the militants to the company appears to be significantly influenced by three factors beyond their own individual values. These are the nature of the unions, the hostility of the management, and the attitudes of the workforce they seek to represent. More specifically, in a situation in which the company questions the role and representativeness of the union, the militants have to ensure that they have the backing of workers. To achieve this they have to 'educate' and mobilize the workers, or adjust their demands, orientations, and actions, as well as continually trying to prove their significance. The consequent union strategy can be divided into a number of key elements: developing their own organization

---

82 Bachy *et al.*, *Représentation et Négociation dans l'Entreprise*, pp. 193ff., found a similar level of hesitancy.

and maximizing their use of legal institutions; maintaining close links to the shop floor, particularly by proving the efficacy of collective action; achieving a balance between union goals and worker democracy; educating the workforce; and fostering unity among the main unions. These various aspects of union strategy will now be considered.

The unions place considerable emphasis upon the importance of the *comité d'entreprise* and the *délégués du personnel*. These have become important channels of union activity in the plant, despite the criticisms of these institutions made by the militants. More generally, it might be asked why class-oriented unions should be prepared to become involved in what, from any perspective, are remarkably weak institutions. Certainly the more *gauchiste* militants accept that there is a 'contradiction' between their ideology and their acceptance of such institutions. However, at its most basic, the reason for accepting these institutions is that they are almost all that the union has, particularly in view of the difficulty of mobilizing workers. Moreover, as the unions point out, these institutions represent, in the French context, significant working-class victories deriving from major periods of struggle, for example 1936 and 1968.[83]

A further reason for accepting these institutions is that they do provide some sort of channel through which workers' grievances may be resolved. These may be of a relatively minor nature, but, as earlier quotes from militants and the unions indicate, a union concerned with workers' interests cannot ignore issues, however unimportant they appear to be. Moreover, as Bachy *et al.* point out, the principles upon which these institutions are founded do not fit easily with the orientations of the *CGT* and the *CFDT*.[84] But where unions are strong they can ensure that the union section in the plant is the key body which controls and directs the activities of *délégués* and members of the *comité d'entreprise*,[85] and this is a strategy fostered by the unions.[86] This strategy is certainly pursued, successfully, in the plants studied, where all the *élus* are trade-union nominees. Hence, the *CGT* holds ten, the *CFDT* two, and the *CGC* one of the posts of *délégués* in plant A (plus corresponding numbers of deputies); on the *comité d'entreprise* the *CGT* has five seats, the *CFDT* two and the *CGC* one (plus deputies). In elections to these posts the *CGT* receives generally about two-thirds of the

---

83 *Le Peuple*, 'Pour une Formation syndicale de départ', p. 14.
84 Bachy *et al.*, *Représentation et Négociation dans l'Entreprise*, pp. 10ff.
85 Martin, 'Les Systèmes de négociation et de représentation dans l'entreprise', *Droit Social*, pp. 94–5.
86 *Le Peuple*, 'Les *Élus CGT* aux Comités d'Entreprise', No. 995, 1976, p. 8; *idem*, 'Pour une Formation syndicale de départ', pp. 14–16; *CFDT*, *La Section syndicale* (Montholon-Services, Paris: 1977); *idem*, *Les Délégués du personnel* (Montholon-Services, Paris: 1977); *idem*, *Le Comité d'entreprise* (Montholon-Services, Paris: 1977).

votes, the *CFDT* about a quarter and *FO* and the *CGC* share the remainder. In plant B the *CGT* obtains almost as many votes as it does in plant A, while the *CFTC* has a portion similar to that of the *CFDT* in plant A. The election results themselves are important, at least for the *CGT*, as evidence of its support and its representativeness.[87]

The *élus*, together with a limited number of union representatives, also have a legal right to time off paid for by the company; the aim of this is to permit them to discuss issues with workers and pursue their grievances. By using the institutions, therefore, the militants can develop their contacts with the workforce. However, the small number of persons with time off and the limited nature of that time, means that the militants do find problems in maintaining a link with the shop floor (see below). Hence, given that the company keeps strictly to the law, the time available to *all* those with a right to time off works out at less than ten minutes with each worker per month. This figure, it should be remembered, includes all the unions, including the *CGC* and *FO*. For the *CFDT* alone, for example, its time off formally works out at less than two minutes per month with each worker. However, in plant A (although not in plant B) militants are often able to take more time off (except when the company tightens up) and, to a degree, the *CGT* will pay its militants lost earnings.

The *élus* and *délégués syndicaux* who have a right to time off form an important base for union organization in the plant. However, the *élus* are meant to represent broad occupational groups and therefore it is possible that major sections of the plant may in practice have little contact with *élus*.[88] This is all the more true in situations where a single militant holds a number of posts (termed in French, '*le cumul*').

In order to reduce these possibilities, stronger unions tend to avoid the use of the *cumul*,[89] and to seek to ensure that they have *élus* in each department in a plant and to share time off between the *élus* and their deputies. For weaker unions, which cannot be sure of winning a substantial number of seats and whose militants may be limited in number, these aims can rarely be achieved. The case of *CGT* in plant B is instructive in this respect.

Until recently in plant B the *CGT* practised the *cumul* but it was found that not only did workers often find it difficult to raise problems with the *élus*, but also that the union organization was highly centralized. This had a number of consequences: the union tended to lose contact with workers, and departments were not encouraged to take action over their own

87 For a national comparison, see J. Dussiot, 'Les Élections aux Comités d'entreprises en 1973', *Révue française des Affaires sociales*, jan.–mars 1975, pp. 145–83.

88 See Linhart, *L'Établi*; P. Bernoux, D. Motte and J. Saglio, *Trois Ateliers d'O.S.* (Editions Ouvrières, Paris: 1973).

89 Bachy *et al.*, *Représentation et Négociation dans l'Entreprise*.

problems. But in addition it became very easy for the company to endanger the position of the union simply by sacking a few key militants. As has been noted, this is exactly what the company did after defeating a lengthy strike. With the help of a full-time official, the *CGT* in the plant is now seeking to develop a more satisfactory form of organization.[90]

Such organization can be seen in the case of the *CGT* in plant A. Those with time off are spread carefully among occupational groups and departments; the number of *élus* in each area is the product of discussions in union meetings. Moreover, the organization and activity of the *élus* is closely linked to the union organization itself. For example, those holding key positions in the union are reserved particular positions such as union representative or secretary of the *comité d'entreprise*. In this way two things are achieved: the time off required for key union activities, and, second, union guidance over elected institutions. In the case of weaker unions, such as the *CFDT*, the post of *délégué syndical* can be used to provide time off for key militants who, due to their jobs, would not be elected to positions with time off.

Developing from the post-1968 legislation, which recognized unions at plant level, the *CGT* in plant A has developed a form of organization that maintains close contact with workers. Instead of being organized solely at plant level, it has developed union sections within departments, each with its full array of officers. Such departments possess autonomy within the confines of policy as determined by the central plant organization and its various committees. At the level of the plant, there exist secretaries concerned with finances, organization, and tracts, and a general secretary and a union bureau. In contrast the *CFTD* simply has an organization at plant level, where issues are occasionally discussed; but in the main each *élu* acts with almost total autonomy and discretion.

The depth of *CGT* organization in plant A can be seen as both the source and the result of its strength in terms of membership and militants; a third of the workforce belongs to the *CGT*, and this is true throughout the occupational grades. The *CFDT* has only a third of this number, a proportion similar to the *CGT* in plant B. The same contrasts are found in terms of numbers of militants: the *CGT* in plant A claims to have about sixty 'real' militants, while the *CFDT* can claim less than half this number. In plant B the *CGT* has only about fifteen militants who are prepared to take anything more than a symbolic role in the union.

Such activism cannot be seen as particularly impressive as compared to the ratio of stewards (let alone other activists) to members of large British plants. However, it does mean that in plant A the *CGT* has not only

---

90 See *Le Peuple*, 'Pour une Formation syndicale de départ'; *idem*, 'Renforcer la CGT et accroître notre Capacité d'action dans les Grandes Entreprises'.

been able to develop a departmental system of organization, but also to use a system of dues collectors to strengthen channels of communication between the union and the workforce. In one especially strong department, for example, there is one collector for every eight members. The collectors meet the union officers to explain the feeling of the shop floor prior to the meetings of all workers.

This organization is important in a number of respects. It is evidence in itself of relative union strength – the level of union membership in plant A is about double that typically found in France. This provides a basis for further recruitment, a theme which is stressed continually in *CGT* tracts and which is a key feature of *CGT* policy nationally. Further, it serves as an important protection for the militants, whose position and freedom depend upon 'the union being a force in the plant'.

As the *CGT* itself continually emphasizes, mobilization and recruitment are intimately related.[91] For, as well as purely bureaucratic purposes (including union competition which is fostered by the election system for *délégués* and the *comité d'entreprise*),[92] the development of union organization had as a basic aim the maintenance of a close relationship with the shop floor. This is perhaps the theme most strongly emphasized in union documents relating to the workplace organization. But despite the depth of *CGT* organization in plant A, there are still severe problems in maintaining close links with workers. Meetings are difficult given a wide variety of starting and stopping times, the dispersed residential pattern of workers and company control of transport for the majority of them, short lunch-hours, and the anti-strike bonus. Hence only one in fifteen *élus* claimed that he met all or most of those represented during the course of a week. Two further strategies therefore assume particular importance: proving the significance of the union, and the tract.

A *CGT* document on plant organization stresses that the way in which militants deal with workers' minor grievances will 'often be a major factor in the judgement that the worker will make of the union and the degree of confidence that he will place on it'.[93] As has been noted, it is in this respect that the legal institutions are of such importance. Andrieux and Lignon point out that many workers admire the militants for their courage and their readiness to fight for the interests of others, even if this imposes significant costs upon themselves.[94] It is exactly this which the militants seek to achieve.

The tract is itself an important means of pointing out to workers what the

91 *Le Peuple*, 'Pour une Formation syndicale de départ'.
92 Gallie, *In Search of the New Working Class*, p. 280.
93 *Le Peuple*, 'Pour une Formation syndicale de départ', p. 22.
94 A. Andrieux and J. Lignon, *L'Ouvrier aujourd'hui* (Editions Gonthier, Paris: 1966).

union has been able to achieve for them. Indeed, in many tracts there exists an uneasy balance between pointing to capitalist exploitation and company intransigence, while at the same time claiming union and collective efficiency. For example, after listing some significant gains, a *CGT* tract continues:

> In these actions the *CGT* has played a role taking as much at national as department level, as well as in the plant a series of initiatives and propositions which have made the bosses and the government retreat from their pretensions ... one must never forget that these demands are the result of the action which workers can undertake. They derive from the strength of the union organization in terms of the members which it represents.

In another case, namely that of wage increases during an incomes policy, a tract declares:

> In fact, since the beginning of the year, the *CGT* has done everything to win the legitimate demands of the workers – tracts in the company, and in the streets [of the town] petitions, delegations to management, demonstrations to the employers' association. We are going to 'strip the beast', for what we have gained since the beginning of the year is worse than useless.

A final example concerns the demands of a particular section. The union declares in a tract that:

> The *élus* of the *CGT* will put forward these demands at the meeting. They will debate and fight for these demands so that they will be satisfied. The *élus* of the *CGT* will do, as always, their utmost but their success will be in direct proportion to the active support that they have behind them.

The *CGT*, as by far the largest union confederation in France, stresses its significance and power in its tracts, which emphasize the value of solidarity and security achieved by organization.[95]

Certainly the *CGT* in plant A makes considerable use of the tract; on average one is produced every other day, and these can be efficiently written, duplicated, and distributed within a matter of hours. The *CFDT*'s rate of output is possibly a tenth of that of the *CGT*: fewer militants are prepared to write tracts and few are prepared to distribute them, particularly if they disagree with their contents. In plant B, the resources of the *CGT* are a similar constraint upon the output of tracts.

Promoting the idea of the efficacy and importance of the union leads to

---

95 *Le Peuple*, 'Renforcer la CGT et accroître notre Capacité d'action dans les Grandes Entreprises', p. 15.

the question of balancing unions' goals and perspectives with those of the workers. For whereas the unions may be class – and politically – oriented, the majority of workers appear not to be so.[96] As a militant explained,

> Most of the men are not interested in collective matters. Whenever I walk through the shop, three or four people always stop me and ask questions. But they are always, 'my father has just died, how many days do I get off?', or 'my son is going into the army, do I get time off?' No one has said anything in the shop about the meeting between Begin and Sadat.

Overall, a slight majority of the militants interviewed thought that 'the majority of workers in the plant are only interested in their wages and see the unions solely as an insurance agency'. There has, therefore, to be some balance achieved between, on the one hand, educating the workforce, and, on the other, accepting its views as constraints.

It has already been noted that the unions, even in their general platforms of demands, claim that they are being reasonable and realistic:

> The dynamics of negotiation depend both on the evolution of the balance of power and on the content of demands. These two elements are linked to the extent that the credibility of the union significantly influences the ability to mobilize and therefore also affects the development of the balance of power. To the extent that union organizations only in practice pose demands that they are sure the company can satisfy, they leave for the future in certain cases the determination of a progressive timetable of implementation (the reduction of working hours for example). The union conception of bargaining objectives is therefore realistic, and will gain nothing be being 'maximalist'.[97]

Nevertheless, the unions cannot be sure of winning the support of workers in anything other than a minimal manner. As a militant noted, 'the men are more ready to strike over make-up than the fifth week's holiday. Make-up is immediate and the worker is very interested. It's not like a national stoppage.' Another commented, in relation to the common platform, that 'the workers certainly accepted it – they always accept demands. The great problem is to get then to fight for these demands.'

It appears that the 'reasonableness' of demands is in part a reflection of the desire to ensure the support of the workforce. In addition, demands such as the common platform are put to the vote by workers, in part as a

---

96   F. Dupuy and D. Martin, *Jeux et Enjeux de la participation* (CRESST, Université Paris-Sud: 1977), p. 95; G. Adam *et al.*, *L'Ouvrier français en 1970* (Des Sciences Politiques, Paris: 1970), pp. 45–8; Andrieux and Lignon, *L'Ouvrier aujourd'hui*.
97   Mercier, 'La Négociation', *CFDT Aujourd'hui*, p. 22.

means of indicating to management that the unions have support. Indeed, in more general terms, both the *CGT* and *CFDT* place great emphasis upon democracy. The *CGT*, for example, distinguishes between trade-union and worker democracy:

> The union members determine the orientation of their union, work out the proposals which will be submitted to the mass meeting to be accepted as demands or the forms of struggle to make them successful; it is this consulting before addressing the whole of the workforce that we call union democracy. But in the last resort it is the workers who decide, also accept, who amend or who reject the propositions of the union which have previously been worked out by all union members. This is worker democracy.

The *CFDT*, while placing rather more stress upon the conditions of democracy, such as equal access to information, similarly emphasizes the need to take account of its historical traditions and orientations. In other words, the unions are prepared to see themselves accepting workers' decisions and inclinations only up to a certain point. And, more generally, they see their role as one of leadership. The strain between being part of the shop floor and accepting its right of decision, and of leading and remaining faithful to an ideology, is the central dilemma of the militant.[98]

While, in terms of broad platforms, the unions may initiate demands, this is less true of issues of a more parochial nature. In these cases, the role of the union and its militants is seen as specifying the nature of the demand, that is, of transforming workers' discontent into demands that can be negotiated and which have some concrete meaning.[99] Hence union documents strongly emphasize the need for care in the formulation of demands.[100] As a militant explained:

> often the workers do not express their position accurately; it is not always easy, right at the start, to explain to them what the problem is and what they are really asking for. It is necessary to work it out for them in an appropriate form, and often the *délégué* who receives their demand rearranges it a little with the help of his own trade union. So, with [a particular problem], really there was the initial position of the workers, that of the *CGT* and that of the *CFDT*. Initially these were very different, and, as a comrade said, over a period of a week or two

---

98 See D. Mothé, 'Le Rapport Militant/Travailleurs dans l'Entreprise', *CFDT Aujourd'hui*, mars–avril 1976; S. Erbés-Seguin, *Démocratie dans les Syndicats* (La Haye, Paris: 1971).

99 For changes in the degree of democracy as this occurs, see S. Bosc, 'Démocratie et Consensus dans les Grèves', *SdT* 4/73 (1973), pp. 440–55.

100 For example, *Le Peuple*, 'Pour une Formation syndicale de départ', p. 22; Mercier, 'La Négociation', *CFDT Aujourd'hui*.

the different positions have become more similar ... Despite the difficulties, we will finally arrive at a set of demands which faithfully reflect the real demand.

It is precisely this belief in the militant's ability to formulate the 'real' demand, given his greater ideological awareness, that legitimizes his leadership, and accordingly his ambivalence. Hence, virtually all of the militants interviewed believed that they should adopt a leadership role; this meant not only calling upon workers to strike, but also being careful to ensure that strikes were only called at opportune moments. A key *CGT* militant explained:

> Unlimited strikes are very, very hard for workers and sometimes there are effects which last for years ... some strikes are so important that they have to be digested. So we make the workers aware that a strike could be tough and that the decision must be taken carefully, that they have to think carefully. But, even so sometimes when they have gone out on strike the workers turn to the union to organize it. They are already fed-up. So, whatever happens, when their anger has risen and risen, it automatically spills over; it is then that we often lose even after our warnings. We in the unions accept our responsibilities, but we cannot say to the workers 'you must not go out on strike', because they are the ones who have to decide.

This uneasy balance between democracy and leadership is seen in the way in which militants claim they have become involved in issues, and how those issues are formulated and pursued. First, the interviews show that virtually all of the militants become involved in issues because workers ask them, rather than other militants, management or due to their own initiative. Over four out of five claimed that all or more than three-quarters of the issues were raised by the workers themselves. However, questions relating to the formulation and processing of demands and grievances show a different pattern of response: for nearly all the militants say that workers, other militants and the union section all play a major role in the formulation of demands, although they claim they themselves never play a key role here. Their personal importance, along with other militants and the union section, becomes clear only in the pursuit of demands. It would appear, then, that the balance between leadership and democracy changes through the course of an issue, this being facilitated by the existence of institutional procedures.

Nevertheless, there is a continual relationship between workers and militants. As one of the latter explained: 'Demands put forward relate either to the aspirations of the workers or what we judge to be vital to help and educate the workers. In each case it is necessary that there is toing and froing between workers and union.' Mothé has noted the way in which this process tends to create a division between militants and workers – by structuring their demands and by 'integrating the reality experienced into an ideological whole which permits better understanding, a better mastery of a situation which appears to them often as a series of inexplicable events: the militant "brings elements of a theory external to the workers" and thereby "affirms his different nature".'[101]

The emphasis upon defending workers' interests and being part of the shop floor means that only a quarter of the militants claim that they *ever* gave up, or refused to pursue, workers' grievances. Similarly, two-thirds of the militants interviewed disagreed with the view that a militant should follow the decisions of his union section if they were contrary to the views of the workers in his section. The crucial task, in such a situation is, of course, the persuasion of workers to accept the approach of the union. In this respect, three-quarters of the militants claimed that opinion leaders existed in their areas, the great majority of these being union members if not militants. Four out of five militants claimed that they could influence the majority of the opinion leaders in their area. If their assessments are correct, then the risk of divisions between union and workers is less, and a 'guided democracy' can exist (see below for an assessment of this).

A major element of this 'guidance' is the attempt to educate the workforce, for this is an essential element in persuading workers to accept the formulation of their grievances into concrete demands. It is also an important activity more generally as the *CGT* emphasizes:

> Ideas are the source of action. That which determines the attitude of a worker or all the workers is that which successfully or not puts over an idea. Thus one pursues a grievance, one decides to strike or to resume work if that demand, that strike or that resumption of work are seen as fair ideas. Union militants therefore find themselves permanently faced with this prime necessity: to convince their comrades at work.[102]

The *CGT* stresses the importance of the union press and of tracts in this endeavour to educate workers and fight the dominant ideas of capitalism. Certainly the unions seek to promote the sale of various union papers; tracts frequently refer to them and on occasion whole tracts are devoted to their importance and their contents. Moreover, the *CGT* in plant A frequently produces tracts which are closely related to the discussion of matters in recent issues of the union's publications, notably in relation to government policy and general strikes.

Table 1 shows the more general pattern of issues raised in samples of tracts of the various unions during a year.

---

101 Mothé, 'Le Rapport Militant/Travailleurs dans l'Entreprise', *CFDT Aujourd' hui*, p. 18.
102 *Le Peuple*, 'Pour une Formation syndicale de départ', p. 17.

Table 1: Issues discussed in union tracts

	CGT Plant A	CFDT Plant A	CGT Plant B
Importance and power of TU	31%	20%	8%
National issues and TU policies	15%	32%	7%
Plant issues (often linked to nat.)	25%	27%	33%
Need to fight and mobilize	29%	21%	52%
Total	100%	100%	100%
N =	134	106	120

A number of features are worthy of comment. The first is the emphasis given in plant A to stressing the role of the union, a feature which has been discussed above (the reason for rather less emphasis on this theme in plant B relates to the problem of political influence – see below). Second, there is a continual emphasis in plant A, particularly in *CFDT* tracts, upon issues of a primarily national nature, such as social security or the forthcoming elections. Indeed, the figures underestimate this theme because plant issues are frequently related to national ones; for example, after showing figures relating to the rise in the cost of living a *CGT* tract points out that wage increases given by the company lag behind. This leads to a discussion of government policy and that 'from the start the *CGT* has condemned the plan Barre' which is the formula of 'everything to profits, nothing to progress'. It then argues that the company 'pretends to pursue the same approach as the government'. In this way, the unions seek to widen the perspectives of the workforce.

Plant issues in fact take up a relatively small proportion of the total issues in the tracts. However, these are treated in two broad ways. The first is the simple reporting of events deemed important, and in such cases the efficacy of union action is often stressed. The second is to raise issues and deduce from them certain conclusions concerning company strategy and the consequent need for workers' action and vigilance. For example, after listing a variety of cases of company intransigence and pressure on militants since the arrival of new managers, one tract continues:

> When one begins to pester the *délégués*, to punish, to reassert discipline over everyone, it is not by chance and it is often only a start as we saw in 1961 with the arrival of the new management – the era of 1,000 redundancies … Yes, it begins with a few disciplinary cases and mild measures for 'reorganization' and then comes, as in 1968, a situation where everybody's load is overflowing. So, advice to workers – let us be vigilant otherwise we're in danger of getting really badly beaten. And always remember this – only united action frightens them.

The theme of struggle and conflict is contained in most tracts and can be seen as underlying the discussion of most issues. It is particularly stressed in plant B where the unions have recently been severely defeated by the company; accordingly the *CGT* is seeking to remobilize the workforce, but primarily on local issues. More generally, tracts in both plants stress such themes as: 'You have to fight'; 'There's no such thing as a miracle: struggle or submit'; 'There is only one way: to struggle, to struggle with all our might; all together.'

The day-to-day activities of the *élus* and other militants are similarly seen as important means of educating the workforce. This is in part consistent with the unions' emphasis upon the workplace as the base for mobilization since it is there that the worker most immediately and concretely experiences the harshness of capitalism. The education process is to be seen clearly in the way in which the militants seek to formulate demands. But the same educational endeavour is pursued, particularly by the more *gauchiste* militants, in relation to individual grievances, even errors in pay. As one *gauchiste* explained: 'When a worker raises an error in his payslip with me, I point out to him that a payslip is a symbol of capitalism, that it means a killing of his real nature.'

As noted, there exists an uneasy relationship between the wider orientations of militants and those of the workforce. The educational endeavours just discussed are one means of seeking to reduce the gap; another is the modification of the union's position, or at least an attempt to ensure that the unions provide a coherent front and one which is seen to be directed towards workers' interests rather than those of a political party.

The *CGT* and *CFDT* have co-operated for a number of years nationally, although this relationship has not been without its problems. In plant A, the *CGT* and *CFDT* have developed a common platform of demands although this was only achieved for the first time last year. As a key *CGT* militant explained:

> We have had this common practice since September. Previously each union had its own platform; these were certainly similar but there were some small differences. The *CFDT* was not completely in agreement with percentage increases while we favoured them ... Because we say that if you are all for equality then there would be a collapse of the hierarchy towards the base. But we came with an agreement ... This was the first time we have had a common platform. In September we could no longer see a real difference or any problem in arriving at a common platform so we worked one out and presented it to the workers.

The discussions to develop the platform lasted three or four months. The stimulus stemmed from two sources. The first was the national agreement between the *CGT* and the *CFDT* 'to have action company by company and branch by branch'. The second was more local awareness that union dissensions led to weakness as workers were provided with differing analyses and recommendations, and the company was able to exploit the differences.

In plant A, such co-operation only exists between the *CGT* and *CFDT*. The essential condition is an acceptance of a class orientation. Hence, relations with the *CFDT* only began to develop, according to a *CGT* militant, 'in 1972 when the *CFDT* adopted a class approach'. But the *CGT* and *CFDT* have no relations with the other unions in the plant because '*FO* and *CGC* favour a policy of collaboration with the employer'.

In plant B, where the *CGT* is much weaker, the pressure for co-operation between the unions is greater. Accordingly, despite the 'collaborationist' approach of the *CFTC*, the *CGT* is prepared to co-operate in the interests of mobilizing the workforce. Clearly there are strains in this relationship, for example due to the *CFTC* supporting the sacking of a *CGT* militant, but in many respects the level of co-operation is greater in plant B than in plant A: joint tracts are common, as are joint meetings and discussions.

In plant A the level of co-operation is in fact limited. For, as a *CFDT* militant pointed out, the important question in relation to the common platform is the source of particular claims. In other words, the agreement relates to specific demands and not to underlying philosophies.[103] Meetings are rarely held between the two unions, and over specific issues arising in the plant the disagreement between them is often considerable. On occasion the focus of action becomes a challenge to the other union rather than to the company. It is not surprising, therefore, that four out of five militants claim that they have more contact with other militants of their own union than those of the other union.

Nevertheless, the aspiration for unity is considerable. Three-quarters of the militants agreed with the view that 'it is necessary to forget the differences between the *CGT* and the *CFDT*, because unity is the most important thing'. An important aspect of this quest for unity and the desire to become more fully accepted by workers is the attempt to remove the influence of political parties. So, for example, all the militants interviewed agreed with the view that 'in the plant it is necessary to put trade-unionism before politics'. As a key *CGT* militant explained:

> Here we are a union – the *CGT* – in the plant where we have amongst the militants all sorts of religious and political views – we have Communists, Socialists, Catholics, Moslems. We meet and we are not always in agreement, but when we come out of the meeting we are in agreement because we bow to

---

103 See E. Maire, 'Dix Questions franches à Edmond Maire', *CFDT Aujourd'hui*, jan.–fév. 1976, pp. 31–42, at p. 35.

the majority and because we have, let us say, made our priority the fact that we are in the enterprise before trade-unionism. But the comrades who came from the *CGT* in the company are able to distribute outside the plant the paper of the *PCF*, or a *PS* [*Parti socialiste*] tract ... for the *CGT* and the *CFDT* now, the basic point is the arrival of socialism.

The limitation on political activity therefore means that all must accept the priority of trade-unionism. But this does not mean that the militants did not actively support the Union of the Left in the elections, even when the *PCF* and *PS* were at each other's throats. However, two-thirds of the militants thought conventional forms of trade-union action were more effective means of promoting workers' interests than were political methods.

The attempt to reduce the importance of political parties can be seen in a number of ways. Despite the association of the *CGT* nationally with the *PCF*, there was no rift between the *CGT* and *CFDT* in the plant during the election period. As a *CFDT* militant said, 'We criticize the *PCF* and the *CGT* approves of it; that's for sure. But here we don't see that difference.' A major problem exists, according to union militants, because of the *gauchistes* who belong to a variety of extreme left parties. These often seek to infiltrate the unions and use time off for political rather than trade-union purposes. The policies of the various unions in the plant differ concerning such *gauchistes*, largely in relation to their strength. The *CGT* in plant A has pursued a policy of refusing to nominate *gauchistes* for positions; indeed they have expelled such militants in the past, for example, for rejecting union policies and workers' decisions in relation to the ending of a strike.

The *CFDT* takes a rather less strong approach. As one of the key militants explained:

> At present we have problems with *gauchistes* in the *CFDT*. The problem is that from a certain point of view – pursuing demands – they do their work very well, defending their colleagues and grieving at department level. But then they say that the union is weak, it is a bureaucracy and they do not agree with a 48-hour strike or whatever because they are for revolution. It is possible that we will exclude [one *gauchiste*], because his union work is no longer being done. As long as they perform their mandate in the plant for their colleagues well, then it is all right. They tend to do this because it increases their popularity and, second, when they fulfil their mandate, the union cannot reproach them. And beyond that they are at liberty to do as they wish. But problems arise when they use their time off to do other things – and this is what is actually happening.

Whereas the *CFDT* has not expelled any *gauchiste* militants, it has refused to accept new *gauchistes* unless they are prepared to agree to the main points of the *CFDT* platform. Ironically, therefore, the *gauchistes* sometimes find themselves becoming militants for 'collaborationist' unions, such as *FO*.

For the *gauchiste* wishes to be involved while the *FO* needs active militants who may become elected as *délégués* or *comité d'entreprise* members.

However, the clearest case of seeking to rid the union of any political element, even of the *PCF*, is to be found in the *CGT* at plant B. One of the major reasons for the defeat of a lengthy strike last year was that workers accepted the company's argument that the stoppage was 'political' rather than in their interests, and the management was also able to sack several militants who were active in the *PCF* cell (for the *PCF*, like a number of Trotskyist groups, form 'cells' within plants[104]). As a *CGT* militant explained:

> The blokes who were sacked were the young *PCF* militants; they were in the *PCF* cell here and were well known in the area as Party members. They were certainly picked on for that reason – they were seen to be working, not for the *CGT*, but for the *PCF*. They were sacked because the strike was seen as a political one. These militants sold *Humanité* [the *PCF* paper] as often as they distributed tracts. There are many workers here who are trade-unionists but don't want to get involved in politics. And it is this which led to the failure of the … strike. Blokes could point to the members of the *PCF* and say the strike was politically motivated. Blokes said they would strike for all of us in the plant, but not for the *PCF*. A large part of the movement was stopped for this reason and management immediately profited, saying, 'look it's not the union, it's political'. And many *délégués* said that if things continued like this, then they would resign because 'we're one with the blokes, not the party'.

In this section, attention has been turned to the ways in which unions attempt to organize and mobilize in order to achieve a favourable balance of power, and thereby impose pressure upon management to achieve concessions. While it is clear that considerable care is taken in the formulations of demands, the primary concerns of the unions appear to be to achieve a balance between their aspirations and the attitudes of the workforce. It is now necessary to attempt to assess the success with which the union endeavours are met.

Union success: grievance handling and mobilization

The previous section has discussed the broad strategies of the militants in order to strengthen their position. It is now necessary to attempt to assess their success. Such an endeavour is clearly difficult if one looks at the extent to which management makes concessions. For, it has been suggested that an important feature of arms'-length bargaining is the attempt by management to deny union influence. In this respect, then, it is only possible to refer to

---

104 See *CFDT*, 'La CFDT et l'Action des partis politiques dans l'Entreprise', *CFDT Aujourd'hui*, juill.–août 1976, pp. 14–26.

the militants' claims, the care with which the company seeks to understand shop-floor feeling and the fact that wage increases in the company tend to be above average for engineering and to exceed (if only marginally) the limits imposed by various incomes policies. In plant A it is also worthy of note that, despite sizeable losses, the company has not yet attempted to introduce any large-scale redundancies. The last attempt was met with strong resistance and the company finally drastically reduced the number made redundant. In plant B the assessment in this respect is less favourable to the unions. Just at the end of the research period the company announced its intention to make several hundred workers redundant. At the time of writing it is not clear whether union reaction will be successful in defeating this plan.[105]

In default of more satisfactory indicators, the main data used has to be patterns of union membership and voting; resort to the union with problems and the extent to which militants negotiate issues; and the frequency of resort to strike action or other forms of collective sanction.

The fact that no elected positions are filled by non-union nominees would suggest that the unions receive a good deal of support from the workforce. However, it has to be remembered that, at least in the first round of elections, the unions do have a monopoly of nominations. Certainly when one turns to union membership (see above) it cannot be said that the unions meet with a great deal of success. Less than half the workforce is unionized; but, on the other hand, this is a considerable achievement in French terms. In other words, within the French context, the unions are remarkably successful in this respect. More generally, the success is rather limited, although it should be remembered that 'membership ... is a voluntary act'[106] as any closed-shop is extremely rare in France.

Nevertheless, the militants claim that they do provide the main channel through which workers pursue grievances. Militants were asked whether in their area workers normally took problems first to them or to the foremen; they were asked this question concerning the organization and pace of work, discipline, job grading, wages and bonuses, and working conditions.

---

105 Ed.'s note: We do not know precisely which plants Eric Batstone researched. However, if it was the Périgny La Rochelle factory, this fell after the *PSA* Peugeot-Citroën 1978 acquisition from 3,000 workers to 2,000 by 1981 and to 950 by 1987. In 1991 it became the Triaxe company, part of the Tersou group, with 544 workers and was finally closed in 1996. If the research was carried out in the two adjacent Lieu-Saint-Amand/Hordain Simca factories in the northern Pas-de-Calais region (the greenfield development dating back to 1969), then after *PSA* changed its name to Talbot in 1978 it became a part of the SEVEL joint venture that *PSA* established with Fiat that lasted until 2012, when the rebuilt factory still employed 700 people.

106 *Le Peuple*, 'Pour une Formation syndicale de départ', p. 11.

Overall, militants claimed that workers were twice as likely to approach them rather than the foremen, although the proportion was somewhat lower in relation to wages and job grading. If this is an accurate reflection of the actual situation, then, again, the militants in the company appear to achieve a fair degree of success. Such use of the union is considerably higher than that indicated by observational studies of plants.[107] Nevertheless, the significance of union action in day-to-day terms is certainly considerably less than in British plants owned by the same company.

Descriptions of the activities of *délégués* by militants give a picture of involvement in relatively minor issues; errors in pay appear to be a major source of activity. One militant described the activities of a *délégué*:

> he looks after the major interests of his fellows, all the little problems which occur in the workshop ... He intervenes in errors in pay ... if a mate has a problem because he is underpaid, he knows how to read the payslip. He intervenes if stop-watches are being used – he sees that the stop-watch is accurate. He intervenes if a window is broken and it is cold in the plant; he intervenes with a maintenance manager to replace window panes. He intervenes if something is likely to fall and is unsafe.

Such activities are, of course, significant but they certainly are not major. Moreover, because of the fear of becoming incorporated the militants fail to play a major role in a central aspect of workers' experience – the organization of work. It is significant that in the quotation the *délégué* simply checks the stop-watch. In the questionnaire militants were asked how frequently they became involved in particular kinds of issues. Only one in eight dealt weekly with any kind of money issue, and half did not do so each month. Half were not involved each month in questions relating to the organization and pace of work, despite the fact that they claimed the company was continually trying to speed up work. However, for nearly a quarter this was a daily issue. Disciplinary issues involved militants about as frequently as organization problems, while job grading was scarcely ever dealt with. The most frequent issue of militant activity was working conditions: half the militants dealt with an issue of this kind at least weekly.

There is, of course, a danger of dismissing such activity too rapidly (and of forgetting that shop stewards in Britain spend a large percentage of their time on similar issues). As one militant argued in the face of such criticism:

> Life is not only about bread but about freedom ... one must pursue both – one is forced to be involved in specific detailed problems of your comrades. If you weren't you would have no meaning and you would not be conforming to your

---

107 Linhart, *L'Établi*; Bernoux *et al.*, *Trois Ateliers d'O.S.*

ideals. One should not conceive of it as being simply an idealist or simply being dominated by little issues of a specific nature. One cannot ignore either aspect.

In terms of the conceptions of the unions themselves, an important indication of support and success would be patterns of collective action and their levels of participation. Overall statistics of any detailed nature were unavailable, but each militant in plant A was asked to give details of every strike or collective sanction in the last year, and union tracts were also studied. In all, thirty stoppages were identified. Of these, sixteen were initiated by the union, or militants, a figure which is only marginally higher than in Britain.[108] However, the levels of participation and of the action are, from a British point of view, especially striking. Half of the strikes initiated by the union were national or industrial stoppages and were generally of only an hour or two in duration. The militants called only two plant-level strikes, and the remainder in specific departments. All but one of the worker-initiated stoppages occurred at departmental level or below. This suggests that the unions in the plant, without instructions from the larger unions, rarely call strikes for the whole of the workforce and those that do are typically of a symbolic nature. Indeed, few strikes (as distinct from go-slows) last more than a day – only two or three in plant A have done so in the last three years.

Moreover, levels of participation in strikes tend to be rather low. According to the figures provided by the militants, eighteen of the thirty strikes mobilized less than a third of the workers involved in the issue, and seven mobilized 10% or less. Only eight mobilized more than two-thirds of the relevant workers. The level of participation tended to be higher in departmental disputes (seven out of eighteen mobilizing two-thirds or more, compared to only one of the twelve other strikes) in worker-initiated stoppages (seven out of fourteen mobilizing more than two-thirds, compared to only one of the union-initiated stoppages).

The difficulties of mobilization and the lack of established procedures for negotiating such matters as the reorganization or speeding up of work prior to their implementation mean that the conditions under which comparable groups work can be very different. This was particularly striking in relation to management attempts to speed up production. Where groups were ready to engage in strike action they frequently achieved a reduction in pace or additional manning. Where they were not ready to do this then their pace of work tended to remain at the new, higher rate. In this respect, the limited, *ad hoc* nature of union influence served to make the frontier of control almost random.

108 E. Batstone, I. Boraston and S. Frenkel, *The Social Organization of Strikes* (Blackwell, Oxford: 1978), p. 74.

In sum, it would appear that the unions achieve only a limited support when they seek to initiate particular stoppages. However, it must be remembered that their educational efforts no doubt play a role in legitimizing the idea of strike action among workers and that the militants quickly become involved in formulating demands and conducting the strike.

Nevertheless, the militants in the plant do demonstrate an awareness of the problems of mobilizing the workforce: this was twice as frequently referred to as the biggest problem for the unions as any other problem. As one militant explained: 'We are never one. A strike of 100% does not exist, but sometimes we get 60 or 70%. Often it is less, but if it is much less then we straightaway try to get them back to work because a minority strike is no good.' Accordingly, the unions seek to use other means to gain workers' support; votes for the platform of demands have already been mentioned. In addition, the militants send round petitions for workers to sign, hold demonstrations inside and outside the plant, and send delegations (largely of militants) both to management and to the employers' association.[109]

The unions may also resort to the law. For in France there is a considerable range of legislation that the unions can use. Particularly where Labour Inspectors are seen as neutral or at least sympathetic to the unions, then militants frequently use this means to resolve grievances. In plant A, for example, it would appear that the Labour Inspector is called in on about as many issues each year as there are strikes. It would appear that he is frequently used in a manner comparable to the way in which shop stewards use external procedure; that is, when workers are not prepared to engage in strike action. Hence, in one situation when workers were not prepared to strike:

> there were days and days of discussion and then we had to get the Labour Inspector to intervene … We saw the danger and tried to prevent it but the workers would not act. If the workers had said they would not work in those conditions [the problem] would have been resolved in ten minutes.

More generally, Adam and Reynaud suggest that the existence of legislation serves as a convenient means for both parties to avoid real bargaining in a context of potential 'anomie'.[110]

---

109 For a more general discussion of union strategies and participation in strikes, see Dubois, *Travail et conflit dans l'industrie*; M. Durand, *Les Conflits du travail* (CRESST, Université Paris-Sud: 1977); D. Weiss, 'Notes sur les Grèves', *Revue française des Affaires sociales* 15:4 (1977), pp. 37–58; Morel, 'Physionomie statistique de grèves', *Revue française des Affaires sociales*, pp. 183–95; Durand and Dubois, *La Grève*.

110 G. Adam and J.-D. Reynaud, *Conflits du travail et changement social* (PUF, Paris: 1978), pp. 63ff.

In sum, it is difficult to assess the overall success of the unions in terms of mobilizing the workforce and successfully pursuing claims. In terms of their grand objectives their success is limited. At a more 'realistic' level any assessment is more difficult, and there are few bench-marks to go by. For example, it is certainly not the case that British shop stewards achieve total success. Nevertheless, the limited participation in strikes and the brevity of most stoppages can scarcely be seen as evidence of great strength. But, in French terms, the union situation in the company studied, and particularly at plant A, would appear to be considerably stronger than in most companies.

Foremen and informal accommodation

The previous sections have looked at the general pattern of arms'-length bargaining and the strategies relating to this method of conducting industrial relations. In effect, these strategies focus upon influencing the reality and appearance of the balance of power. Two other methods of accommodation exist, however. The first, resort to the law, does not need further discussion. The second is the existence of informal deals and forms of accommodation which occur largely at shop-floor level. In order to investigate this area it is useful to start with a brief consideration of the position of the foreman.

The foreman is, as always, in the 'hot seat', confronted on the one hand with a variety of instructions from management, and on the other with the workforce. A number of the position's features are significant for present purposes. First, in the face of a growing centralization within the company, the foreman has a decreasing amount of formal discretion. He has, in particular, to achieve the programmes of production and at the same time work within fairly limited budgets. These points were especially emphasized by the militants. Hence, in the questionnaire they were asked at what level of the management structure they were usually able to resolve particular, relatively minor, issues. On such matters as discipline, increased bonuses or job regrading, only one in seven of the militants referred to the foreman whose discretion was seen to be somewhat greater in terms of problems relating to safety and speed of work. These elements are important for the later discussion.

Second, the foremen are encouraged by management not to become closely involved with militants. Their role as observers of union and worker activity has already been noted. In addition, according to the militants, they are encouraged by management to ensure that they take up any workers' grievances and thereby exclude the unionized *élus*. Finally, particularly in the more weakly organized plant B, the militants claim that higher management view with a good deal of suspicion any foreman who is discovered talking at any length to a militant.

On the other hand, if they are to achieve their production programmes foremen have to ensure the co-operation of the workforce and this may not always be possible within the confines of the constraints laid down by higher management. Moreover, in the more strongly organized plant A about a third of the foremen are themselves unionized (mainly *CGT*); these and some others are sympathetic to the militants.

In many issues, the *délégués* first approach the foremen. Two-thirds of the militants interviewed say they discuss problems with the foremen daily, while only one in seven even meet the departmental manager this frequently: the majority of militants meet the higher plant management less than monthly. Moreover, while almost half say that it is very easy to meet the foremen to discuss a problem, only one militant says this as far as higher management is concerned, and almost half say that it is positively difficult. Similarly, through the questionnaire an attempt was made to see whether strong bargaining relationships existed between militants and members of management. About a quarter of militants appear to have such strong relationships with foremen but none with higher members of management (as indicated by the receipt of tips and informal information and the making of deals on any regular basis). *Some* degree of wheeling and dealing is found between most militants and foremen, and in some cases with higher management. But while only half of the militants have this type of informal relationship with foremen, this is true of only one in seven of them in relation to managers above this level.

The pressures of such relationships are obvious given the union emphasis on *rapports de force*. The ability to reach compromises to satisfy these pressures derive from three sources as far as the sections of the plant investigated are concerned – namely assembly-line production (in plant A) and piecework areas, notably welders and machinists in plant B. These sources were prior consultation, informal reorganization of tasks and the payment of make-up.

Prior consultation formally exists through the *comité d'entreprise* but, as has been seen, this is of little significance. Moreover, in the assembly department, it was clearly of importance to keep small groups of workers fairly happy in order to prevent the whole line grinding to a halt. Despite higher management's attempts to limit the role of the union, and also some suspicion on the part of workers of militants closely engaged in discussions with foremen, informal meetings are held between foremen and militants. From the foremen and other groups (for example, those in production planning), the militants receive information on the details of production plans and, in addition, they are able to sort out particular problems. Discussions with foremen are generally held away from the line and, it seems, on major issues, may occur outside the plant. However, it is clear that the scope for such informal dealing is limited; with new models, for example, resort to strike action has been the main method to improve manning. On a less grand scale, for example, increases in speed or awkward combinations of models, custom and practice have grown up with regard to manning.

This can be seen as similar to the informal reorganization of tasks. Workers themselves often, of course, develop short-cuts in their tasks and in the main foremen are happy to turn a blind eye to this for it ensures output without problems. But important means of reorganization derive from the relationship between work-study and foremen.

Work-study is relatively undermanned in both plants, and in the main methods and speeds are calculated without going onto the shop floor where they often create a strong reaction (there being no prior discussion of changes). Foremen frequently reorganize tasks on the basis of their local and detailed knowledge in such a way as to make the situation acceptable to workers, for example by combining two jobs the handling time between them can be 'given' to the workers. Work-study staff often either remain ignorant of such changes or are happy to turn a blind eye to them. Their 'scientific' skills appear to remain credible, and everyone else is happy.

The main problem appears to arise in plant B, in a department where there is a high turnover. What this means is that workers unfamiliar with the tasks, and frequently foreign and with no French, are unable to match even the 'amended' times. Consequently conflicts are common between foremen and work-study staff who defend their timings and blame turnover for production problems. However, in the more unionized plant A this problem does not appear to occur: work-study staff have often been recruited from the shop floor and are familiar with the short-cuts used. But, according to the militants, these staff 'do not betray their comrades'.

The third meaning of 'dealing' by foremen is largely confined to piecework areas. The piecework system operates on the following basis: the norm for output is set at 100, and workers receive bonuses up to a rate of 150. Above that rate, they receive no additional bonus. But in addition foremen have a budget for make-up. What, according to militants, frequently happens is that foremen expect workers to exceed a rate of 150 on loosely timed jobs as a condition for make-up on higher jobs, for the maximum of 150 has become the real norm. Moreover, as has been noted, militants argue that some foremen distribute make-up preferentially to those who act 'responsibly' and are not unionized; in such cases the militants are not slow to demand a greater fairness of distribution. But in addition, it seems that make-up is used by *CGT* foremen in particular as a means of meeting worker/union demands. Informal accommodations and concessions are therefore largely confined to the lower levels of organization.

Two arguments may be put forward concerning this role of ambivalent mediator. The first is that management is aware of this informal accommodation and welcomes it as a means of preventing the escalation of problems and hence more frequent confrontation. The second is that this accommodation is an essential and inevitable consequence of managerial endeavours at centralization. The second appears the more valid argument, as has recently been argued in the French context.[111] And, in terms of the first argument, it seems that management wishes to give a *limited* discretion to foremen, but to discourage union activism rather than to reach compromises with it.

In sum, in the face of management's production programmes on the one hand, and potential worker disruption on the other, more junior levels of management, and foremen in particular, frequently resort to informal deals with militants and workers. For while the company as a whole may be able and prepared to withstand stoppages, this is less true of the individual foreman whose assessment by higher management depends upon reaching production targets. Therefore, where co-operation from workers is a continuous requirement and where stoppages by a few men can lead to significant disruptions (such as on assembly lines), there is pressure for foremen to deal with workers' representatives – the militants – rather than maintain the company strategy of arms'-length bargaining. While some militants, notably in the *CFDT*, are hesitant concerning such relations, they find themselves drawn into them because they do facilitate the resolution of many grievances. Many *CGT* militants are less hesitant, particularly where the foremen concerned are members of the same union. It might therefore be suggested that informal deals are not only important for the maintenance of production but also as a further safety valve (in addition to the law) for the postures which go to make up the dominant pattern of arms'-length bargaining.

Some concluding thoughts

The theme of this paper has been that the pattern of industrial relations in French companies can best be described as one of arms'-length bargaining. That is, the use of power is less institutionalized than in many other countries so that what happens at the bargaining table is of far less significance than a more direct demonstration or indication of force. Consequently, particularly for management, the subtle game of taking hints and cues is dependent far more upon understanding what is happening at the point of production

---

111 C. Morel, 'Les Stratégies de négociation dans l'Entreprise', *SdT* 4/77 (1977), pp. 362–82.

rather than upon the statements of union negotiators. At the same time, both parties concentrate their efforts upon a longer-term strategy of influencing the militants of the workforce and the position of the union. The range of strategies has been discussed at some length.

A number of reasons can be put forward to explain this pattern of industrial relations. It can be argued that a more institutionalized means of dealing with grievances and demands cannot exist where the two parties so manifestly reject the legitimacy of the existence of the other party. This is certainly a partial explanation, but given that a similar basic hostility has existed in other countries that now have more institutionalized systems, this is far from a totally satisfactory answer. The case of multi-national companies, such as the one studied here, suggests that employers will seek to avoid a more routinized system of dealing with the unions if this does not seem to be the best means of achieving their particular ends. Clearly this attitude is strongly influenced by a variety of cultural and historical factors which have both a direct effect and an indirect one through the development of particular kinds of institutions. But the latter are not inevitable, and are likely to change when one or both parties believe there are advantages in different forms of organization and have the power to achieve the desired changes. In other words, when unions achieve a closer relationship with the workforce, when workers are more ready to challenge management decisions, especially in a favourable economic situation, then management is likely to give fuller recognition (possibly due to government pressure).

It might therefore be argued that employers in France do not recognize the unions more fully precisely because of the 'patchiness' of their influence with the workforce. The weak legal institutions and rather sterile management–union meetings are sufficient formalities to channel much disgruntlement. Further, the pattern of formal unilateral decisions (rather than concessions) serves to preserve the image of managerial autonomy, particularly with the further safety valves of resort to the law and informal accommodation.

Similarly, while the unions cannot be said to be overjoyed with their position, they gain a number of advantages from the existing pattern. They have a relatively secure legal base for activity in the plant and at the same time they are able to claim victories without generally being tied down by signing agreements. They are, in other words, able to achieve some reasonable balance in action between their two potentially contradictory goals of protecting the worker in the short term and rejecting the system of capitalism in the longer term. Arms'-length bargaining, therefore, assumes a particularly significant role precisely because it permits short-term accommodation without formally compromising long-term ends and basic philosophies. This is almost as true of the unions as of management.

For the unions the situation is, of course, rather more difficult precisely because they are the ones seeking dramatic change. Further, there are difficulties in balancing the acceptance, if only grudgingly, of, for example, the *comité d'entreprise* and their radical goals. The means of making the two coherent appears to be not only the double function of the union discussed above but also the necessity of gaining the support of the workforce. Given the awareness of the importance of power, unions have to gain the support of the workforce. At least at company level this would appear, generally, to require some moderation to their goals. In other words, the need to prove union relevance and its commitment to workers (in order to gain their support) may lead to a modification of union goals or to a greater gap between day-to-day action and ideology.

Clearly it is difficult to check such a thesis without considerably more data than is available from this study. Moreover, while such changes may have occurred, one might also add that such trends may be simply reversed in the face of economic crises when the radical statements of the unions appear to have more meaning.[112] Similarly, while workers may not generally accept a radical perspective, they may do so in such situations as strikes as they work out the implications of their situation.[113] Certainly the major advances in the position of the union have tended to come from occasional 'explosive' situations, although afterwards their main impact appears to have been in the shape of legislation rather than stronger unions, for example in terms of membership (which, after a period, has tended to fall back to its old levels). Similarly, the results of elections in companies since the general election indicate that the *CGT* has been losing support because of its leader's support of the *PCF*.

Moreover, one can identify trends which may encourage employers to recognize the unions more fully. These relate primarily to the changing nature of industry. But, on the other hand, economic crises and high unemployment may encourage employers to adopt an even more aggressive approach. From the almost daily accounts in the French press of occupations or the forceful eviction of strikers from companies it would seem that at present the pattern has been away from any greater institutionalization. It is as yet too early to see if the newly re-elected government's policy of encouraging discussions will bear any fruit.

Much of the immediately preceding discussions is necessarily speculative. But it should, hopefully, be enough to point to the dangers of assuming that French industrial relations will inevitably become more institutionalized, that at present their 'system' is 'less developed' but

---

112 See A. Mercier, 'Les Conflits de longue durée', *CFDT Aujourd'hui*, nov.–déc. 1976, pp. 4–13; Adam and Reynaud, *Conflits du travail et changement social*, pp. 295ff.

113 G. Lorant, Fédération Services CFDT, N. Mandray and D. Anselme, *Quatre Grèves significatives* (EPI, Paris: 1972).

will inevitably become more 'mature'. Moreover, the French experience provides important warnings concerning the conventional view of the institutionalization of class conflict.

A good deal of the literature on systems of collective bargaining tends to focus upon procedures and negotiating skills. There is therefore a tendency to forget the essential element which continually underlies bargaining in the Anglo-Saxon style: namely, power. For power is important in establishing collective-bargaining institutions. Both parties have to be convinced that the other is sufficiently strong to justify it being recognized and being dealt with. Similarly, bargaining is not solely – or often even mainly – about logical argument, but about power. While argument may provide legitimacy for concessions, while some bargaining may be integrative, much bargaining is simply a process of assessing power and commitment. In this sense, the French emphasis upon negotiation as merely one stage in a larger process is perfectly correct. The point is that in France the background conditions and strategies of bargaining are that much more obvious in part because of the orientations of the parties, but also because those conditions appear to be unstable and uncertain. Even so, it is important for unions in all countries to ensure that they have the support of workers on many issues.[114]

One can usefully pursue this theme of power and institutionalization further. For example, there are some signs in Britain that, in the current economic crisis, patterns of institutionalization may be collapsing. There have been some cases of employers adopting strategies in Britain which are common in France. One might also see the wave of occupations of recent years in the same way. In other words, in changing circumstances employers and workers may not believe that institutionalized routes are the most effective; in other words, conventional forms of negotiation and limited strike action are once more seen more clearly as tactical devices.

In France, it has also to be remembered that there is some institutionalization of industrial relations – the *comité d'entreprise*, the *délégués du personnel*, management–union meetings, and some agreements, even at company level. These facts raise a number of questions concerning the commonly accepted conditions for institutionalization, such as an acceptance of certain common values, an acceptance of rules of the game, and so on. Basic among these is that each party accepts the legitimacy of the other side.

These conditions scarcely apply to the French situation. It has been argued that neither employers nor unions accept the other and yet the institutions

---

114 See E. Batstone, I. Boraston and S. Frenkel, 'Principles in Work-Place Bargaining', in E. Coker and G. Stuttard (eds), *Industrial Studies 2: The Bargaining Context* (Arrow: 1976); 1978); Batstone *et al.*, *The Social Organization of Strikes*.

exist. It might be suggested that the *CGT*'s concern with 'realism' is, in fact, a recognition of the employer: but this is a recognition of its power rather than its legitimacy. A similar argument has been put forward by Adam and Reynaud: that the unions and employers are really in agreement that power should remain with the employer in the capitalist context.[115] This is perfectly true, but whether this can be termed legitimacy is doubtful. Moreover, it is a somewhat convoluted argument that this meets the condition for institutionalization, for the unions do not recognize the legitimacy of the social structure in which the employers' position rests.

Similar questions can be raised with regard to other aspects of the conventional arguments concerning institutionalization. The unions are very critical of the powers that the law provides them with; the employers are seeking to remove the favoured position of the union in the *comité d'entreprise*. And yet the institution continues to function. The unions also made frequent resort to the law despite their criticism of it. It might be argued that the 'rules of the game' are accepted but it is in a pragmatic manner consistent with arms'-length bargaining rather than any deeper commitment to the rules. It is a case of 'it's all we've got' rather than anything else. Moreover, it has been suggested that the unions use the position of *élu* as a means of pursuing their own goals. Again, therefore, the reasons underlying the acceptance of the institution are scarcely supportive of the *comité d'entreprise*.

The unions used the statutory work-based institutions as a means of mobilization, given the time allowance which *élus* obtain. The existence of institutionalized agencies therefore becomes a way by which manifest conflict may become more frequent. More generally, Dubois and Durand have argued that institutionalization can lead to greater levels of strike activity.[116] They argue that the creation of new rules means that there are more to argue and fight about. This is no doubt part true. But another reason may be suggested. The establishment of institutions that provide a base for union activity, and which possibly also recognize by their very existence that there is conflict, may serve to foster the expression of that conflict outside the institutionalized channels. This may occur not only for reasons relating to change,[117] but also because of the legitimacy of conflict is recognized and the organizations that 'feed into' the institutionalized channels have therefore become more developed. But there is no reason to assume that those organizations will make use only of the institutionalized

115 Adam and Reynaud, *Conflits du travail et changement social*, p. 101.
116 P. Dubois and C. Durand, 'Sociologie des Conflits sociaux', *L'Année Sociologique* 24 (1973), pp. 535–54.
117 See E. Batstone, 'The Organization of Conflict', in G. M. Stephenson and C. J. Brotherton (eds), *Industrial Relations: A Social Psychological Approach* (Wiley, New York: 1978).

channels. Nor is this argument applicable only to France: recent survey research in the Industrial Relations Research Unit can be seen as supporting this contention, as can also the work of Turner and his colleagues.[118] Most obviously, the level of strike action is higher in many countries with highly complex and 'deep' forms of institutionalization than in countries where institutions are less 'developed'.

If these arguments are correct, then it seems reasonable to conclude that institutionalization is simply a means of accommodation to a particular balance of power. Any legitimacy which attaches to the institutions that develop is conditional and pragmatic. If they appear to be the most convenient means of pursuing issues then they will be used, but otherwise they will be rejected or manipulated in a variety of ways. This is perhaps particularly true when institutions are created by law by a government seeking to play a mediating role between two warring parties.

This is not to deny that negotiators in particular may become firmly attached to the institutions and that therefore these may gain a greater degree of legitimacy. But this is by no means inevitable. While the contacts fostered by institutionalized means may improve understanding, this may lead to greater conflict. While institutions may make contact between the two parties easier, this may have little relevance if the gains achieved are seen as consistently unsatisfactory. Indeed, the parties may seek to maintain the institutions precisely because their failure to produce results can be used as evidence of the aggression and intransigence of the other partner. Institutions may therefore be used to fuel the flames rather than reduce them.

Further, if it is accepted that the existence of institutions is primarily a routinization of power relations, the hesitancy of the French unions concerning the signing of agreements in fact has only a limited significance. For, as the concept of arms'-length bargaining indicates, the unions accept in a *de facto* sense that, say, wages will be increased by only a certain amount. It is true that they can then roundly condemn the company. But how significant is this in comparison with a situation, such as might be found in Britain, where after a lengthy strike the unions are forced to sign an agreement which they in fact do not accept. Those actually signing the agreement may feel committed to it, but other union officers and workers may feel no such obligation. The experience of some companies after forcing changes in the payment system upon stewards and workers are particularly instructive in this respect. More generally, the nature of many strikes in Britain would suggest that in practice such agreements have a

---

118 H. A. Turner, G. Roberts and D. Roberts, *Management Characteristics and Labour Conflict: A Study of Managerial Organisation, Attitudes and Industrial Relations* (Cambridge University Press: 1977).

limited and conditional legitimacy. The position and status of agreements often seems to be preserved more by skilful manipulation, reinterpretation, and ensuring that contrary actions do not become too well publicized than by anything else.

Nevertheless, this is not to deny that institutions may serve to reduce the expression of conflict. The rhetoric of peaceful negotiation may lead to more subtle ways. More importantly, where institutions have sufficient coverage in terms of issues and depth that go further than a superficial consultation, they may facilitate agreement. This is of particular importance for trade unions since, for example, in many British companies, the assumption by management is that the unions do represent workers. In other words, they do not have to prove their representativeness continually. This contrasts with the French situation where meaningful discussions or concessions seem to be much more piecemeal precisely because the union is required to prove that it represents a strength of feeling among the workforce on each issue. Nevertheless, on crucial issues the unions in Britain still do have to prove their support.

This brings us back to the starting point. The reason for the assumption of union strength and representativeness in many British companies is that they have proved this so often in the past. And it is precisely this problem that the French unions face. But in Britain this evidence from the past means that in practice they do not necessarily always have that representativeness on a specific issue in the present. This is, of course, precisely the basis of criticisms of union incorporation.

The pattern of industrial relations in France at plant and company level has been described as arms'-length bargaining. This pattern has been explained in terms of the orientations of the actors and the balance of power. At one level the nature of French industrial relations can be seen as in marked contrast to the British pattern. But at another level it can be seen as similar, and as a useful case study for questioning the conventional assumptions concerning institutionalization. The discussion in this section has not been intended as anything approaching a full analysis of the latter question. But hopefully enough has been said to indicate that, at the minimum, much of the debate in this area has been rather one-sided. The argument here has purposely sought to be biased in the other direction in order to point up weaknesses in the conventional argument.

In conclusion, it might be suggested that it would be useful to pursue the analysis of institutionalization along lines comparable to the analysis of bureaucracy and organization. In these latter areas, one can identify a movement in the theoretical debate away from ideal-types emphasizing co-operation and consensus to an awareness, at least by some, of the importance of power, conflict, and basic disagreements. In other words, the analysis has shifted from the formal logic of bureaucracy to the reality of organizational behaviour. The same sort of analysis is required with the question of institutionalization. It is particularly ironic that this should need to be said about the analysis of a type of structure which is based upon recognition of conflict. But the main thrust of the conventional analysis has been the peace-making nature of institutionalization; in other words, an acceptance of its declared aim, to the (partial) detriment of an understanding of the context in which it operates and how it works in practice. While weaknesses in a particular institutional system may be recognized, the reason is generally attributed to failures of detailed organization rather than being seen as endemic to institutionalization itself. The former explanation may often be in part valid, but this does not deny the need to study the latter.

Terms and abbreviations

CGC	*Confédération générale des cadres*
CGT	*Confédération générale du travail*
CFDT	*Confédération française démocratique du travail*
CFTC	*Confédération française des travailleurs chrétiens*
FO	*Force ouvrière*
PCF	*Parti communiste française*
PS	*Parti socialiste*
Comité d'entreprise	Works council
Délégués du personnel	Personnel delegates
Élus	The workers' elected representatives, i.e. members of the *comité d'entreprise* and *délégués du personnel*
Militant	Union activist: a union member who is prepared to do rather more than merely be a member. The definition is loose; in the paper it is used primarily as a general term to refer to *élus* and those holding official union positions. Questionnaire data relating to militants derives from interviews from sixteen *élus* and union officials in plant A belonging to the *CGT* and *CFDT*. This is equivalent to about one-half of the total. In addition, interviews of a less structured form were held with ten militants.

doi:10.3828/hsir.2015.36.5

In Praise of Collective Bargaining: The Enduring Significance of Hugh Clegg's *Trade Unionism under Collective Bargaining*

Keith Sisson

I have a very strong personal interest in highlighting Hugh Clegg's *Trade Unionism under Collective Bargaining* (*TUCB*).[1] I have spent most of my working life grappling with some of the 'Unfinished Business' it identified. But that's not why I urge people to read or reread it. I have three much more important reasons for them doing so. The first is *TUCB*'s approach. It is unparalleled in its clarity and succinctness, running to no more than 121 pages, including index and very few footnotes – something the reviewer in *Economic Journal* found especially praise-worthy.[2] There is none of the algebra, models, and complicated jargon that have come to characterize so much social-science work, let alone the seemingly infinite varieties of 'pluralism' of some industrial relations literature. There are just a few very clear and straightforward propositions in plain language. But they are very challenging and give considerable food for thought.

The second reason is the importance of its subject matter. *TUCB* deals with the main influences on trade-union behaviour, the significance of the structure of collective bargaining and the role of employers and their organizations in shaping it. Academic texts are quoted either because they're very bad (and offer an easy sacrificial straw person) or very good

I'm extremely grateful for the help I've had in preparing this article from Willy Brown, Paul Edwards and Paul Marginson. The editors (Paul Smith and Dave Lyddon) have also made many pertinent suggestions for its improvement.

1 H. A. Clegg, *Trade Unionism under Collective Bargaining: A Theory Based on Comparisons of Six Countries* (Basil Blackwell, Oxford: 1976).
2 S. McDowell, 'Book Review', *Economic Journal* 87 (1977), p. 388.

and have to be referred to. *TUCB* falls into the latter category. Put simply, *TUCB* has become the perennial starting point for anyone dealing with union behaviour and the practice of collective bargaining. A measure of the interest that the book has stimulated is that, at the last Google Scholar count, it had been cited more than 500 times. Even more to the point is that almost seventy of these citations have been since 2010, more than thirty years after publication. *TUCB* has also been translated into Italian and Spanish.

The third reason is that *TUCB* implicitly raises fundamental questions about the importance and sustainability of collective bargaining in every country – issues that are matters for deep reflection today not in the least for policy-makers interested in matters of performance and productivity, the development of human and social capital, and democratic governance. In particular, it forces us to think about the role of collective bargaining in society, what has been lost as a result of its decline and what might be done to restore its practice.

So if you have never read it, please do. It won't take you long, but shows what can be done with bold approach. If you haven't looked at it for many years, please revisit it. Not just for old times' sake, but because of the thoughts it is likely to stimulate about the current state of trade unions and collective bargaining.

Trade Unionism under Collective Bargaining: argument and unfinished business

In its own words, *TUCB* aims 'to expound a theory of trade union behaviour under collective bargaining and test it against the evidence available from six countries' – Australia, France, Germany, Sweden, the UK, and the USA (p. 118). Chapter 1 is a summary of the argument. Its starting point, which draws on the work of Sidney and Beatrice Webb and H. A. Turner,[3] is that the methods by which trade unions seek to regulate the terms of employment of their members are the foremost influences on their behaviour. It follows that, where collective bargaining is the main method of action, it is the variations in the dimensions of the structure of collective bargaining that are key. The main dimensions comprise:

- extent – the proportion of employees covered by collective bargaining
- level – whether collective bargaining takes place between workplace representatives and local managers, or between district/regional/

---

3 S. Webb and B. Webb, *Industrial Democracy* (Longmans, Green and Co.: 1897); H. A. Turner, *Trade Union Growth, Structure and Policy: A Comparative Study of the Cotton Unions in England* (Allen and Unwin: 1962).

national/confederal trade unions and their employers' organization counterparts

- depth – the extent to which local trade unions are involved in the administration of collective agreements
- degree of control – the extent to which the collective agreements establish obligatory standards
- scope – the number of aspects of employment that collective agreements cover
- union security – the degree of support given by employers to union efforts to recruit and maintain members.

Chapter 2 demonstrates how union density reflects the extent and depth of collective bargaining and the degree of union security offered by collective bargaining. Chapter 4, on government, and chapter 5, on workplace organization, show how these features of union behaviour, along with the strength of factionalism, are accounted for by the level of collective bargaining. Chapter 6 describes how the long-term pattern of strikes similarly depends on the level of collective bargaining, together with the degree of control exercised by collective agreements and their disputes procedures. Chapter 7 also explains differences in union attitudes to industrial democracy in terms of the level of collective bargaining. It is only the external structure of trade unions, that is their coverage in terms of types of occupations and industries, which are not directly shaped by the dimensions of collective bargaining: chapter 3 argues these are largely a product of the period in which trade unions were formed.

In chapter 8, *TUCB* argues that the main influences on the various dimensions of collective bargaining are the structures of management and employers' organizations. But it adds the rider that, where the law intervened at an early stage, it could be equally or even more important. In chapter 9, appropriately entitled 'Unfinished Business', *TUCB* argues that the evidence for five of the six countries confirms the theory. It has less explanatory power for France, however, because the main method of union action is not collective bargaining. Rather it is political action and, in particular, the pursuit of statutory regulation. For this reason, *TUCB* does not claim to amount a general theory of trade unions, let alone industrial relations. Before these can be attempted, it argues, further work needs to be completed. For a general theory of trade unions, the circumstances that promote collective bargaining must be compared to those that lead unions to prefer political action. For a theory of industrial relations, there is a need for more information about the behaviour of employers' organizations, managers, and governments.

Criticisms and comments

Hardly surprisingly, given its approach and ambitions, *TUCB* has had no shortage of critics. An early example is the *British Journal of Industrial Relations* reviewer, who was very unhappy that it did not adopt 'a more systematic approach to model-building, involving explicit conceptualization and measurement, as well as a clearly hypothetico-deductive tack'.[4] His counterpart in the Sydney-based *Journal of Industrial Relations* felt that Clegg had not supplied enough 'detailed factual data to support his case' and did not fully understand the relationship in Australia between collective bargaining and the arbitration system.[5] The book's treatment of strikes also came under attack,[6] though, in this case, others came to its defence.[7] More generally, the approach has been criticized as 'almost tautological … the direction of causality is not always clear … For example, does widespread collective bargaining lead to high union density or does unionization encourage collective bargaining, or are the two processes reciprocally connected?'[8]

Rather than catalogue the criticisms, however, I want to focus here on issues that I think are of general significance – either because of the debate and further research they encouraged or because they can now be seen to have been an important landmark in the development of the subject. These are what *TUCB* said, or rather didn't say, about the other influences on union behaviour and, in particular, what might be described as the 'political dimension': its treatment of the role of employers in shaping the structure of collective bargaining and whether they were as decisive as *TUCB* suggested. And, perhaps most important and yet unintended, there's its contribution to the development of industrial relations thinking about theory.

4   M. Warner, 'Book Review', *British Journal of Industrial Relations* (*BJIR*) 15:2 (1977), p. 297.
5   M. Rimmer, 'Book Review', *Journal of Industrial Relations* 19 (1977), pp. 442–3.
6   J. E. Cronin, *Industrial Conflict in Modern Britain* (Croom Helm: 1979), p. 25; W. Korpi and M. Shalev, 'Strikes, Industrial Relations and Class Conflict in Capitalist Societies', *British Journal of Sociology* 30:2 (1979), pp. 164–87, pp. 167–70; S. Scheuer, 'A Novel Calculus? Institutional Change, Globalization and Industrial Conflict in Europe', *European Journal of Industrial Relations* (*EJIR*) 12:2 (2006), pp. 143–65, pp. 144–5.
7   Scheuer, 'A Novel Calculus?' *EJIR* p. 145.
8   C. Frege and J. Kelly, 'Union Revitalization Strategies in Comparative Perspective', *EJIR* 9:1 (2003), pp. 7–24, p. 11.

Limited application?

Importance of the political dimension

Arguably, given his aims, Clegg was being no more than realistic in emphasizing that *TUCB* was about trade unions under collective bargaining and had less explanatory power for countries where the main method of union action was political action. Effectively, however, he gave critics an 'open goal', which many have been unable to resist. One of the very first was Everett Kassalow in *Industrial and Labour Relations Review*.[9] *TUCB* was 'most welcome' but limited on two accounts. First, it did not give enough attention to what he termed the 'political dimension'. He specifically mentioned unions' interest in workers' participation in the then Federal Republic of Germany, which he argued was more than just a substitute for lack of workplace bargaining. Second, he questioned whether the argument had much relevance to developing countries – implicitly raising the issue of the requirements for effective collective bargaining discussed later.

There were similar comments from reviewers in other countries. As well as Australia, they came from India,[10] Italy, and Spain. In the case of Spain, for example, Faustino Minguélez Lobo was prompted to conclude politely:

> Possibly Clegg overestimates the role of negotiation. Greater importance should be given to the socio-political context of each country and thus the tradition of each union to reach a deeper understanding of different union behaviour. The political factor is quite determining of the behaviour of unions and also the type of negotiation that has developed since 1975.[11]

More generally, Carola Frege and John Kelly have suggested that *TUCB*'s 'emphasis on collective bargaining seems too embedded in an Anglo-American understanding of industrial relations'.[12] That may be so, but *TUCB* has by no means been dismissed as irrelevant in countries with a strong 'political dimension'. Far from it. In two of them, Italy and Spain, industrial relations scholars were instrumental in getting foreign-language editions published. Also, in introducing the book to an Italian audience, Gian Primo Cella regrets that Italy was not included. This is not just because of the importance of the 'political' dimension in Italy, including the

---

9 E. Kassalow, 'Book Review', *Industrial and Labor Relations Review* 31:1 (1977), pp. 115–17.

10 M. S. Ashaf, *Indian Journal of Industrial Relations* 12:4 (1976), pp. 537–40.

11 F. Miguélez Lobo, *Reis* 38 (Centro de Investigaciones Sociologicas: 1987), pp. 296–9, pp. 298–9.

12 Frege and Kelly, 'Union Revitalization Strategies in Comparative Perspective', *EJIR*, p. 11.

different ideological positions of the main trade-union confederations and their manual and non-manual membership, but also because *TUCB* helps to illuminate many of the features of his country's industrial relations. He discusses the relevance of each of the dimensions of collective bargaining, with what he has to say about the development of autonomous workplace bargaining being especially insightful in understanding attitudes to other forms of industrial democracy.[13] Arguably, largely because it uses *TUCB* as the framework, the discussion, brief though it is, is one of the most insightful introductions to the situation in Italy at the time.

Its terrain being generally accepted as reasonable in this way, it's not unfair to suggest *TUCB* also helped to stimulate further thinking about the influences on trade-union behaviour. One example is Ross Martin's *Trade Unionism: Purposes and Forms*.[14] In the first part of the book, Martin presents a comprehensive account of the conflicting objectives, responsibilities, and functions that trade unions have aspired to. He then constructs, with reference to twenty-seven countries, a fivefold typology by which the institutional forms of trade-unionism can be ordered and categorized on a transnational basis. He also develops a theory which explains their major differences in terms of political parties and party systems.

Another work that has to be mentioned is Colin Crouch's *Industrial Relations and European State Traditions* with its detailed analysis of the development of industrial relations systems in fifteen European countries.[15] Crouch does not mention *TUCB*. Intentionally or not, however, the book does a grand job in dealing with one of the two main items of *TUCB*'s unfinished business, in its exploration of the circumstances in which unions incline towards political action rather than collective bargaining.

TUCB is also a starting point for Richard Hyman's insightful discussion of trade-union identities, positioning different European union movements between what he refers to as the 'eternal triangle' of market, class, and society. Briefly, he identifies 'three ideal types of European trade unionism each associated with a distinctive ideological orientation. In the first, unions are interest organizations with predominantly labour market functions; in the second, vehicles for raising workers' status in society more generally and hence advancing social justice; in the third, "schools of war" in a struggle between labour and capital.' Hyman presents these three

---

13 G. P. Cella, *Sindacato e contrattazione collettiva* (Franco Angeli Editore, Milano: 1980), pp. 15–18.

14 R. M. Martin, *Trade Unionism: Purposes and Forms* (Clarendon Press, Oxford: 1989).

15 C. Crouch, *Industrial Relations and European State Traditions* (Clarendon Press, Oxford: 1993).

ideal-types diagrammatically as a triangle of competing orientations.[16] UK trade unions are placed on the side between market and class, close to the apex of market and society. By contrast, French trade unions are situated on the side between class and society.

Interestingly, most of these critics and commentators have been primarily concerned with the links between the 'political dimension' and trade-union behaviour. There has been very little discussion of the implications for collective bargaining. Yet it is perhaps the relationship between the 'political dimension' and collective bargaining that makes the UK and the USA the 'exceptions'. Fundamentally important are the coverage and legal status of collective agreements. In the UK, the statutory right of recognition first introduced in the 1970s is essentially workplace- rather than sector- or nationally-based as it is in most other major EU-member countries.[17] Effectively, like their counterparts in the USA, where recognition is also workplace-based, UK trade unions are faced with a 'Catch 22' situation – they can't secure recognition without members, but they can't demonstrate the benefits of membership without recognition. Also in the UK, collective agreements are grounded in procedural rules and are voluntary in status. In many other EU-member countries, collective agreements are rooted in substantive rules that are sector-wide and legally enforceable. Crucially, because they are sector-wide, and therefore inclusive in coverage, collective agreements benefit the unorganized as well as the organized, which is not the case in the UK[18] and the USA, outside the public sector.[19]

---

16 R. Hyman, 'Changing Trade Union Identities and Strategies', in R. Hyman and A. Ferner (eds), *New Frontiers in European Industrial Relations* (Blackwell, Oxford: 1994); *idem, Understanding European Trade Unionism: Between Market, Class and Society* (Sage: 2001), pp. 1–2, 4.

17 Under the Industrial Relations Act 1971 and the Employment Protection Act (EPA) 1975, bargaining units were not necessarily workplace-based; the EPA explicitly refers to 'an employer or two or more associated employers'. The EPA's statutory union-recognition procedure was repealed in 1980 and not replaced until the Employment Relations Act 1999, whose provisions became effective in 2000. In principle, the bargaining unit did not have to be workplace-based but anything above was made difficult.

18 From 1940 until 1980 (under various statutes) there was a provision for extending recognized terms and conditions to non-conforming employers. It was an indirect mechanism through unilateral arbitration, however, and so hardly comparable to multi-employer bargaining.

19 Clegg's explanation (pp. 23–7) as to why public-sector workers in the UK remain relatively well organized and benefit from sector agreements continues to have validity. First, most public services consist of a small number of undertakings – in some instances with a single body in charge of a whole industry or service. Second, most public services are subject to a degree of government control; once it becomes public policy to recognize trade unions, it is difficult for individual establishments to withhold recognition. Third,

There is also an important technical point to this 'political dimension'. Collective bargaining in the form that it developed in most countries offers an alternative to statutory intervention in regulating the employment relationship. In the language of legal discourse, the law can be 'reflexive' and 'procedural'.[20] It does not have to come up with one-size-fits-all solutions to problems; and maintaining the status and membership of trade unions and employers' organizations creates the platform for their greater involvement in, and deliberation of, economic and social policy-making, along with the networks for achieving greater social cohesion. Paradoxically, far from giving employers in the UK greater flexibility, the decline of collective bargaining has meant more 'juridification', that is the greater involvement of the law and the courts in employment relations matters. This is because 'law's allure' can be seen as part of a wider process in society in which legal rules are introduced to help deal with risks and uncertainties that might otherwise result in conflict if actors were left to their own device.[21] The ongoing significance of the points in these last two paragraphs will become clearer in the final section.

A very formal perspective

Something that quickly became clear was that the framework of *TUCB* did not do justice to the many forms that collective bargaining can take. France didn't fit in not just because trade unions in France put more weight on statutory regulation rather than collective bargaining. It was also because *TUCB* prioritized formal at the expense of informal processes.

This was as much the fault of his colleagues, I hasten to add, as it was of Clegg himself. I certainly have to put my hand up. In the year that *TUCB* was published (1977), I spent the last three months in France working on its 'unfinished business'. In the first week I was fortunate to get an interview with Jean-Daniel Reynaud, who was roughly Hugh Clegg's equivalent based at the *Conservatoire nationale des arts et métiers* in Paris. I don't think he had yet read *TUCB*, but was more than happy to respond to a question about French 'exceptionalism'. It was very important not to get

being large undertakings and subject to public scrutiny, public undertakings find it difficult not to operate other than on the basis of bureaucratic rules, and sector-wide collective bargaining is a simple and effective means of providing them. Fourth, in contrast to senior managers in most private companies, there is a high degree of unionization among senior officials in most public services.

20 C. Barnard and S. Deakin, 'In Search of Coherence: Social Policy, the Single Market and Fundamental Rights', *Industrial Relations Journal* 31:4 (2000), pp. 331–45, p. 341.

21 G. Silverstein, *Law's Allure: How Law Shapes, Constrains, Saves, and Kills Politics* (Cambridge University Press, New York: 2009).

too hung up about formal agreements, he was at pains to emphasize. In the words of his book published the year before:

> discussion and compromise takes place often not on a global text which claims to cover the relations and rules of work in their entirety, but piece by piece: one day on a rise in wages, and then on a formula for holidays, and then on the amount of work and the forms of remuneration. This piecemeal negotiation does not have the ambitions of a comprehensive negotiation or a signed contract. But it corresponds better to a changing situation where the pressure of demands cannot be anticipated and where it is better to be able to regulate fairly quickly the incidences of conflict which appear even if it is the heat of the moment.[22]

As soon as he started to develop the point about 'piecemeal negotiation' and the form of the daily interaction between managers and the workers' representatives, I could have kicked myself. In the early 1970s I had been running negotiating exercises for our MA and MBA students at Warwick based on Richard Walton and Robert McKersie's *A Behavioral Theory of Labor Negotiations*.[23] Indeed, the then Institute of Personnel Management was to publish a collection of them in 1977. But, in ignorance of the detailed situation in France, I had not made the connection with Walton and McKersie's 'attitudinal structuring' discussed in detail in their chapters 6 and 7. In other words, much of collective bargaining in France was not about exchange or, indeed, making decisions: it was about structuring attitudes.[24]

The situation is not dissimilar to that in some industrializing countries. One example I came across in preparing this article is that of Chris Chan and Elaine Hui, where *TUCB* is the starting point for discussing the development of collective bargaining in China. Collective bargaining, the authors point out, was a term that had only recently gained currency (in 2008, in Shenzhen province) – 'collective consultation' had been the

---

22 J.-D. Reynaud, *Les Syndicats en France, Vol. 1* (Editions de Seuil, Paris: 1975), pp. 195–6.
23 R. E. Walton and R. B. McKersie, *A Behavioral Theory of Labor Negotiations* (McGraw-Hill, New York: 1965).
24 More discussion of the situation in France at the time will be found in the hitherto unpublished 1978 paper by Eric Batstone, available in this issue of *Historical Studies in Industrial Relations* (*HSIR*). Entitled 'Arms'-Length Bargaining: Industrial Relations in a French Company', it draws on empirical research undertaken in 1977 and 1978 involving interviews with union activists (*militants*) in two large workplaces belonging to a foreign-owned multi-national company. The title says it all: even if there were very few formal agreements, positions were adopted and compromises made just as they were in the UK workplaces that Eric and his colleagues had explored: E. Batstone, I. Boraston and S. Frenkel, *Shop Stewards in Action: The Organization of Workplace Conflict and Accommodation* (Blackwell, Oxford: 1977).

dominant expression largely because of collective bargaining's connotations with industrial conflict. They further suggest that there was also very little resembling *TUCB*'s portrayal of collective bargaining in the other countries. Echoing the earlier discussion about collective bargaining in France, however, they suggest that it was possible to identify four different patterns of negotiation: 'collective consultation as a formality', 'collective bargaining by riot', 'party state-led collective bargaining' and 'worker-led collective bargaining'.[25]

The informal co-ordination of collective bargaining was another issue whose importance was only to be revealed in subsequent research.[26] Take Germany and Sweden. Formally the levels of collective bargaining were very different. In Sweden, collective bargaining was highly centralized, with negotiations taking place between the respective confederations. By contrast, in Germany negotiations were seemingly relatively decentralized – the confederations did not negotiate with one another and in the large metalworking sector, collective bargaining even took place at the level of the state (the *Land*) rather than national level. In practice, however, the situation was not as it seemed. Not only were the *Land* negotiations in metalworking centrally co-ordinated by employers, but also the settlements in other sectors. Effectively, in other words, there was a form of 'pattern bargaining' with metalworking the 'pilot' for negotiations.

Pattern bargaining has a long history in the USA.[27] The more general significance of 'co-ordinated bargaining', however, surfaced in the debate over the connection between structures of collective bargaining and macro-economic performance.[28] As David Soskice pointed out, it was not so much the *level* at which collective bargaining took place that was important in explaining different inflation and unemployment outcomes, but the extent to which it was co-ordinated.[29]

---

25 C. King-Chi Chan and E. Sio-Ieng Hui, 'The Development of Collective Bargaining in China: From "Collective Bargaining by Riot" to "Party State-led Wage Bargaining"', *The China Quarterly*, First View Article (December, 2013), pp. 1–22, pp. 5ff.

26 F. Traxler, S. Blaschke and B. Kittel, *National Labour Relations in Internation-alized Markets: A Comparative Study of Institutions, Change and Performance* (Oxford University Press: 2001). K. Sisson and P. Marginson, 'Co-ordinated Bargaining: A Process for Our Times?', *BJIR* 40:2 (2002), pp. 197–220.

27 G. Seltzer, 'Pattern Bargaining and the United Steelworkers', *Journal of Political Economy* 59 (1951), pp. 319–31.

28 M. Bruno and J. Sachs, *Economics of Worldwide Stagflation* (Blackwell, Oxford: 1985); L. Calmfors and J. Driffill, 'Bargaining Structure, Corporatism and Macroeconomic Performance', *Economic Policy* 3:6 (1988), pp. 13–61.

29 D. Soskice, 'Wage Determination: The Changing Role of Institutions in Advanced Industrialized Countries', *Oxford Review of Economic Policy* 6:4 (1990), pp. 36–61.

The role of employers over-estimated?

TUCB can certainly be credited with putting the role of employers firmly on the industrial relations map. I started the chapter on management in each edition of the Industrial Relations Research Unit textbooks[30] by saying that, until the 1980s, most commentators had paid no more than perfunctory attention to their role. By comparison with trade unions and the state, management seemed to be a relatively unproblematic, if not unimportant, actor. It was management, defined as a group of people with responsibility to the board of directors or its equivalent for running the organization, which exercised the discretionary rights that are the employment contract's distinguishing feature. To paraphrase John Dunlop,[31] management was one of a number of actors working within an *industrial relations system* of institutions, processes and rules shaped by technology, markets, and the balance of power in the wider society: it was assumed to share the same interests or 'ideology' of the state and trade unions in having a relatively stable framework within which it could get on with the tasks of planning, controlling, and co-ordinating the business's activities.

Focusing on collective bargaining, employers were certainly fundamentally important in influencing the level. Collective bargaining can be single-employer or multi-employer; single-employer bargaining can also be single- or multi-establishment, and multi-employer bargaining single-industry or multi-industry. It is also the case that in the formative phase in industries such as printing and engineering, it was very often employers which more or less imposed this multi-employer level of collective bargaining on trade unions. If this sounds strange today, it must be remembered that not only had employers organized themselves before trade unions emerged, collective bargaining was a mechanism for combating the unilateral regulation of craft-based unions. Multi-employer bargaining brought two main benefits. It not only provided a degree of 'market' control by putting a floor under competition on wages and working time, it was also important in maintaining their 'managerial' control. It pooled their strength *vis-à-vis* organized labour, enabling them to counter trade-union 'whipsawing' tactics with the threat of lockouts that raised the costs of industrial action considerably; and it helped

---

30 J. Purcell and K. Sisson, 'Strategies and Practice in the Management of Industrial Relations', in G. S. Bain (ed.), *Industrial Relations in Britain* (Blackwell, Oxford: 1983), pp. 95–120; K. Sisson and P. Marginson, 'Management: Systems, Structures and Strategy', in P. K. Edwards (ed.), *Industrial Relations: Theory and Practice in Britain* (Blackwell, Oxford: 1995), pp. 89–122; *idem*, 'Management: Systems, Structures and Strategy', in P. K. Edwards (ed.), *Industrial Relations: Theory and Practice* (2nd edn, Blackwell, Oxford: 2003), pp. 157–88.
31 J. T. Dunlop, *Industrial Relations Systems* (Holt, New York: 1958).

to neutralize the workplace from trade-union activities by exhausting or setting limits to the scope for negotiation there. Collective bargaining, in other words, involved a form of mutual recognition in which management's right to manage was implicitly – and in some cases such as the engineering and metalworking industries in Sweden and the UK explicitly – recognized.

It is nonetheless not unfair to suggest that *TUCB* did overstate the role of employers. As several authors emphasized, this is especially true of developments in the 1960s and 1970s when trade unions were successfully pushing for decentralization and the extension of collective bargaining. Tom Johnston put it like this:

> Given the way in which he deploys his argument, Clegg comes precious close to saying that trade unions are a dependent variable, reacting and adapting to these two independent variables. Is it entirely satisfactory to suggest that management and employers' associations somehow determine the structure of collective bargaining? Do unions never pressure employers? Swedish employers, trying to adapt to the recent onslaught of union-inspired legislation which fundamentally alters the balance of management prerogative, must raise an eyebrow at such a thought.[32]

As Cella emphasized in the case of Italy, it was very difficult to attribute recent developments in the structure of collective bargaining to employers – certainly private-sector employers.[33] The development of national bargaining was pioneered by the state-sector employers under pressure from governments responding to trade unions' demands. Likewise the explosion of workplace bargaining at the end of the 1960s/early 1970s was the responsibility of the equivalent of local shop stewards (*delegati*). By contrast, *Confindustria* (the employers' confederation) and *Federmeccanica* (the metalworking employers' association) were finding it very difficult to adapt to the changing circumstances.

Some qualification is also needed about the role of employers in shaping collective bargaining in its formative years. As several early reviewers suggested, it was the interaction between trade unions, employers and governments that was important. In Johnston's words, even if it would have made for 'greater unwieldiness', it might have been 'better to recognize active interdependence among the actors on the industrial relations stage from the start'.[34]

To draw on my own stab at the 'Unfinished Business',[35] the structure of

---

32 T. L. Johnston, 'Book Review', *Scottish Journal of Political Economy (SJPE)* 24:2 (1977), pp. 188–90, p. 190.
33 Cella, *Sindacato e contrattazione collettiva*.
34 Johnston, 'Book Review', *SJPE*, p. 190.
35 K. Sisson, *The Management of Collective Bargaining: An International Comparison* (Blackwell, Oxford: 1987).

collective bargaining was not the result of the parties (employers, trade unions or governments) making a rational choice from a number of possible options, any more than did the recognition of trade unions occur in a piecemeal and *ad hoc* fashion. Rather both recognition and the structure of collective bargaining were deeply rooted in a historical compromise at 'critical junctures', reflecting the timing, pace, and degree of concentration of industrialization, together with the state tradition. In the UK and Western Europe, multi-employer bargaining emerged as the predominant pattern largely because employers, above all in the metalworking industries, were confronted with the challenge of national unions organized along occupational or industrial lines.[36] In Britain, the procedural bias of multi-employer has its origins in the engineering industry's 'Provisions for Avoiding Disputes' of 1898 and implicitly recognized that craft trade unions, such as the Amalgamated Society of Engineers, had already established a firm foundation in the workplace, with its district committees having the power to impose their own regulations.[37] In Sweden, the national agreement reached in engineering in 1905 was, by contrast, rooted in the substantive terms and conditions, and reflected the relative weakness of employers at local level and the centralization of the trade-union movement. In France and Germany, where the crisis in the years immediately after the First World War was on a much larger scale, the government was involved as well as employers and trade unions. In both cases, the compromise was underwritten by compulsory rules – government and trade unions were anxious lest the large metalworking employers, which hitherto had been able to resist trade-unionism with little difficulty, would revert to their previous position once the immediate crisis was over.

Only in the USA and Japan did single-employer bargaining emerge as the predominant pattern. By the time legislation was introduced requiring employers to recognize trade unions in the 1930s and 1940s respectively, the relatively large individual employers that had emerged at an early date in industrialization in both countries had already exerted a profound influence on the trade-union movement.[38] In the circumstances, employers and governments did not come under strong pressure to introduce multi-employer bargaining, and most employers opted for dealing with trade unions at enterprise or establishment level largely out of the desire to maintain their internal systems of job regulation and, especially in Japan, to deny the trade unions the platform from which to push for more effective national unionism.

Also important to remember is that, although they set countries on a particular course, the compromises were not as fixed or immutable as may

36 *Ibid.*, ch. 6.
37 J. Jeffreys, *The Story of the Engineers, 1800–1945* (Lawrence and Wishart: 1946).
38 Sisson, *Management of Collective Bargaining*, ch. 7.

appear from a present-day perspective. In the language of institutional analysis, which *TUCB* could be said to have reinvigorated, further 'critical junctures' punctuated any 'equilibrium' that may have seemed apparent. In the UK, developments in the 1920s such as the engineering lockout of 1922 and the failure of the Mond–Turner talks after the 1926 General Strike help to explain why the parties stayed on the path of 'voluntarism' – employers were in the ascendancy and saw no good reason to disturb the status quo. In Sweden, by contrast, growing industrial conflict led to the passage of the Collective Agreements Act and Labour Court Act in 1928 and the long-standing desire of Swedish employers to confirm the legal status of their substantively based collective agreements.

Theory 'in' or theory 'of'?

There has been much said about Clegg's humility when it comes to making any theoretical contribution[39] – he usually deferred to Allan Flanders in this respect, in the case of *TUCB* suggesting that 'The architecture of his theory would have been nobler and more substantial' (p. ix). He was certainly very clear about the theoretical limitations of *TUCB*. He did not claim that it offered a full-blown theory of trade unions, remember, let alone a theory of industrial relations. It nonetheless gave considerable legitimacy to the view that the subject should be searching for a theory of industrial relations. It also seemed to confirm the view that trade unions and collective bargaining should be the focal point for such an endeavour.

Some colleagues, notably Bruce Kaufman, have clung on to what Hyman later was to describe as the theory 'of' industrial relations approach,[40] drawing on Dunlop's seminal 1958 *Industrial Relations Systems* to do so.[41] But most of us have followed Hyman in going for the alternative theory 'in' industrial relations. In a much-used phrase, employment relations is 'multi-disciplinary'. Roughly translated, this means two things: first,

---

39 See P. Ackers, 'Collective Bargaining as Industrial Democracy: Hugh Clegg and the Political Foundations of British Industrial Relations Pluralism', *BJIR* 45:1 (2007), pp. 77–101, pp. 77–8; W. Brown, 'Clegg, Hugh Armstrong', in *The IEBM Handbook of Human Resource Management* (International Thomson Business Press: 1998), p. 848.

40 B. Kaufman, 'Employment Relations and the Employment Relations System: A Guide to Theorizing', in *idem* (ed.), *Theoretical Perspectives on Work and the Employment Relationship* (ILR/Cornell University Press, Ithaca, NY: 2004); R. Hyman, 'Is Industrial Relations Theory Always Ethnocentric?', in Kaufman (ed.), *Theoretical Perspectives on Work and the Employment Relationship*, p. 265.

41 Dunlop, *Industrial Relations Systems*.

building on and seeking to integrate the often contending insights from the traditional disciplines of economics, sociology, psychology, law, and politics; and, second, focusing on what is sometimes described as 'middle range' theorizing, that is achieving greater understanding of the causes and consequences of the key institutions involved in governing the employment relationship – for example, the enduring features of work organization or the structure of collective bargaining.

I don't recall anyone specifically mentioning *TUCB* in their intellectual journeys. Looking back, though, I think it was an important watershed. Even though *TUCB* talked in terms of a theory 'of' industrial relations, everything about the book points in the direction of theory 'in' industrial relations. Consider Colin Hay's framework for contrasting the different dimensions of 'positivism', 'constructivism' and 'critical' or 'scientific realism'.[42] *TUCB* did not see the *role of theory* to be the discovery of laws dealing with empirical regularities. Rather it was about achieving a better understanding of trade-union behaviour. In terms of its *values*, it was certainly concerned with simplicity and succinctness but not at the expense of the realism of its assumptions. In terms of its *theoretical assumptions*, the main actors were groups rather than individuals, and their rationality was very much context- and time-dependent rather than universal. Even critics recognized that *TUCB* 'alerts us to the powerful argument that industrial relations institutions shape the structures and behaviours of the actors — in other words, "institutions matter".'[43] In terms of its *analytical approach*, *TUCB* was very much characterized by induction rather than deduction; it privileges evidence and observation and, on the basis of these, tries to draw some generalizable conclusions. Last, but by no means least, were *TUCB*'s *methods*. As already indicated, it was not concerned with modelling as Martin was to attempt in *Trade Unionism: Purposes and Forms* – that is, developing ideal-types that seek to portray the essential features of a situation.[44] Rather the emphasis is very much on comparative and historical analysis. Arguably, *TUCB* became an exemplar for what developed into a rich stream of comparative industrial relations analysis engaged in middle-range theorizing inspiring directly or indirectly such works as Harry Katz and Owen Darbishire's *Converging Divergences: Worldwide Changes in Employment Systems*, and Kathleen Thelen's *How Institutions Evolve: The Political Economy of Skills in Germany, Britain, the United States, and Japan*.[45]

---

42 C. Hay, *Political Analysis: A Critical Introduction* (Palgrave, Basingstoke: 2002), pp. 29, 49.

43 Frege and Kelly, 'Union Revitalization Strategies in Comparative Perspective', *EJIR*, p. 11.

44 Martin, *Trade Unionism: Purposes and Forms*.

45 H. Katz and O. Darbishire, *Converging Divergences: Worldwide Changes in Employment Systems* (ILR Press, Cornell Studies in Industrial and Labor

More than a matter of antiquarian interest – further food for thought

In this concluding section, I'd like to argue that *TUCB* is more than a matter of antiquarian interest. I believe it implicitly raises two questions that contribute to its enduring significance. The first involves the wider roles of collective bargaining, which is perhaps best put by asking what has been lost as a result of the decline of collective bargaining in the forty years since its publication. The second question concerns the sustainability of collective bargaining – the conditions necessary for the practice of collective bargaining and the enjoyment of its benefits.

The importance of collective bargaining

The decline in union membership and collective bargaining in the UK means the loss of many things. Most obviously is their role as Flanders' 'sword of justice'.[46] As the same author emphasized, trade unions are not 'labour cartels' and collective bargaining is not the collective equivalent of individual bargaining. Crucially, collective bargaining is not just about wages, but issues such as 'discipline and dismissal, promotion, and training, together with the promotion of a rule of law'.

> Stated in the simplest possible terms these rules provide protection, a shield, for their members. And they protect not only their material standards of living, but equally their security, status and self-respect; in short their dignity as human beings.[47]

In the UK, collective bargaining has been able to provide little such protection in recent years, with living standards for many being in decline – even in the public sector where it continues to cover the overwhelming majority of employees. There are more people in jobs than ever before but the gap between prices and pay has been widening, with household incomes declining by more than 8% since 2008 and unlikely to get back to where they were until 2016.[48] Other benefits associated with employment such

---

Relations: 2002); K. Thelen, *How Institutions Evolve: The Political Economy of Skills in Germany, Britain, the United States, and Japan* (Cambridge University Press: 2004).

46 A. Flanders, 'Trade Unions in the Sixties', in *idem* (ed.), *Management and Unions: The Theory and Reform of Industrial Relations* (Faber: 1970), p. 15.

47 *Idem*, 'Collective Bargaining: A Theoretical Analysis', in *idem*, *Management and Unions*, p. 215.

48 Resolution Foundation (Gavin Kelly), *The Outlook for Living Standards: Sunshine and Clouds Ahead* (2014), available at www.resolutionfoundation. org.uk; see also ONS, *Annual Survey of Hours and Earnings 2014: Provisional Results, Key Points* (2014), available at www.ons.gov.uk.

as pensions have also been reduced: there has been a massive decline in the number of defined-benefit pension schemes, with many having to work longer to qualify for any pension.

Recent years have also witnessed a considerable reduction in the security traditionally associated with the employment relationship.[49] Many full-time permanent jobs have given way to part-time and temporary ones, with a big growth in agency working as well.[50] There has also been a sizeable increase in the number of the self-employed as the returns from waged jobs have declined. Especially notable is the rise of so-called zero-hour or 'non-standard' contracts – the Office for National Statistics estimates suggest that more than 1.4 million people are involved in contracts with no guaranteed hours.[51]

It cannot be emphasized enough that it is not just individual social justice that is at stake. The relative decline of wages and of labour's share has considerable implications for macro-economic performance. Levels of pay are critical in maintaining consumer demand and the government's tax take. Ironically, the main reason why the Coalition government that came to power in 2010 has not been able to reduce the deficit as fast as it intended is that tax revenues have been declining.

Another effect has been an increase in inequality, with a raft of international bodies such as the International Monetary Fund, the Organisation for Economic Co-operation and Development, and the United Nations highlighting the knock-on effects for society at large in terms of a sense of social injustice, inefficiency, and impediments to growth.[52] Inequality has been growing in most countries. It is no coincidence, however, that inequality is greater in the UK and the US than it is in other comparable countries. As some econometric evidence confirms, inequality is correlated

---

49 See D. Marsden, *A Theory of Employment Systems: Micro-Foundations of Societal Diversity* (Oxford University Press: 1999).

50 See D. Grimshaw, M. Marchington, J. Rubery and H. Willmott, 'Introduction: Fragmenting Work across Organizational Boundaries', in *idem* (eds), *Fragmenting Work: Blurring Organizational Boundaries and Disordering Hierarchies* (Oxford University Press: 2004).

51 ONS, *Analysis of Employee Contracts that do not Guarantee a Minimum Number of Hours* (2014), available at www.ons.org.uk.

52 International Monetary Fund (J. D. Ostry, A. Berg and C. G. Tsangarides), 'Redistribution, Inequality, and Growth', *Staff Discussion Note* (2014), available at www.imf.org; Organisation for Economic Co-operation and Development, *Focus on Inequality and Growth* (2014), available at www.oecd. org; United Nations Development Programme (UNDP), *Human Development Report 2005. International Cooperation at a Crossroads: Aid, Trade and Security in an Unequal World*, ch. 2 'Inequality and Human Development' (United Nations, New York: 2005); *idem, Inequality Matters: Report on the World Social Situation* (2013), available at www.un.org.

with the structure of collective bargaining – the more decentralized the bargaining, the greater the inequality and vice versa.[53] This is because, as already explained, a decentralized structure benefits only the unionized, whereas a centralized one benefits both unionized and non-unionized. In most other member-states of the European Union (EU), the framework of inclusive sector agreements has been maintained – any decentralization to company and workplace level has been largely 'organized'.[54] In the UK decentralization in the 1960s and 1970s was largely 'disorganized', with the inclusive structure enshrined in national agreements giving way to fragmented single-employer agreements. As well as being much more vulnerable to the changes in employment and business structures outlined above, single-employer agreements mean that the unorganized do not benefit from collective agreements.

It may not be as obvious, but also important is the contribution that trade unions and collective bargaining make to the democratic process. This has also considerably diminished in recent years. This is because one of the things that collective bargaining brings is the opportunity for employee 'voice' not only in the making of the rules but also their administration. From this involvement comes ownership and from ownership a measure of commitment. Not for nothing did many of the pioneers of employment relations study in the UK and the USA talk about 'private systems of governance', 'industrial jurisprudence', 'industrial self-government', 'secondary systems of industrial citizenship', 'industrial democracy' and the like.[55] In Dunlop's words, 'a great deal of the complexity and beauty of collective bargaining involves the process of compromise and assessment of priorities within each side'.[56] As Peter Ackers reminds us, Clegg certainly saw collective bargaining in this vein.[57]

Again, it's not just workers who have lost out. Society at large suffers too. David Coats puts the argument most forcibly in discussing the wider significance of employee 'voice'. Democracy, he argues, 'is about more

---

53 See K. Sisson, 'Why Employment Relations Matter', *Warwick Papers in Industrial Relations* 92 (Industrial Relations Research Unit, Coventry: 2009).

54 F. Traxler, 'Farewell to Labour Market Associations? Organized versus Disorganized Decentralization as a Map for Industrial Relations', in F. Traxler and C. Crouch (eds), *Organized Industrial Relations in Europe: What Future?* (Avebury, Aldershot: 1995), pp. 3–21.

55 See S. Slichter, J. J. Healy and R. E. Livernash, *The Impact of Collective Bargaining on Management* (Brookings Institute, New York: 1960); T. E. Marshall, *Citizenship and Social Class*, ed. T. B. Bottomore (Pluto Press edition: 1991).

56 J. T. Dunlop, 'The Social Utility of Collective Bargaining', in L. Ulman (ed.), *Challenges to Collective Bargaining* (Prentice-Hall, Englewood Cliffs, NJ: 1967), p. 173.

57 Ackers, 'Collective Bargaining as Industrial Democracy', *BJIR*.

than periodic elections on a one-person-one-vote universal franchise ... Citizenship has to be learned. It depends on discussion, debate, the assessment of alternative points of view, a democratic decision by majority vote and a willingness by the losers to live with the outcome.'[58] It is here that union membership and involvement in collective bargaining is to be seen as fundamentally important. Trade unions not only ensure an independent voice, but also an opportunity to be involved in the democratic processes of argument and voting, while collective bargaining means involvement in both making and administering the rules governing the employment relationship. Coats's conclusion does not pull any punches: 'If worker voice institutions are weak then the public domain is weakened. If the public domain is weakened then the quality of our democracy is diminished.'[59] Sadly, the wider case for trade unions and collective bargaining has rarely appeared on the policy-makers' agenda in the UK in recent years.

The sustainability of collective bargaining

A re-reading of *TUCB* in the light of what has happened subsequently also raises questions about the conditions necessary for the survival of collective bargaining. *TUCB* does not specifically deal with these – and, indeed, is open to the criticism that it assumes collective bargaining would carry on much as it had done in the past. Clear from his earlier work, however, is that Clegg understandably put considerable store by industrialization. It is this that was the basis of what might be described as trade unions' 'coercive' or 'structural power'[60] – the ability to offer countervailing power by taking or threatening to take some form of industrial action imposing costs on employers.

Clearly, this 'structural' power has declined significantly in recent years. Much attention has focused on the changing patterns of employment, in particular, the decline of manufacturing and the growth of services, and the hollowing out of many semi-skilled jobs due to changing technology.[61] Also important, though, is intensifying competition. In recent years, the nature and extent of competition has changed dramatically, spreading beyond the boundaries of the national state to become global and so beyond

58 D. Coats, *Speaking Up! Voice, Industrial Democracy and Organizational Performance* (Work Foundation: 2004), p. 11.
59 *Ibid.*, p. 40.
60 M. Simms and A. Charlwood, 'Trade Unions, Power and Influence in a Changed Context', in T. Colling and M. Terry (eds), *Industrial Relations: Theory and Practice* (3rd edn, Wiley, Chichester: 2009), p. 128.
61 See H. Lesch, 'Trade Union Density in International Comparison', *CESifo Forum* 4/2004; J. Visser, 'Union Membership Statistics in 24 Countries', *Monthly Labor Review* (January 2006).

the scope of nationally based collective bargaining. The result in the case of domestically based companies is that there are much smaller 'rents' for employers to share with trade unions in the form of higher levels of wages. In the words of William Brown and his colleagues, drawing on the UK's *Workplace Employment Relations Survey*: 'The growth of collective bargaining in the twentieth century had been nurtured by imperfect competition. Tightening product market competition suffocated it.'[62] In the case of multi-national companies, it is not that there are smaller rents; rather it is that these are beyond the reach of trade unions and, indeed, national governments, as the debate over tax illustrates.

Moreover, intensifying competition is no longer just a product-market phenomenon. The liberalization and deregulation of capital markets in the 1980s and 1990s did not just promote mobility in terms of the geographical location as well as the content of investment. It also encouraged the growth of much more active/aggressive investors such as hedge funds, private-equity groups and sovereign-wealth funds, primarily concerned with 'buy' and 'sell' decisions which may be made many times a day. Coupled with the greater availability of capital to finance merger and acquisition activity, this has made for a redefinition of the nature of competition itself, which has come to be known as 'financialization'.[63] As well as encouraging fundamental changes in the role of banks, the result has been to intensify the pressure on managers to increase returns to shareholders and also to make it difficult for trade unions to use collective bargaining to hold the line. If capital cannot secure the returns it wants or cut costs to fund its very often heavily in-debted takeovers, it simply moves on.

However, comparing the fate of collective bargaining in the UK and other EU member-states such as France, Germany and Italy suggests that the sustainability of collective bargaining does not just depend on 'coercive power'. Also important is its 'legitimacy power' – the extent to which society legitimizes the wider roles it fulfils.[64] Fundamentally important here is the

---

62 W. Brown, A. Bryson and J. Forth, 'Competition and the Retreat from Collective Bargaining', in W. Brown, A. Bryson, J. Forth and K. Whitfield (eds), *The Evolution of the Modern Workplace* (Cambridge University Press: 2009), pp. 40–1.

63 K. Sisson and J. Purcell, 'Management: Caught between Competing Views of the Organization', in Colling and Terry (eds), *Industrial Relations*; J. Froud, C. Haslam, S. Johal and K. Williams, 'Shareholder Value and Financialization: Consultancy Promise, Management Moves', *Economy and Society* 29:1 (2000), pp. 80–111; *idem*, 'Restructuring for Shareholder Value and Its Implications for Labour', *Cambridge Journal of Economics* 24 (2000), pp. 771–97; E. Stockhammer, 'Financialization and the Global Economy', *PERI Working Paper* 240 (University of Massachusetts, Amherst: 2010).

64 M. Simms and A. Charlwood, 'Trade Unions, Power and Influence in a Changed Context', in Colling and Terry (eds), *Industrial Relations*, p. 128.

relationship between collective bargaining and the 'political dimension' discussed earlier, in particular the way the law deals with the coverage and status of collective agreements. In France, Germany and Italy, the coverage of collective agreements has been 'fraying at the edges' and their contents 'hollowed out', reflecting very similar changes in employment and business structures. But because the decentralization has been 'organized' rather than 'disorganized' as it was in the UK, collective agreements continue to play a major role in setting minimum standards of pay and conditions of employment. Moreover, in many cases such sector agreements are being supplemented by social pacts at the economy level, reflecting the value policy-makers place on involving trade unions and employers' organizations in setting the minimum standards that it would otherwise fall to government to grapple with.[65]

The policy conclusion to be drawn from this discussion is pretty clear. If UK policy-makers wish for society to enjoy the benefits of collective bargaining, they will have to legislate to give it the greater legitimacy it enjoys in many other EU countries. They could do so by improving the current arrangements for the statutory recognition of trade unions or by implementing the EU's national-level Information and Consultation Directive as it was intended, that is requiring employers to introduce collective information and consultation processes rather than putting the onus on employees to 'trigger' a request, and coupling that with the stronger provisions of the 'recast' European Works Council Directive giving employee representatives rights to obtain the financial and material resources needed to carry out their duties, call special meetings, hold pre-meetings, seek external advice, and undertake training.

Arguably, however, this is not going to help much with the 'Catch 22' problem of trade unions needing members to secure recognition, but recognition to secure members. It also means that the benefits of collective bargaining will be largely reserved to the well-organized, with little more than a 'trickle-down' effect on those not covered. The alternative is to think in terms of revitalizing an inclusive structure of sector collective agreements as the Mather review has done recently in its report for the Scottish government:

> The benefits of a sectoral approach come from an ability to address challenges and determine strategies that affect all organisations and workers in a sector. They also come from an ability to determine agreed standards on pay, terms and conditions and other matters such as investment in training. A sectoral

---

65 K. Sisson, 'Private Sector Employment Relations in Western Europe: Collective Bargaining under Pressure?', in J. Arrowsmith and V. Pulignano (eds), *The Transformation of Industrial Relations in Europe: Institutions and Outcomes in the Age of Globalization* (Routledge: 2013).

approach maximises efficiencies in the consultation and negotiation process and establishes a level playing field that marginalises firms seeking an advantage through 'undercutting' the competition – either by paying lower wages and offering poorer terms and conditions or poaching skilled workers from those who invest in workforce training.[66]

Keith Ewing and John Hendy, in their 'manifesto for collective bargaining', have suggested what might be involved.[67] In such industries as manufacturing, they argue for the promotion of multi-employer bargaining, with employers being cajoled with 'carrots and sticks' as they were in the formative stages of collective bargaining in many sectors at the end of the First World War. In industries that are highly fragmented and where this was not feasible, such as care and retail, they propose a modern version of multi-party wage councils. Either way, the outcome would be inderogable terms and conditions.

Clearly, such recommendations fly in the face of prevailing views, which favour the breaking up even of the long-standing public-sector national agreements that remain. Those with long memories are also likely to respond that these recommendations run contrary to those Clegg made to the Donovan Commission in 1968; it was he who set the tone for the Commission's final report and its stress on voluntarism and the greater formalization of company and workplace activity.[68] In so changed a world, it's perhaps idle to speculate what Clegg might think now. My feeling, though, is that he would have agreed that collective bargaining was an institution well worth saving even if it required statutory underpinning.

Emeritus Professor of Industrial Relations
Industrial Relations Research Unit
University of Warwick
Coventry CV4 7AL

66 J. Mather, *Working Together Review: Progressive Workplace Policies in Scotland* (2014), para 4.2, p. 34; available at www.scotland.gov.uk.
67 K. D. Ewing and J. Hendy, *Reconstruction after the Crisis: A Manifesto for Collective Bargaining* (Institute of Employment Rights, Liverpool: 2013), available at www.ier.org.uk; see also UNITE, Unite submission to Labour Party Low Pay Review, January 2014; available at www.yourbritain.org.uk.
68 P. Ackers, 'Game Changer: Hugh Clegg's Role in Drafting the 1968 Donovan Report and Redefining the British Industrial Relations Policy-Problem', *HSIR* 35 (2014), pp. 63–88.

HSIR 36 (2015) 159–180

doi:10.3828/hsir.2015.36.6

The Trade Disputes Bills of 1903: Sir Charles Dilke and Charles Percy Sanger

Paul Smith

Introduction

No paper trail exists in The National Archives to cast light as to how the Trade Disputes Act (TDA) 1906 emerged in its final form. No departmental memoranda, replete with comments by ministers, civil servants, and parliamentary draftsmen and counsel are to be found in the files of the Board of Trade, the Home Office, the Attorney-General's department, or the Lord Chancellor's department. This was not how the Act was formulated, though the lacuna is still surprising. One would have expected some memoranda by the various departments that would be responsible for the Act's implementation and oversight.

Given this, it has proved necessary for historians to use a range of sources to reconstruct the legislative process which,[1] even though it took place in

---

Thanks to Dave Lyddon for help with newspaper research.

1 K. D. Brown, 'Trade Unions and the Law', in C. Wrigley (ed.), *A History of British Industrial Relations, 1875–1914* (Harvester, Brighton: 1982); R. Kidner, 'Lessons in Trade Union Law Reform: The Origins and Passage of the Trade Disputes Act 1906', *Legal Studies* (*Leg. Stds*) 2:1 (1982), pp. 34–52; G. Lockwood, 'Taff Vale and the Trade Disputes Act 1906', in K. D. Ewing (ed.), *The Right to Strike: From the Trade Disputes Act 1906 to a Trade Union Freedom Bill 2006* (Institute of Employment Rights, Liverpool: 2006); N. McCord, 'Taff Vale Revisited', *History* 78:253 (1993), pp. 243–60; D. Nicholls, *The Lost Prime Minister: A Life of Sir Charles Dilke* (Hambledon Press: 1995), pp. 284–8, 299–300; J. Saville, 'The Trade Disputes Act of 1906', *Historical Studies in Industrial Relations* (*HSIR*) 1 (1996), pp. 11–45;

plain sight in the House of Commons, also left little trace. There is of course the succession of private members' bills, many sponsored by the Trades Union Congress (TUC), and the Liberal government's bill and associated parliamentary debates, but the record is limited to *Hansard*. The process of negotiation within Parliament that produced the finished statute is obscure. For example, the important amendment to the Trade Disputes Bill 1906 proposed by Sir Charles Dilke in the House of Commons committee, which gave immunity for inducement of breach of a contract of employment in a trade dispute, was accepted by the Attorney-General, Sir John Walton, and Dilke waived his right to speak.[2] No record of any kind survives of the meeting beforehand where this must have been discussed. The amendment defining a trade dispute was first introduced at the bill's report stage by Walton on behalf of the government, but the wider definition was only inserted in the Commons, again by Walton, after the bill had returned from the Lords, so as to embrace sympathetic industrial action.[3] No records of the discussions that must have preceded this have ever been found.

The reports of the TUC Parliamentary Committee are a valuable source, but they are cryptic at times. For example there is no record of the discussion of the delegation which met the Attorney-General, Sir John Walton, on 23 October 1906, although some detail is given of the meeting with him on 24 October.[4] Here is reported the Parliamentary Committee's recommendation that Dilke's proposed amendment to the clause on picketing ('and such attending shall not be held to be a nuisance'), which it had hitherto supported, be not proceeded with in the face of the Liberal government's opposition. What is not reported is that Dilke (referred to as 'a member' in the Parliamentary Committee's report) had earlier pushed his amendment to a vote in the committee stage where it was narrowly defeated by 127 votes to 122.[5] Dilke is referred to five times in the Parliamentary Committee's 1907 report,[6] but his innovative role in promoting legislation to reform trade-union law is glossed over. In particular, his role in formulating and then amending clause 3 in relation to inducement of breach of contract of employment, and interference, is ignored (see below).[7] It is clear from

J. Thompson, 'The Genesis of the 1906 Trade Disputes Act: Liberalism, Trade Unions, and the Law', *Twentieth Century British History* (*TCBH*) 9:2 (1998), pp. 176–200.

2 *Parliamentary Debates* (*Hansard*) (HC), 4th ser., vol. 162, cols 1677–8.

3 *Ibid.*, 5 November 1906, cols 232–3; *Ibid.*, vol. 167, 17 December 1906, col. 1144.

4 Trades Union Congress (TUC), *Trades Union Congress Report 1907*, 'Parliamentary Committee's Report', pp. 50–67, at pp. 51–2.

5 *Hansard* (HC), vol. 162, 3 August 1906, cols 1656–61.

6 TUC, 'Parliamentary Committee's Report' (1907), pp. 51, 52, 58, 59.

7 Dilke's importance in the Trades Disputes Act (TDA) is stressed by Kidner, 'Lessons in Trade Union Law Reform', *Leg. Stds*; Nicholls, *The Lost Prime*

David Shackleton's speech,[8] 19 December 1906, that Robert Reid, former Liberal MP and by then the Lord Chancellor, Lord Loreburn, had acted as an adviser to the TUC at many points.[9]

The documents published here for the first time[10] thus have an importance that belies their brevity in that they provide evidence of Dilke's position in 1903 on the reform of trade-union law, which came to fruition with the TDA. His view is expressed in a letter by his secretary (H. H. Wilson) to Miss Mona Wilson, secretary to the Women's Trade Union League (WTUL),[11] who had forwarded a comment by Charles Sanger, a barrister,[12] on two draft bills to reform the law on trade unions. Bill I refers to Bill 141 [2 Edw. 7.], introduced by Dilke in 1902, which after minor amendments suggested by Sanger became Bill 55 [3 Edw. 7.], 1903. Bill II is an early draft of what became, after amendment, Bill 7 [3 Edw. 7.], introduced in the Commons by Shackleton, supported by a joint sub-committee of the TUC Parliamentary Committee, the General Federation of Trade Unions,[13] and the Labour Representation Committee.[14] The bills are reproduced, with

---

Minister, pp. 284–8, 299–300; P. Smith, 'Unions "naked and unprotected at the altar of the common law". Inducement of Breach of Contract of Employment: *South Wales Miners' Federation and Others* v. *Glamorgan Coal Co. and Others* [1905]', *HSIR* 35 (2014), pp. 33–61, at pp. 55–60; Lord Wedderburn, 'History of British Labour Law', *HSIR* 17 (2004), pp. 127–38, at pp. 133–5. In his entry in the *Oxford Dictionary of National Biography, Vol. 16* (Oxford University Press: 2004), pp. 181–6, Roy Jenkins cannot bring himself to discuss Dilke's role with regard to the TDA.

8 For Shackleton, see J. M. Bellamy and J. Saville (eds), *Dictionary of Labour Biography, Vol. 2* (Macmillan: 1974), pp. 335–9.

9 TUC, 'Parliamentary Committee's Report' (1907), pp. 61–7, at p. 63. Reid's role was recognized by Kidner, 'Lessons in Trade Union Law Reform', *Leg. Stds*, n. 57, p. 43, but missed by Saville, 'Trade Disputes Act', *HSIR*, n. 23, p. 18.

10 Gertrude Tuckwell Papers, TUC Library Collection, London Metropolitan University. Thanks to Christine Cousins, former archivist, TUC Library Collections, for bringing the documents to my attention.

11 Lady Dilke was the Women's Trade Union League (WTUL)'s chair: see J. M. Bellamy and J. Saville (eds), *Dictionary of Labour Biography, Vol. 3* (Macmillan: 1976), pp. 63–7.

12 Charles Sanger was also an author and economist, and sometime member of Trinity College, Cambridge: *The Collected Writings of John Maynard Keynes. Vol. 10: Essays in Biography* (Macmillan St Martin's Press for the Royal Economic Society: 1972), pp. 324–5; W. C. Lubenow, *The Cambridge Apostles, 1820–1914: Liberalism, Imagination, and Friendship in British Intellectual and Professional Life* (Cambridge University Press: 1998).

13 A. Prochaska, *History of the General Federation of Trade Unions, 1899–1980* (Allen and Unwin: 1982).

14 See F. Bealey and H. Pelling, *Labour and Politics, 1900–1906: A History of the Labour Representation Committee* (Macmillan: 1958).

others, below. Included also is a letter from Richard Bell, general secretary of the Amalgamated Society of Railway Servants, to Dilke; and a draft letter (which contains crossed-out material) from Mona Wilson to Shackleton (who was WTUL treasurer) and obviously a central person in the conference organized for 11 March 1903. Mona Wilson's letter puts forward some of Dilke's points in his commentary on Sanger's document, with the addition of a convoluted draft clause on the immunity of trade-union funds in trade disputes.

Sanger pointed out that neither of the proposed bills sought to deal with picketing as a common law nuisance, and therefore the law on nuisance had to be amended if peaceful picketing were to be lawful. Dilke did *not* amend his bill to take account of this but later he fought hard for its inclusion in the 1906 bill, forcing the issue to a vote after the joint sub-committee had accepted the Liberal government's assurance that it was unnecessary (see above). Dilke accepted Sanger's suggestion as to minor changes in the wording of clause 4 on picketing, which were included in clause 2 of Bill 55, 1903.

In relation to conspiracy, Sanger argued that the issue was one of defining the limits of a trade dispute, and then excluding the common law. At this date, Dilke believed it was better to leave the definition 'vague and wide': in the event the TDA s. 5(3) was determinably wide.[15] In all likelihood, given the scope of the wording, Dilke played some role in this. The draft of Bill II contained a clause to protect newspapers, that is union newspapers, from being enjoined to civil action for conspiracy when they offered support in a trade dispute. This was later deleted, presumably on the grounds that it was unnecessary.

Sanger questioned whether clause 3 of Dilke's bill (which gave tort immunity to unions and their representatives in any trade dispute) 'would stand any chance of becoming law as it goes so far; and therefore I think clause 3 of Bill II is on more practicable lines but it seems to me to go to an unreasonable length as it stands. What I should think is wanted is to protect a Trade Union against the unauthorized acts of its members rather than officers.' Dilke's comment on the paper is terse: 'I think that we should leave the limitations to the govt' and 'I oppose *unions* being responsible for this limitation' (original emphasis). The letter is more explicit: 'N. Browne's objection to Dilke's Bill is that it goes "to an unreasonable length". Dilke's view is the exact opposite: we must state in our Bills the full extent of our

---

15 S. 5(3) TDA 1906 reads: 'the expression "trade dispute" means any dispute between employers and workmen, or between workmen and workmen, which is connected with the employment or non-employment or the terms of employment, or with the conditions of labour, of any person, and the expression "workmen" means all persons employed in trade or industry, whether or not in the employment of the employer with whom a trade dispute arises'.

desire, and leave limitations to the Govt. when they try to legislate. Otherwise we weaken our hands in criticising them.' This confirms the record as to Dilke's belief that the TUC and many Labour MPs were too modest as regard the reform of trade-union law. 'Too easily satisfied' was his view.[16]

With regard to refusing to work with non-unionists – boycotting – Sanger argued that if clause 1 of Bill I were implemented, and if the definition of a trade dispute were sufficiently wide, then 'the question arises whether Quinn v Leathem[17] is not rendered harmless because that case went on the footing that there was a conspiracy'. But Dilke had a wider concern: it was not the case itself, which had proved difficult for many trade-unionists to support, but the dicta of the judges which could then be applied in other cases. In this he was prescient as to the ever-present threat to trade unions and industrial action from the common law interpreted and developed by the judiciary.

Finally, Sanger argued that the issue in dispute in the Denaby case – where the payment of benefit by the Yorkshire Miners' Association during an unauthorized strike had been successfully challenged in the courts (going to the House of Lords in 1906) by a member (financially supported by the company in dispute and the local coalowners' association) – had to be treated with care because of the wider impact on unlawful expenditure.[18] In his letter, Dilke agreed.

⚜ ‡ ⚜

At first many unions had been cautious in their reaction to the *Taff Vale* decision in 1901 but the award of £42,000 in damages and costs in January

---

16 Mary Macarthur, WTUL secretary, commented: 'Nor after this major issue [reversal of the *Taff Vale* judgment] was settled triumphantly did his [Dilke's] anxiety and watchfulness abate. He scrutinized the provisions of the Bill with jealous care. He desired to exclude every ambiguous word. "Too easily satisfied," he scribbled on a note to me after Labour members had neglected to press an amendment he considered of importance and as the Bill moved slowly forward several such criticisms came into my hands': S. Gwynn and G. M. Tuckwell, *The Life of the Rt. Hon. Sir Charles W. Dilke, Bart., M.P., Vol. 2*, Appendix 2 to ch. 52, 'Labour, 1870–1911', p. 367. See also Nicholls, *The Lost Prime Minister*, p. 300.

17 *Quinn* v. *Leathem* [1901] AC 495 (HL); J. McIlroy, 'The Belfast Butchers: *Quinn v Leatham* after a Hundred Years', in K. D. Ewing (ed.), *The Right to Strike: From the Trade Disputes Act 1906 to a Trade Union Freedom Bill 2006* (Institute of Employment Rights, Liverpool: 2006), pp. 31–67.

18 *Howden* v. *Yorkshire Miners' Association* [1903] 1 KB 308; [1905] AC, 256. See R. G. Neville, 'In the Wake of Taff Vale: The Denaby and Cadeby Miners' Strike and Conspiracy Case, 1902–06', in J. Benson and R. G. Neville (eds), *Studies in the Yorkshire Coal Industry* (Manchester University Press: 1976).

1903 alerted them to the danger.[19] This was compounded by the *Glamorgan* ruling and damages in 1905.[20] The TUC Parliamentary Committee proceeded to sponsor a series of bills to restore unions' tort immunity for industrial action to the position understood to have been that created by the 1870s' legislation, with the caveat of its restriction to action authorized by a union's executive. These bills were narrower in aspiration and design compared to those introduced by Dilke,[21] whose views the Parliamentary Committee rejected (though he had spoken for the TUC in the Commons, 1900–02).[22]

As drafted by Edmond Browne, the TUC's standing counsel, its bill, Bill 82 1902 (see below) was, according to Kidner, 'a rather puny affair'.[23] In contrast, Dilke's radicalism stands out. Drafted before the *Taff Vale* costs award, his Bill 141 (presented 25 March 1902) proposed a very wide immunity in trade disputes for interference with business and contract, conspiracy, trade-union funds, and picketing, in many ways prefiguring the TDA. In clause 1 he had proposed:

> Where an act is done in contemplation or furtherance of a trade dispute, the person doing the act shall not be liable to an action on the ground that by that act he interfered, or intended to interfere, either with the exercise by another person of his right to carry on his business, *or* with the establishment of contractual relations between other persons: Provided that nothing in this section shall exempt such person from liability on any other ground. (emphasis added)

In addition to putting *Allen* on a statutory footing,[24] the clause, in encompassing all contracts (contracts of employment and commercial

---

19 *Taff Vale Railway Co.* v. *Amalgamated Society of Railway Servants* [1901] AC 426; H. A. Clegg, A. Fox and A. F. Thompson, *A History of British Trade Unions since 1889, Vol. 1: 1889–1910* (Clarendon Press, Oxford: 1964), pp. 315–16, 323.

20 *South Wales Miners' Federation and Others* v. *Glamorgan Coal Co. and Others* [1905] AC 239 (HL); Smith, 'Unions "naked and unprotected at the altar of the common law"', *HSIR*, p. 55.

21 Nicholls carefully marshals the available evidence to reconstruct Dilke's role: Nicholls, *The Lost Prime Minister,* pp. 284–8, 299–300. See also Saville, 'Trade Disputes Act', *HSIR*, pp. 22–37; Kidner, 'Lessons in Trade Union Law Reform', *Leg. Stds*, pp. 42–52. Dilke also sponsored the Parliamentary Committee's bills: R. Kidner, 'The Development of the Picketing Immunity, 1825–1906', *Leg. Stds* 13 (1993), pp. 103–20, at pp. 115–17.

22 R. Bell, general secretary of the Amalgamated Society of Railway Servants, to Sir C. Dilke, 2 February 1903.

23 Kidner, 'Lessons in Trade Union Law Reform', *Leg. Stds*, p. 43.

24 No legal liability could lie against a trade union when it acted lawfully: *Allen* v. *Flood* [1898] AC 1 (HL).

contracts), would have immeasurably strengthened unions. It reappeared in Dilke's second bill (Bill 55 1903), but in his third bill (Bill 91 1904) the immunity was widened so as to read 'or with the establishment *or continuance* of contractual relations between other persons' (emphasis added). This clause was also contained in the Trade Unions and Trade Disputes Bill (Bill 32), introduced by Dilke and Keir Hardie in February 1906. None of the bills sponsored by the TUC Parliamentary Committee contained anything resembling this.

Clearly Dilke did not persuade the Parliamentary Committee to support his preferred wording in relation to 'interference' (see above) in its 1906 bill, but clause 3 of the government's Bill, which had no parallel in Labour's bill, was indebted to Dilke. It stipulated that

> An act done by a person in contemplation or furtherance of a trade dispute shall not be actionable as a tort on the ground only that it is an interference with the trade, business, or employment of some other person, or with the right of some other person to dispose of his capital or his labour as he wills.

It was in the bill's committee stage on 3 August that Dilke formally moved his amendment to clause 3 so as to encompass *Glamorgan*.[25] He did not reintroduce the language of his earlier bills as he may have thought that this would prove a step too far for those many Labour and Liberal MPs who retained more modest views as to how the law should be changed, or, given *Glamorgan*, he may have wanted to make explicit reference to *inducement* of breach of contract of employment.

As amended the clause read:

> An act done by a person in contemplation or furtherance of a trade dispute shall not be actionable as a tort on the ground only *that it induces some other person to break a contract of employment* or that it is an interference with the trade, business, or employment of some other person, or with the right of some other person to dispose of his capital or his labour as he wills. (emphasis added)

Given Dilke's silence and Walton's obfuscation, it fell to Llewellyn Atherley-Jones, Radical Liberal MP for North West Durham, and counsel for the Miners' Federation of Great Britain,[26] to state without equivocation that 'What the Committee had to do was to make an exception in the case of trade unions, and say that whereas all other persons might not advise breaches of contract with impunity trade unions might so advise.' [27]

---

25 See *Hansard* (HC), vol. 162, 3 August 1906, cols 1677–92.

26 H. V. Emy, *Liberals, Radicals and Social Politics, 1892–1914* (Cambridge University Press: 1973), pp. 65, 136.

27 *Hansard* (HC), vol. 162, 3 August 1906, cols 1686–8.

The spirit and wording of Dilke's bills, and we must assume his discussions and lobbying with MPs and the TUC, were a powerful factor in the final formulation of the TDA 1906. This has been obscured by the lack of documentation and the self-serving myth that the TDA was the child of the Labour Representation Committee (in 1906 renamed as the Labour Party). This began with the official report of the 'Complimentary Banquet to Mr D. J. Shackleton', 19 December 1906, held to celebrate the imminent passage of the Trade Disputes Bill, which contains only one reference to Dilke (by Shackleton) but together with other Liberal MPs.[28] It is more valid, however, to see the TDA as a product of Liberal radicalism, of which Dilke was the prominent spokesman. The Liberals held the Commons majority, after all. Many Liberal MPs had been elected in 1906 pledged to support the reform of trade-union law;[29] this was accepted by the Prime Minister, Sir Henry Campbell-Bannerman.[30] A forensic search of the existing archives, and for new ones, may disclose additional evidence of Dilke's role.

Management School
Keele University
Staffordshire
ST5 5BG

---

28 Parliamentary Committee's Report, TUC, *Report 1907*, pp. 61–7, at p. 63.
29 Thompson, 'The Genesis of the 1906 Trade Disputes Act', *TCBH*, pp. 176–200, but Dilke's contribution is not discussed.
30 Kidner, 'The Development of the Picketing Immunity, 1825–1906', *Leg. Stds*, pp. 107, 117, attributes the Liberal government's support for the TDA to political expediency; for a contrary view see Saville, 'Trade Disputes Act', *HSIR*.

[C. P. Sanger, 'Memorandum of Proposed Bills affecting Trade Unions', annotated by Sir Charles Dilke][1]

Memorandum of Proposed Bills
affecting Trade Unions

Peaceful Picketing

To watch and beset a man's house with the view to compel him to do or not to do that which it is lawful for him not to do or to do is, unless some reasonable justification for it is consistent with the evidence, a wrongful act (1) because it is an offence within S7 of the Conspiracy & Protection of Property Act 1875 and (2) because it is a nuisance at common law for which an action would lie.

Who says it him?

       Section 3 of the Conspiracy & Protection of Property Act 1875 has nothing to do with civil remedies.

       In order to legalise peaceful picketing it is necessary

(1) To amend section 7 of the Conspiracy etc Act 1875

(2) To amend the Common Law as to nuisance.

Why? It was never interference before the Lyon v Wilkins case

E   Neither of the proposed Bills before me attempt to deal with (2) & I consider that it is necessary that the law as to nuisance must be amended if peaceful picketing is to be legalised. Section 7 of the Conspiracy Act

E   1875 is a section imposing penalties for certain acts – it legalises nothing

E   expressly & it does not touch civil causes of action. I think that if either or both of the proposed bills were passed that an injunction could still be

L E You can't stop all holes re justification

F   granted (though in a somewhat different form) in a case like that of *J. Lyons & Sons* v *Wilkins* (1899 1 Ch 255). It is not easy to draw a section to deal with this but I have made an attempt.

On the other point Bill I is much better than Bill II. It is [illegible] hard

but E

[illegible comment] to limit the amendment of sect 7 of the Conspiracy etc Act 1875 to acts done in 'trade disputes'. There is no such limitation

L L δ

in the Act of 1875. I therefore think that Bill II should adopt clause 4 of Bill I subject to the following criticisms of such clause.

(α) The word 'peacefully' is in the wrong place it should come before

G

'to persuade'. *Yes, if you like* [illegible word]

(β) Perhaps it would be better to have 'any' person instead of 'such'

H

person. *I'm convinced in this.*

E & H L "Surely"

Law of Conspiracy

Both Bills aim at doing away with conspiracy as a cause of action when the conspiracy is 'in contemplation or furtherance of a trade dispute'.

Better left vague & wide

The difficulty is to determine & define the limits of a trade dispute.

L

There are a good many cases.

(α) dispute between the employer & his workmen.

(β) Strike or lock-out in the trade because of a dispute in one shop.

(γ) Sympathetic strike or lock-out because of a dispute in another trade.

(δ) Strike at instance of employers association because the employer undersells the others. I think this occurred in the Birmingham Metal bedding Trade

(ε) Demarcation disputes.

---

1   Underlining in the text of Sanger's document is by Dilke.

L, Surely

I do not feel clear that the Courts would hold that (γ) or (δ) perhaps (ε) were trade disputes. They have inclined to a very narrow construction of the words 'trade dispute between the employer & workmen'. If possible all the cases should be thought of & then a very comprehensive definition added to the draft bill. *Can't stop every hole L, & F*

M 7 years

I don't fully understand the object of the section about newspapers & consequently I can't criticise it much.

I do not think it clear as it stands. If the object is to permit black lists being published in newspapers I think the clause should be amended so as to make the point clear.

M Papers may be lliable for conspiracy if they take their side. Hornidge interview

Actions against Trade Unions

L, Leave it wide

Surely

Clause 3 of Bill I would practically do away with the decision in the Taff Vale case if 'Trade Dispute' is defined very widely but the definition would need to be very wide. I question, for instance, whether there was a trade dispute in the *Glamorgan Coal Coy Ld* v *South Wales Miners Federation* (1903) 1 KB 118. I doubt also whether clause 3 of Bill I would stand any chance of becoming law as it goes so far; and therefore I think clause 3 of Bill II is on more practicable lines but it seems to me to go to an <u>unreasonable length</u> as it stands. What I should think is wanted is to protect a Trade Union against the unauthorized acts of its members rather than officers. Until judgment is given in the Taff Vale it is not possible to say what the true state of the law is. I have tried to draw a clause to make unions responsible only for the acts of their officers or authorised acts of their members.

(~ Browne)

N I think [leave?] *the limitations to the govt*

N I oppose <u>unions</u> being <u>responsible for this</u> limitation

Boycotting – refusing to work with other non-unionists

O

Clause I of Bill is I understand aimed at *Quinn* v *Leathem* but so far as I can see it does not <u>meet</u> *Quinn* v *Leathem* because in that case there was no trade dispute of any sort or kind. On the other hand, *Quinn* v *Leathem* apparently makes it impossible for unionists to bring pressure on non-unionists by threatening to strike if the employer does not dismiss the non-unionists. If the law as to conspiracy is amended in the way suggested & trade dispute is given a meaning sufficiently extended to cover such a case the question arises whether Quinn v Leathem is not rendered harmless because that case went on the footing that there was a conspiracy.

Not the case but the wordding of the judges

Explain points O

(i) If A induces B to break his contract with C that may give C a right of action against A

(ii) but if A alone induces B not to enter into a contact with C that does not (I think) give C a right of action against A

(iii) a conspiracy for combination of X, Y & Z to induce B not to enter into a contract with C may (I think) give C a right of action against X, Y & Z. If the law of conspiracy is altered so that (iii) no longer gives a right of action I think that (ii) will apply & that unionists will be able to refuse to work with non-unionists (but not to make employers break existing contracts) and that Clause 1 of Bill I will not be needed. But my view of the law may be wrong.

Illegal payment of strike pay

The recent case of Denaby mines (judgment of the Court of Appeal is reported in The Times of 28 Jan. 1903) must be considered very carefully. Is the result of it objectionable to Unionists, if so it is worth while considering how it can be met by legislation.

P It cant neither, P

Summary of suggestions

I think Bill II should be altered as follows.

Clause I should be replaced by clause 4 of Bill I. A new clause should be added as follows:

E. G. H

& [illegible word] to wait nearby some limitations as [illegible word]

—"Attending at or near the house or place where a person resides or works or carries on business or happens to be in the approach to such house or place in order to obtain or communicate information or peacefully to persuade or attempt to persuade any person to do or abstain from doing that which he has a legal right to do or abstain from doing shall not give a right of action or to any relief by damages or injunction to any such person.

2. Clause 2. The parts as to newspapers should be clearer. !

3. Clause 3. Either clause 3 of Bill I should be adopted or a clause to the following effect

"A trade Union shall not be liable for the acts of any of its members other than the secretary, treasurer and members of any committee or other officer of the Trade Union unless such act is expressly authorized by the rules of the Trade Union or is authorized, adopted or ratified by some officer of the Trade Union.

The following clause should be added

4. "The words 'between employers & workmen' in Section 3 of the Conspiracy & Protection of Property Act 1875 are repealed."

5. Trade dispute" in this Act & in the Conspiracy & Protection of Property Act 1875 include not only strikes, lock-outs and other disputes between an employer and his workmen but any dispute, disagreement or difference between members of a trade union and workmen who are not members of that union, or between workmen engaged in different trades or employment.

"Trade Union" means Trade Union as defined in section 16 of the Trade Union Amendment Act 1876."

6. "This act may be cited as the Trade Disputes Act 1903."

?

The definition of trade dispute is of the highest importance; the one I have suggested requires extending and amending.

D Yes It is best to keep to the old definition of Trade Union & not to add anything about any association. *Yes*

D Yes If the old definition is objected to it should be amended in the Trade Union Acts so that it should have the same meaning in all cases.

C. P. Sanger

[Letter: Richard Bell, secretary Amalgamated Society of Railway Servants, to Sir Charles Dilke, 2 February 1903]

2nd Feb 1903

Dear Sir Charles,

I duly received your communication of the 24th Jan the content of which have had my fullest consideration. Three days after the receipt of your letter we had a meeting of the Parl Ctte. I did not bring your letter forward, thinking that you might have sent copies to the other members, or to Mr. Woods, the Secretary. It was not mentioned by either of them, and so I did not bring mine forward. The principles contained in your letter were thoroughly discussed, but the Ctte seemed to differ, to some extent from your views. The details, however, are too great to be discussed in a letter, and I hope to have an opportunity of seeing you shortly.

Yours faithfully

Richard Bell

꙳꙳ ⚘ ꙳꙳

[Letter: H. K. Hudson, secretary to Sir Charles Dilke, to Miss M. Wilson, secretary, Women's Trade Union League, 4 February 1903]

76, Sloane Street SW

Feb. 4 :03

Dear Miss Wilson,

Sir Charles Dilke returns your papers with this note. The letters apply to those put at the side of your papers.

A. It is useless to write to any of them, except for the purpose of putting your views, as he did in his letter to Bell.[1]

B. Not clear. Cl 3 is not argued against and not given up by Browne.[2] It is given up by Haldane,[3] but it is clause 3 in both Bills.

C. The page sent to Ll. Davies[4] for advice.

D. Dilke is against new definitions, but this is not intended for a new one, but only for a note.

E. He hardly sees that your man has met his own suggestion as to stopping up the gap of possible other forms of injunction, based for example on the common law of nuisance. But under the Act specifically legalising peaceful persuasion before '71, after the repeal of that Act in '71, under the words of '71, as explained in the Cabinet makers Recorder's charge,[5] and the judgment, and under the Act of '75, peaceful persuasion picketing was not interfered with in this way up to the Lyons v. Wilkins series of judgments. For some 60 or 70 years no such law was used against the unions. You may remember the explanation given in Parliament in 1875, quoted by Dilke in introducing the deputations last year, and by Beaumont in his speech on the motion.

---

1 Richard Bell, general secretary, Amalgamated Society of Railway Servants, MP Derby.
2 Browne, counsel to the TUC Parliamentary Committee.
3 Richard Haldane, Liberal MP, barrister.
4 Arthur Llewelyn Davies, barrister, Radical Liberal.
5 *R.* v. *Hibbert and Others* (1875) 13 Cox CC 82; M. Curthoys, *Governments, Labour, and the Law in Mid-Victorian Britain: The Trade Union Legislation of the 1870s* (Clarendon Press, Oxford: 2004), pp. 159–60.

F. Dilke thinks that you can't stop all the holes. The judges can always find fresh points. He is however mentioning E. to Ll. Davies.

G. Grammar only. Accepted.

H. He will consult Ll. Davies.

I & J are omitted.

L. He thinks it better to leave vague than to define, on account of fresh legal decisions, probably making bad law. He does not think that the particular decisions suggested would be likely to be given, at all events, for some years.

M. He strongly agrees. But Hornidge,[6] Chairman of the P.C. and of the special Committees on the Bill, in an interview says that the newspapers are run in for conspiracy now if they side with the unions. This shows the object of the words.

N. Browne's objection to Dilke's Bill is that it goes "to an unreasonable length". Dilke's view is the exact opposite: that we must state in our Bills the full extent of our desire, and leave limitations to the Govt. when they try to legislate. Otherwise we weaken our hands in criticising them.

O. Dilke's clause 1 in not aimed at the decision, but at the Judge's words.

P. It is probably impossible to deal with Denaby.[7] 3 points were decided: (1) that the action was not prohibited by sec 4 of the Act of '71: (2) that there had been a breach of the society's rules: (3) that it was a case for injunction. The only point on which there could be legislation would be on the first; as the others are facts. Now (1) seems legally correct: that an action to restrain expenditure contrary to the rules is not an action to enforce an agreement for benefits. Are we prepared to extend sec. 4 so that no action can be brought to restrain the misapplication of trade union funds further than is provided in Dilke's cl 3? It seems difficult to lay down the principle that officials shall not be liable to restraint if they mis-spend funds?

Yours very truly,

H K Hudson.

---

6 W. Boyd Hornidge, general secretary, National Union of Boot and Shoe Operatives; president, Trades Union Congress, 1903.

7 *Howden* v. *Yorkshire Miners' Association* [1903] 1 K.B. 308.

꜀꜀꜀꜀ ¿ ꜀꜀꜀꜀

[Letter: Miss M. Wilson, secretary, Women's Trade Union League, to D. Shackleton MP, March 1903]

[Draft of a letter: handwritten, amended text]

Women's Trade Union League

March 1903

Dear Mr Shackleton

I am sending you one or 2 suggestions by the instruction of my Committee about the bill dealing with Trade Union Law which is to be considered by the Conference on March 11. Of course aware that there is no immediate prospect that the bill will be passed, but it is important it should embody all the points which Unionists wish to be considered & that it should be so worded that Labour members should be able to support it in detail in the House of Commons. The present bill, although I agree with its main intentions, does not appear to me to fulfil these conditions.

The backwardness of trade organisation among women generally makes it indispensable to them the use of methods of warfare which some to the stronger unions can afford to consider old fashioned.

My excuse for troubling you with the enclosed notes on the bill is that

I am,

Yours faithfully

Mona Wilson

[Secretary, Women's Trade Union League]

Clause I

It is unwise to limit the legalisation of peaceful picketing to 'Trade Disputes'. The tendency of the courts has been to put a narrow construction on the terms 'trade disputes', & there is the necessity for its introduction as the limitation is not contained in the Conspiracy & Protection of Property Act 1875. For this reason I think that Clause 4 of Sir Charles Dilke's bill is preferable with two small alterations –

   a) 'peaceably' should precede instead of following persuade.
   b) 'any person' is better than 'such person'.

Further I should like to point out that Section 7 of the Conspiracy Act 1875 does not touch civil causes of action. An injunction could, therefore, in certain cases, still be granted against a union, even if Clause I were passed. To meet this difficulty a new clause is required on the lines of the roughly drafted clause which follows –

'Attending at or near the house or place where a person resides or works or carries on business or happens to be in the approach to such house or place in order to obtain or communicate information or peacefully to persuade any person to do or abstain from doing that which he has a legal right to do or abstain from doing shall not give a right of action or to any relief by damages or injunction to any such person.'

Clause II

What does Mr. Sanger think of Hornidge's explanation as to newspapers?

The latter part of this clause referring to actions against newspapers is surely very obscure. I should have taken it as referring to 'black-listing', but I see that Mr Hornidge, the Chairman of the Parliamentary Committee, has explained it as intended to protect newspapers siding with a union during a dispute against a charge of conspiracy. Should not the intention of the clause be more definitely expressed?

Is there no way of overcoming the difficulty with trade dispute without defining it – e.g. some periphrasis[8] conditions of labour –

---

8 Ed.'s note: Oxford Dictionary defines periphrasis as 'The use of indirect and circumlocutory speech or writing.'

Clause III

The intention of the Parl. Comm. not to ask for the complete repeal of the Taff Vale decision is presumably due to the desire to put forward only the most moderate demands. The exemption from suability, which was the deliberate intention of the legislators [...] to some extent compensated for the unequal conflict with the employers undertaken by the worker organisations (& I have in my mind women's organisations in particular). Its loss is therefore to be deplored. But if the position is to be accepted it is surely desirable fully to recognize its responsibilities. It is impossible that the rules of a trade union should provide for all the consequences & it is necessary that the executive should have power to act for welfare of the union. I would therefore suggest instead of clause III that a new clause should be drafted.

It should throw the full responsibility on the executive but it should at the same time protect the executive against responsibility for the direct disobedience of its officials. The following is a rough draft to shew my meaning –

'A trade union shall not be liable for acts of any of its members other than the secretary, treasurer & members of any committee or other officer of the Trade Union, unless such act is expressly authorized by the rules of the Trade Union or is authorized, adopted, or ratified, by some officer of the Trade Union. If it shewn that any officer or member of committee has acted in direct contravention of the instructions of the executive, or in direct contravention to the rules of the union, unless such contravention was sanctioned by the executive, the unions shall not be liable for his acts.'

Additional Clause

The bill not attempted to deal with interference with contracts. It is of course undesirable that Trade Unionists should be able freely to persuade workmen to break contracts but unless they are permitted to persuade blacklegs who are under contracts but have not begun to work, to refuse to begin work, it could be easy for employers to make legalised picketing of very little use, cf. in the Taff Vale case. I should suggest, therefore, in the interests of weak organisations, that an additional clause should be added dealing with this point.

Clause IV

Add clause to all contracts in view of Commission.

Ask Mr. Sanger all actions of employers' assoc. with a view to speech.

[Trade Union Bills, 1902–1903]

Bill 84, sponsored by the TUC Parliamentary Committee, 1902 (Browne).

[2 EDW. 7.]   Trade Unions

A BILL to Amend the Law relating to Trade Unions 1902.

Be it enacted by the King's most Excellent Majesty, by and with the advice and consent of the Lords Spiritual and Temporal, and Commons, in this present Parliament assembled, and by the authority of the same, as follows:–

1. No action or other proceeding at law or in equity shall be maintainable against any trade union, or against any persons in their representative capacity as officers or trustees of any trade union, for any wrongful act or acts committed by any officer, trustee, servant, agent, or member of such trade union in furtherance, or purporting to be in furtherance, of any strike, lock-out, or any trade dispute between employers and workmen, unless it be proved that the council, committee, or other governing body of such trade union expressly authorised or were privy to such wrongful act or acts.
2. For the purposes of this Act, the term "trade union" means a trade union defined by section sixteen of the Trade Union Amendment Act, 1876.
3. This Act may be cited as the Trade Unions Act, 1902.

Bill 141, sponsored by Dilke, 1902.

[2 EDW. 7.]   Trade Disputes

A BILL to Legalise the peaceful conduct of Trade Disputes.

Be it enacted by the King's most Excellent Majesty, by and with the advice and consent of the Lords Spiritual and Temporal, and Commons, in this present Parliament assembled, and by the authority of the same, as follows:–

1. Where an act is done in contemplation or furtherance of a trade dispute, the person doing the act shall not be liable to an action on the ground that by that act he interfered, or intended to interfere, either with the exercise by another person of his right to carry on his business, or with the establishment of contractual relations between other persons: Provided that nothing in this section shall exempt such a person from liability on any other ground.
2. An agreement or combination by two or more persons to do or procure to be done any act in contemplation or furtherance of a trade dispute shall not be a ground for an action, if such act when done by one person is not a ground for an action.
3. An action shall not be brought against a trade union, or against any person or persons representing the members of a trade union in his or their representative capacity, for any act done in contemplation or furtherance of a trade dispute.
4. Attending at or near the house or place where a person resides, or works, or carries on business, or happens to be, or the approach to such house or place, in order merely to persuade such person peaceably to do or abstain from doing that which he has a legal right to do or abstain from doing, shall not be deemed a watching or besetting within the meaning of section seven of the Conspiracy and Protection of Property Act, 1875.
5. This Act may be cited as the Trade Dispute Act, 1902.

Bill 7, supported by the TUC Parliamentary Committee, Labour Representation Committee, and the General Federation of Trade Unions, 1903.

[3 EDW. 7.]   Trade Disputes

A BILL to Legalise the Peaceful Conduct of Trade Disputes.

Be it enacted by the King's most Excellent Majesty, by and with the advice and consent of the Lords Spiritual and Temporal, and Commons, in this present Parliament assembled, and by the authority of the same, as follows:–

1. It shall be lawful for any person or persons, acting either on their own behalf or on behalf of a trade union or other association of individuals, registered or unregistered, in contemplation of or during the continuation of any trade dispute, to attend for any of the following purposes at or near a house or place where a person resides, or works, or carries on his business, happens to be:–
(1) For the purpose of peacefully obtaining or communicating information:
(2) For the purpose of peacefully persuading any person to work or abstain from working.
2. An agreement or combination by two or more persons to do or procure to be done any act in contemplation or furtherance of a trade dispute, shall not be ground for an action if such act when committed by one person would not be ground for an action.
3. This Act may be cited as the Trades Disputes Act, 1903.

Draft Bill adopted by the National Labour Conference re Trades Disputes Bill (TUC Parliamentary Committee, Labour Representation Committee, and the Management Committee of the General Federation of Trade unions), Wednesday 11 March 1903.

[This is the post-conference version.]

Trades Dispute

A Bill to Legalise the Peaceful Conduct of Trade Disputes, 1903.

Be it enacted by the King's most Excellent Majesty, by and with the advice and consent of the Lords Spiritual and Temporal and Commons, in this present Parliament assembled, and by the authority of the same, as follows:–

Legalisation of Peaceful Picketing
1. It shall be lawful during the contemplation and continuance of a trade dispute for any person or persons, whether by or on behalf of a trade union or any other association of individuals, whether registered or unregistered or not, to attend at or near a house or place for the purpose of obtaining or communicating information, or of peacefully persuading any person to work, or to abstain from working, or for any combination of these purposes, and any attendance, communication, or persuasion as aforesaid, without using violence, shall not be deemed a watching or besetting within the meaning of section 7 of the Conspiracy and Protection of Property Act, 1875.

Amendment of Law of Conspiracy

2. An agreement or combination by two or more persons to do, or procure to be done, any act in contemplation or furtherance of a trade dispute, shall not be a ground for an action, if such action, when done by one person, is not a ground for an action, and no action shall be brought against any newspaper, periodical, or other publication which deals with the circumstances of such trade dispute, provided that nothing in this section shall exempt such newspaper, periodical, or other publication from liability on any other ground.

Action Against Trade Unions and other Associations

3. An action shall not be brought against a trade union or other association aforesaid for the recovery of damage sustained any person or persons by reason of the action of a member or members of such trade union or other association aforesaid, unless it be proved that such member or members of such trade union or other association aforesaid acted with the directly expressed sanction and authority of the rules of such trade union or other association aforesaid.

Short Title

4. This Act may be cited as the Trades Dispute Act, 1903.

Bill 55, sponsored by Dilke, 1903.

[3 Edw. 7.]   Trade Unions and Trade Disputes

A Bill to Legalise the peaceful conduct of Trade Disputes, and to alter the Law affecting the Liability of Trade Union Funds.

Be it enacted by the King's most Excellent Majesty, by and with the advice and consent of the Lords Spiritual and Temporal, and Commons, in this present Parliament assembled, and by the authority of the same, as follows:–

1. Where an act is done in contemplation or furtherance of a trade dispute, the person doing the act shall not be liable to an action on the ground that by that act he interfered, or intended to interfere, either with the exercise by another person of his right to carry on his business, or with the establishment of contractual relations between other persons: Provided that nothing in this section shall exempt such a person from liability on any other ground.

2. An agreement or combination by two or more persons to do or procure to be done any act in contemplation or furtherance of a trade dispute shall not be a

ground for an action, if such act when done by one person is not a ground for an action.

3. An action shall not be brought against a trade union, or against any person or persons representing the members of a trade union in his or their representative capacity, for any act done in contemplation or furtherance of a trade dispute.

4. Attending at or near the house or place where a person resides, or works, or carries on business, or happens to be, or the approach to such house or place, in order peaceably to persuade any person to do or abstain from doing that which he has a legal right to do or abstain from doing, shall not be deemed a watching or besetting within the meaning of section seven of the Conspiracy and Protection of Property Act, 1875.

5. This Act may be cited as the Trade Dispute Act, 1903.

HSIR 36 (2015) 181–203

doi:10.3828/hsir.2015.36.7

Review Essays Symposium:
The Winter of Discontent

The Trade Unions and the 'Winter of Discontent': A Case of *Myth*-Taken Identity?

Colin Hay

J. Shepherd, *Crisis? What Crisis? The Callaghan Government and the British 'Winter of Discontent'* (Manchester University Press: 2013) xii + 205pp., £70, ISBN 978-0-7190-8247-4.

T. Martin López, *The Winter of Discontent: Myth, Memory and History* (Liverpool University Press: 2014) 252pp., £70, ISBN 978-1-7813-8029-1.

> *Sorrow breaks seasons and reposing hours,*
> *Makes the night morning and the noontide night.*

> (Brakenbury, *Richard III*, Act 1, Scene 4, ll. 76–7)

A lot can change in a season, especially if that season is winter and one is the Prime Minister of a minority Labour government seeking to extricate the economy from an unprecedented and seemingly intractable condition of 'stagflation' by imposing on the trade unions a ceiling on wage increases at around half the prevailing rate of inflation. So it was as autumn turned to winter in 1978. The story is well known. Indeed, it has long since entered into British folklore – and strangely perhaps it seems to have done so even as the events themselves were unfolding. Over three decades later and with historians and political scientists now enjoying the access to the public record afforded by the thirty-year rule, the evidence is available for a more systematic appraisal and reappraisal of the 'Winter of Discontent'.

Yet it is perhaps naive to think that a perfect sifting of fact from folklore and fiction is ever possible. And, with such an intensely mythologized and symbolically significant historical episode, that inherent difficulty is compounded by the powerful sense that to understand the Winter of Discontent is, precisely, to understand the role of folklore, fiction, and mythology in the unfolding of historical events.

It is in this context, I will argue, that we should read, engage with and evaluate the recent contributions of John Shepherd and Tara Martin López. Theirs are, in effect, the first book-length, detailed historical accounts of the events of the Winter of Discontent and the narratives both with which they became suffused and to which, in turn, they gave rise to be written since the opening of the archives. As such, and albeit in rather different ways, they provide the evidential basis for a reappraisal or benchmarking of what we know – or think we know – about this almost legendary episode.

My aim in what follows, then, is not just to review critically the contribution of each book to the existing literature but, and perhaps more significantly, to begin to use the evidence they assemble to adjudicate between the many contending perspectives which still fight over the interpretation of this most highly charged and contested historical juncture. That I seek to do so – and that there might be value in so doing – is at least in part because, for reasons that we will come to presently and perhaps somewhat surprisingly, neither of these books seeks to take stock of the Winter of Discontent in this way. Shepherd is certainly closer to declaring this as his at least ostensibly stated ambition. But, somewhat frustratingly, his analyses typically stop just short of adjudicating between contending claims in the existing literature and even of establishing what precisely is at stake for the wider debate in resolving the series of questions that he seeks to answer. His perspective, forensically detailed and richly evidenced though it certainly is, often remains rather implicit – and it would appear that, despite some ostensible claims to the contrary in the introductory chapter, his task is rather more to bring the evidence to light than it is to establish a definitive account of what happened and its enduring significance. There is a refreshing honesty and disarming modesty about this, but it does make the book feel at times more like a route-map through the archives (supplemented, of course, by copious references to witness testimony, biography, and his own and others' interviews with direct participants) than it does the direct intervention in the debate that it could have been. That said, it is undoubtedly a very fine work of (predominantly) archival contemporary political history that is destined, quite rightly, to become the primary reference point for all subsequent scholarship on the Callaghan government, the demise of the Social Contract and the immediate pre-history of Thatcherism. But fine though it is, it is also very traditional and at times one almost feels the need to blow the dust of the archives from the pages of the text.

Yet superficial impressions can be misleading and even here all is not quite what it seems. The text certainly reads and feels very much like a traditional piece of archival history. But Shepherd is, in fact, quite wide ranging, even unconventional, in his use of sources and his analysis draws (albeit sparingly) on close to fifty interviews with key protagonists in the drama while relying extensively (in the end, perhaps *too* extensively) on the biographies of a number of Cabinet ministers and their advisers. As such, the book is less conventional than it appears. Indeed, there is a certain irony here. For where Martin López's rather more obviously iconoclastic text and Shepherd's part company, it is typically Martin López who provides either the prescient insight from the archive or the telling quote from sources rather closer to the core of the action to trump, in effect, one of Shepherd's many anecdotes from a key protagonist's biography or from one of his own interviews. One example, among many, concerns the crucial question of where the 5% wage limit at the heart of the dispute between the unions and the government originated in the first place. Shepherd, true to form, cites Shirley Williams from an interview with the author in 2008. In it she suggests, quite credibly, that the figure was 'probably based on Treasury models' (p. 37).[1] Yet Martin López's greater triangulation of sources would lead us to contextualize this observation rather differently. For, drawing on the comments of Bill Rodgers (as Secretary of Transport at the time, a figure rather closer to the action), she shows that the Treasury in fact held back its latest inflation projections (which were, in fact, rather higher than those it chose to share with Jim Callaghan) and that, as a consequence, the 5% figure, though certainly informed by Treasury models (as Williams suggests), was not informed by the Treasury's then current thinking (p. 59).[2] Callaghan, in effect, acted on the basis of Treasury misinformation. The additional context is extremely valuable and, time and again, and despite (or conceivably because of) the seemingly greater archival immersion of Shepherd, it is Martin López who provides it.

As this perhaps already serves to suggest, Martin López's book, while drawing on many of the same sources, is very, very different in ambition, style, and content to Shepherd's. Where his remains almost stubbornly conventional, hers is engagingly and infectiously unconventional. It is also much more ambitious and the nature of that ambition is fundamentally different from that of Shepherd. For, as its subtitle ('myth, memory and

---

1 For a similar observation see her autobiography, published the year after, S. Williams, *Climbing the Bookshelves: The Autobiography* (Virago: 2009).

2 W. Rodgers, 'Government under Stress: Britain's Winter of Discontent', *Political Quarterly* (*PQ*) 55:2 (1984), pp. 171–9.

history') subtly hints, this is above all a work of remembrance, recovery, even of *restitution* – a social (as distinct from political) history which arises from an unapologetically normative and dispositionally empathic relationship towards the everyday participants in the events which have come to characterize and constitute the Winter of Discontent. Her history is, in a sense, their history, a social and an oral history that she seeks to piece together from their own testimony. In so doing, she seeks to reclaim from the mythology in and through which these events are typically viewed, the experiences, the motivations and, above all, the authentic voices of the genuine participants – and to juxtapose these to the palpable fiction of the accepted narrative. It is for precisely this reason that Martin López's aim is not to revisit and to resolve existing controversies in the light of the new evidence she brings to light. For, in a sense, the implication of her approach is that the existing literature has been posing the wrong questions and gathering its evidence in the wrong way – it is, in effect, an elite political history of elite political conduct that is incapable of the kind of remembrance and reclamation that Martin López seeks.

Here, too, initial perceptions can be misleading. For, as I have already hinted at, Martin López has a lot to say about many of the issues that have divided historians and political analysts of the (elite) politics of the period. One might even suggest that, important though it clearly is to contextualize politically the situation in which rank-and-file union members found themselves, at times Martin López traps herself in precisely the same kind of elite political history that Shepherd exemplifies and that she ostensibly rejects.

Yet that is perhaps just a little too harsh. For this, too, is a very fine book and most of the history it contains, whether conventional and elite political, or less conventional and socially recapitulative, is fresh, insightful and innovative. Indeed, if I have a central analytical gripe with the account she offers it is not about providing too much contextualization, but too little. It is, in fact, precisely the same gripe I have with Shepherd's analysis – the failure to provide a sufficiently detailed *economic* or, more accurately, *political-economic* contextualization of the struggles of the Winter of Discontent. As I will suggest presently, I think this leads both Shepherd and Martin López to fail to appreciate adequately the corner into which the terms of the International Monetary Fund (IMF) loan, on the one hand, and the Callaghan administration's management of the Social Contract, on the other, backed the unions. Appropriately contextualized in this way it becomes clear, I contend, that the crisis, when it came, was almost bound to take the form of the withdrawal of rank-and-file union members' support for an ever more regressively redistributive incomes policy from which they got less and less in return. Indeed, by early 1979 all that the Callaghan government could offer union members in the hope that they might be persuaded to return from the picket lines and suffer (in silence) an accelerating reduction in their real earnings was the thought that things could only get worse under a Conservative administration. The tragic irony is that, in this at least, it was proved right. This, I think, should be integral to any attempt to reclaim and give voice to the hidden history of the winter of 1978–79.

In fact there is one other issue that I have with both of these accounts, though to call it a gripe would be putting it too strongly. Indeed, one of the things that I like so much about both books is that they take so seriously, certainly in comparison to much of the preceding debate, the mythology of the Winter of Discontent and its significance for the legacy of this (retrospectively) ruptural moment.[3] But, ultimately, I think both get the mythology of the Winter of Discontent – and perhaps the role of mythology in the process of historical change, more generally – wrong. And they do so in a remarkably similar way.

This is a point that I will elaborate in much more detail, below. But, in brief, there are two elements to this. First, I think Shepherd and Martin López are misguided in seeing the mythology of the Winter of Discontent as, in effect, a *retrospective* construction conveniently placed upon events *once they had happened* and crystallized in the Conservatives' 1979 general election campaign. In fact neither presents very much evidence for this view and I would suggest that there is plenty of evidence that the crisis was lived, experienced, and responded to *in real time* – by direct participants as much as by more distant observers – in and through what we would now term the 'mythology' to which it gave rise. As such, myth and mythology were integral to what the Winter of Discontent was, and the events themselves are no less real for this. This is what I mean by a 'constructed crisis', though the term has been widely misinterpreted, not least by both Shepherd and Martin López, as I will seek to explain.[4] Second, and relatedly, such a view of the mythology of the Winter of Discontent as chronologically subsequent to and hence independent of the events themselves, leads both authors to attempt some kind of 'debunking' or 'demystification' – the

---

3 Retrospective, in the sense that it was far from clear at the time that the Winter of Discontent was or would become, in effect, the point of inception of Thatcherism, and that Thatcherism would endure and evolve for so long afterwards. Thus, it is only with the benefit of both hindsight and the (politically contingent) unfolding of the history that was to follow, that one can fully appreciate the significance of the moment in which Thatcherism itself was born.

4 On the Winter of Discontent as a 'constructed crisis', see C. Hay, 'Narrating Crisis: The Discursive Construction of the Winter of Discontent', *Sociology* 30:2 (1996), pp. 253–77; *idem*, 'The Winter of Discontent Thirty Years On', *PQ* 80:4 (2009), pp. 545–52; *idem*, 'Chronicles of a Death Foretold: The Winter of Discontent and the Construction of the Crisis of British Keynesianism', *Parliamentary Affairs* 63:3 (2010), pp. 446–70.

sifting of fact from fiction. But, if we accept that the mythology was not chronologically subsequent to, *but simultaneous with*, the events then no such corrective demystification is possible. Put differently, the Winter of Discontent unfolded in the way in which it did precisely because of the myths in and through which it was lived, experienced, and responded to at the time. We can correct, after the fact and after the careful sifting of the evidence, the misinterpretations and misinformation on which such myths were predicated, but to understand what happened is to understand the effects at the time of precisely such misinterpretations and misinformation.

My reflections, in what follows, are split into two parts. In the first of these I seek to develop a fuller appreciation of the (many) strengths and (fewer) weaknesses of these important new studies of the Winter of Discontent. In the second I seek to take stock of the place of the Winter of Discontent in the wider political and economic history of the post-war period, in a way that neither book does, by reconsidering some of the major unresolved disputes in the literature in the light of the new evidence that each study unearths.

The Winter of Discontent: myth-contextualized, myth-understood

Given that they draw on so many of the same sources and deal ostensibly with the same subject, it is remarkable how different these two books are in focus, style, and analytical content. Martin López's book, as I have already sought to suggest, is an almost restorative and redemptive work of normative social history. It seeks, above all else, to piece together and thereby to retrieve the experiences, subjectivities, and identities of rank-and-file union members from their pervasive depiction in the folklore of the time as instrumental, self-serving 'wreckers' bent on 'holding the country to ransom' to extract more than their fair share of the country's meagre economic resources, with wanton disregard for the consequences for others. In this way, Martin López uses oral history to restore to the otherwise silenced direct participants in the events themselves a voice and an identity largely effaced by the mythology in which the Winter of Discontent has come to be shrouded. She seeks, in other words, to give back to the strikers and pickets their, quite literally, *myth*-taken identity. And, in so doing, she sets out to correct a systematic bias in the elite political history of the period by juxtaposing the conventional view, reconstructed from the perspective of those whose voices are recorded in the official archives, the witness seminars, the biographies, and the autobiographies of the period with the subject-position of the pickets and strikers themselves.

Yet this would suggest that Martin López offers us a radical alternative social history of the Winter of Discontent, strikingly different from that of Shepherd, for instance. But, though perhaps inherent in the logic of her approach, that is in the end not quite what we get. For her book starts and finishes in much more familiar territory, in the well-worn elite political history of the winter of 1978–79. In between, to be sure, she strives – at times, quite brilliantly – to reconstruct and give a voice to rank-and-file union members and, indeed, their leaders and she unearths, in the process, a range of extremely important factors almost entirely overlooked in the existing literature (most notably, perhaps, the rapid organizational and generational changes underway in British trade unions at the time). But the questions that she seeks to answer with this new material are, in the end, perhaps all too familiar and all too conventional: whether Callaghan was right to decide against an early election in the autumn of 1978, whether he should have declared a State of Emergency early in 1979 and so forth. And her answers, though supremely well informed and invariably extremely persuasive, are actually quite conventional too.

There are, of course, different ways of interpreting this: (1) that Martin López merely shows (with recourse to valuable new evidential material) that the revisionist history of the Winter of Discontent associated with authors such as Steve Ludlam, Paul Smith, Nick Tiratsoo and, perhaps even myself, is broadly correct;[5] (2) that she reminds us that, although not consciously intended as a redemptive reconstruction of the events from the perspective of the direct participants, that literature always contained within it a much more credible and sophisticated view of the motivational dispositions of rank-and-file union members (than in the popular mythology of the time); and (3) that one does not need a redemptive reconstruction of the identities and motivations of the strikers and pickets in order to answer the questions that Martin López poses herself and that, partly as a consequence, she is in danger of not making the best use of the new oral testimony she gathers.

Perhaps unremarkably, I see some mileage in all three responses. In a way, the first two can be taken together. Martin López's careful and sensitive reconstruction of the motivations of rank-and-file union members involved in the Winter of Discontent is not principally intended as a critique of the existing scholarly history of the period, except in the sense that it reminds us (usefully) of the dangers of presuming to know the motivations of political actors (especially where the option exists of asking them directly). As such,

5 See S. Ludlam, '"Old" Labour and the Winter of Discontent', *Politics Review* 9 (2000), pp. 30–3; P. Smith, 'The Winter of Discontent: The Hire and Reward Haulage Dispute, 1979', *Historical Studies in Industrial Relations* (*HSIR*) 7 (1999), pp. 27–54; *idem*, *Unionization and Union Leadership: The Road Haulage Industry* (Continuum: 2001), ch. 7; N. Tiratsoo, 'You've Never Had It So Bad: Britain in the 1970s', in *idem* (ed.), *From Blitz to Blair: A New History of Britain since 1939* (Weidenfeld and Nicolson: 1997); Hay, 'Narrating Crisis', *Sociology*; *idem*, 'Chronicles of a Death Foretold', *Parliamentary Affairs*.

and particularly since her oral testimony largely verifies the more complex motivational assumptions made in that literature, it is hardly surprising that she reaches similar conclusions to it.

There is perhaps an additional point to be made here. If the weakness of the existing literature (which Martin López seeks to correct) lies in its failure to treat the motives and motivational dispositions of the direct participants as an open empirical question, then there is perhaps an inverse weakness in Martin López's own account – and one to which I have already alluded. For motivations are contextual, and Martin López, I would suggest, fails adequately to contextualize the behaviour of the strikers and pickets. In a way her interviews, sensitively and sympathetically redemptive though they undoubtedly are, tell us more about the *agency* exhibited by the union members she talks to in the invention and performance of the rituals of protest that characterized the Winter of Discontent than they tell us about the underpinning *motivations* informing such agency. For to get at these, Martin López would almost certainly have had to adopt a more inquisitorial and interrogatory mode of intervention – pushing respondents to relate their agency (what they did) back to their perception of the political and economic context in which they found themselves (getting them, in effect, to explain how and why they felt that what they did was justified).

An alternative strategy, rather closer in fact to the existing literature, would have been to relate the narratives of the participants she retrieves through oral history to her own understanding of the context in which union members found themselves. But to do this adequately would require rather more political economy than Martin López's book ultimately delivers. In order to make sense of the behaviour of strikers and pickets, and even to make sense of the narratives they offer retrospectively of their behaviour, I argue, would require placing them in the appropriate political and, above all, economic context. Martin López brings us significantly closer to the point where we might be able to do that – by furnishing us with the narratives that we might relate to our understanding of the context in which the Winter of Discontent took place – but she does not provide it herself.

This brings us directly to the third point identified above, that is the suggestion, hinted at again in the preceding paragraph, that Martin López does not make full use of the opportunity to engage directly with union members that her interviews afford her. Again, I think there is something in this, and, laudable though it is, it might well be that construing her interviews as part of a process of redemption is part of the problem here. For there remain a number of unresolved and even unasked questions in the political and economic history of the Winter of Discontent that urgently need to be addressed. But this is hardly a critique of Martin López. For reading her work makes one more aware of those questions. Indeed, arguably she is perhaps better placed that anyone to pose and to answer them, since she is one of the very few analysts of the period to talk directly to rank-and-file union members. The key question here, it strikes me, is 'what *was* the alternative to Thatcherism?' This is, of course, a phenomenally difficult question to answer with any authority.

But some things are clear. First, as almost all commentators agree, the attempt to control inflation by binding public-sector unions and their members to a degree of wage moderation that could not be secured in the private sector was untenable. But, second, and as we shall see in more detail presently, from 1975 onwards the Labour government (under first Wilson and then Callaghan) was in fact remarkably successful in bringing down inflation while holding unemployment essentially stable (see Figure 1).

In this respect its record was, of course, much better than that of the government of Margaret Thatcher which replaced it. As Figure 2 shows, during the years of 'crisis' (between the first quarter of 1974 and the second quarter of 1979) the British economy grew by around 12%, whereas the putative 'solution' to the crisis (from the first quarter of 1979 to the end of 1982) saw it shrink by 2.2%. The medicine may very well have been worse than the condition.

This suggests that there was a tenable alternative to Thatcherism, if only it could have been found. But, and this is the crux of the matter, to get a credible sense of what that might have been requires an assessment not only of the extent of the gulf of ideas separating union members, union leaders, and the government (which, to some extent we already have), but also a sense of what the former might have deemed acceptable in return for a binding agreement to a degree of wage moderation consistent with the management of inflation. The answer to that question still evades us. If we are ever to find it, it can only be through the kind of oral history that Martin López's work exemplifies.

Thus far I have tended to emphasize the striking differences between these two works. But no less striking are their similarities. Indeed, given that one is primarily a work of archival elite political history (ostensibly concerned with the Callaghan government's role in, and culpability for, the Winter of Discontent), the other primarily a work of redemptive oral social history (ostensibly concerned with retrieving a 'counter-memory' from the long-forgotten subjects of that winter), it is staggering how much they have in common. Perhaps most surprising of all is their shared chronology, which even extends to the rather quirky ordering of the narrative they both present. Thus, both books start their substantive analysis (after a fair bit of set up and framing) not with the Winter of Discontent at all but with the 1979 general election campaign. This, as I have already suggested, is largely – and both strangely and problematically, to my mind – because they see the mythology of the Winter of Discontent (with which both, refreshingly, are interested) as originating not in the events themselves but

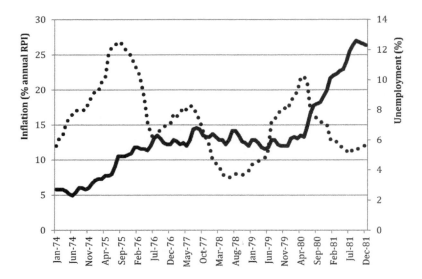

Figure 1: Managing the problem of 'stagflation'

Source: HM Treasury, *Economic Trends* (various years).
Key: unemployment (–); inflation (• • •)

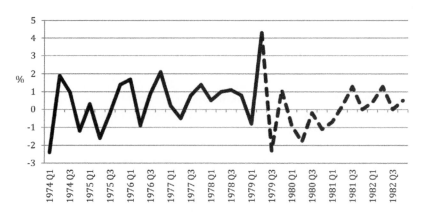

Figure 2: Economic output growth, 1974–82

Source: HM Treasury, *Economic Trends* (various years).
Key: Labour tenure (–); Conservative tenure (- - -)

in the election campaign that was to follow. This is a point to which I return below. But, having overturned the well-established chronology of the Winter of Discontent at the start, both authors return to a very conventional, and rigidly chronologically ordered, narrative in subsequent chapters. Thus, even if the content of the narrative is rather different, the episodes recounted and the order in which they are recounted are both extremely familiar and almost identical to those in the existing literature. Accordingly, after a little contextualization in the politics and industrial relations of the 1970s (arguably too little, in both cases), the Winter of Discontent is seen to begin with the dispute at Ford, followed by the road haulage strike and the oil tanker drivers' overtime ban before we turn to the public-sector National Day of Action on 22 January 1979, and thence to the series of disputes and strikes involving public-sector workers (notably the infamous Liverpool gravediggers' strike, and stoppages and strikes by other local government and National Health Service staff) that would rumble on until the devolution referendum and the vote of no confidence in the Callaghan government. Things come full circle as we return to where we started with the 1979 general election campaign and, ultimately, to Thatcher standing on the steps of Downing Street quoting St Francis of Assisi.

What are we to make of this familiar and highly conserved narrative? Well, once again there are two rather different readings possible. On the one hand, we might take the seeming consensus as a simple vindication and verification: Shepherd and Martin López, benefiting from their access to the public records and to a rich and diverse array of other primary and secondary materials, are able to confirm that the existing literature (most of which did not enjoy the same access to such sources) is right in its chronology and sequencing of the key events, and perhaps even that it gets the linkages between them right too. But, tempting though such a reading is, this is perhaps just a little too convenient. Indeed, there is, I think, an important methodological point to make here, though it relates rather more to Shepherd than it does to Martin López (whose aim is far less to establish the sequence of events and whose principal sources are non-archival).

It strikes me that, in the most general terms, there are two rather different approaches that one can take to archival evidence (and, indeed, to other primary data sources). One is more inductive than the other. At the more inductive end of the spectrum (for, in the end, this is perhaps better seen in terms of a continuum rather than a simple binary), the historian enters the archive without a strong sense of the historical narrative and precisely in order to construct or reconstruct that narrative from the sources themselves. At the other end of the spectrum, the historian enters the archive with a narrative already in place and is seeking (merely) additional insight and detail to elaborate, augment, and further enrich an account which already exists in at least outline form. Shepherd, I suggest, is far closer to this (the latter) end of the archival historians' spectrum – and, in a way, that might be something of a shame.

There is a general point to be made here and a more specific one. The general point is that, as the first detailed book-length study of the Winter of Discontent to benefit from full access to the public records, one might perhaps have anticipated a more open and sceptical attitude to the conventional chronology and to the identification of the key episodes around which the established narrative is invariably structured. It is not impossible, I think, to imagine that a different historian, perhaps less versed in the literature, might have come to infer and reconstruct from the archival record a rather different history, placing the emphasis on different moments and different strategic choices in the unfolding drama. And that leads to the more specific point. For, at times, Shepherd's account in fact hints – albeit very subtly – at precisely such an alternative account. For there are at least three moments or episodes to which Shepherd refers, albeit briefly and in passing, that are scarcely mentioned in the existing literature and which just might be potential candidates for key moments in a newly revisionist history of the disintegration of the Social Contract and the birth of Thatcherism.

The first of these is the first significant strike in the public sector during the winter of 1978–79, namely that at the BBC. What makes this particularly interesting, and hence potentially worthy of the kind of detailed scrutiny that Shepherd chooses not to afford it, is that this was hastily resolved by the government (ostensibly so as to prevent a television blackout over Christmas), with a pay settlement of 12%: that is at over twice the 5% ceiling. This, as far as I can tell, is the only reference to this dispute in the entire literature on the Winter of Discontent and, sadly, Shepherd gives us only a sentence (p. 61). His source is, in fact, not from the public records at all but from the *Financial Times* on the 22/23 December 1978, immediately after the dispute's resolution. Yet what would, of course, be fascinating to explore in more detail are the ministerial papers from the public records on this intriguing episode. How was the deal brokered and with what degree of opposition from around the Cabinet table? What advice did the government receive and from whom? To what extent was the deal seen as precedent setting and to what extent, if any, did it influence the negotiations, still underway at the time, to avert the public-sector unions' National Day of Action planned for the New Year? What was the rationale for this seemingly major concession made before the then almost inevitable clash between the public-sector trade unions and the government? How might things have proceeded differently if the terms of the BBC settlement had been taken as paradigmatic for the public sector as a whole? Some (if not all) of the answers to these questions undoubtedly lie in the public record; but they have yet to be unearthed.

The second such episode comes, ironically, from just a couple of days later in the unfolding saga. It relates to the attempt, orchestrated by the General and Municipal Workers' Union (GMWU) – but ultimately with the support of the other public-sector trade unions including, crucially, the National Union of Public Employees (NUPE) – to avert the National Day of Action and the ensuing dispute. On Christmas Eve 1978, Larry Whitty (head of the GMWU's research department) and Derek Gladwin (the secretary of the GMWU's southern region and a close personal friend of Callaghan) presented to Number 10 a potential deal. What makes this all the more interesting – and, with the benefit of hindsight, all the more tragic – is that its terms were in fact less generous to the unions than those which would ultimately be agreed over two months later (and, in the case of NUPE, rather later still). To be fair, the episode itself is not new to the literature. It is mentioned by Steve Ludlam, whose doctoral thesis (despite being completed in 1991, nearly two decades before the opening of the public records), arguably still remains the most authoritative study of the period and it is something to which I also give some prominence.[6] And it is to her credit that Martin López, in fact, gives rather more detail than Shepherd, though, like myself, she draws in so doing largely on Ludlam's work (pp. 115–16). Interesting and incisive though they are, Shepherd's comments on the subject are confined to a single footnote and his source is, once again, not from the public record but from a personal interview with Larry (now, Lord) Whitty (p. 85, n. 12).

Here, as with the BBC dispute, we need to know more – and that information is only likely to be found in the public record. Why, by whom, and on what basis, was the deal rejected and to what extent was the resolution of the BBC strike two days earlier seen as precedent setting? How close did Whitty come to brokering a deal and to what extent did the government resign itself, in rejecting the deal, to a continuation of the Winter of Discontent in the public sector into the New Year? Finally, to what extent were Denis Healey's attempts both in Cabinet, and in the House of Commons the next day, to augment the 5% ceiling on wage rises with an across-the-board £3.50 increase in weekly pay and an acceptance of a permanent mechanism to monitor and ensure wage comparability a direct result of the failed deal? Again, we do not have answers to these, arguably crucial, questions but at least we now know where to look.

The final element of a potentially new revisionist history of the Winter of Discontent is not, strictly speaking, an episode so much as a text, the 'Stepping Stones' programme produced, in effect, by the Centre for Policy

---

6 S. Ludlam, Labourism and the Disintegration of the Postwar Consensus: Disunited Trade Union Economic Policy Responses to Public Expenditure Cuts, 1974–79 (Ph.D., University of Sheffield: 1991); Hay, 'Chronicles of a Death Foretold', *Parl. Affairs*, p. 455.

Studies for Thatcher and her closest advisers. This, of course, has generated its own literature.[7] But its implications for our understanding of the Winter of Discontent have, to date at least, typically remained un- or under-explored. Here, I think, Shepherd and Martin López deserve rather more credit, for both clearly see the link and spend some time discussing it. But, arguably, they do not explore it quite enough and, from my perspective at least, they don't get the link quite right (though I freely accept that, in the end, this is a matter of historical interpretation and not simply something that can be resolved evidentially).

What is interesting about Stepping Stones is that it resolves (or might credibly be taken to resolve), in a way, a long-standing dispute in the literature on Thatcherism (a literature with which, of course, neither book engages). That dispute concerns the question of whether the first Thatcher government was elected with an ideological 'blueprint' for office – an animating policy script, in effect, which would inform the unfolding of a Thatcherite 'project' over time.[8] Clearly no such script ever existed and it is much better to see Thatcherism, if it can be seen as a project at all, as a unfolding script made and re-made over time in the light of changing circumstances, although animated throughout by a common and central moral-cum-political 'instinct' or disposition.[9] What is interesting about Stepping Stones is that it shows that although Thatcherism lacked an ideological or a policy blueprint and was not, as such, pre-scripted, it had – and benefited massively from – a communications strategy blueprint. Indeed, what it also shows is that, before the Winter of Discontent, those who were ultimately to define what Thatcherism was to become (and, notably, *not Thatcher herself*, who remained stubbornly sceptical and unconvinced until the Winter of Discontent itself) had targeted the unions as public enemy number one for the new Thatcher administration (should the Conservatives prevail at the polls). The point is that it was the Winter of Discontent which made Stepping Stones credible as a communications strategy, not least for Thatcher herself; and as soon as it was credible it became defining of what Thatcherism was to become. In other words, the targeting of the unions, which arguably made much of the Thatcherite

---

7 A. Taylor, 'The "Stepping Stones" Programme: Conservative Party Thinking on Trade Unions, 1975–79', *HSIR* 11 (2001), pp. 109–33; P. Dorey, 'The Stepping Stones Programme: The Conservative Party's Struggle to Develop a Trade-Union Policy, 1975–79', *HSIR* 35 (2014), pp. 89–116.

8 Most vociferous in their criticism of such a view of Thatcherism are D. Marsh and R. A. W. Rhodes (eds), *Implementing Thatcherite Policies: Audit of an Era* (Open University Press, Buckingham: 1992), and P. Kerr, *Postwar British Politics: From Conflict to Consensus* (Routledge: 2001).

9 On which see S. Farrall and C. Hay (eds), *Thatcher's Legacy: Exploring and Theorizing the Long-Term Consequences of Thatcherite Social and Economic Policies* (Oxford University Press: 2014).

agenda possible, was contingent on the Winter of Discontent itself. This neither Shepherd nor Martin López see – though it is an interpretation quite consistent with the evidence they present.

The importance of this can scarcely be understated. For it suggests that, in the absence of the Winter of Discontent, the first Thatcher administration would not have been able to, and would not even have chosen to, target the unions (and perceived union 'power') in the way in which it did. And without that, it is impossible to imagine that the consequences of its brutal monetarist offensive in terms of unemployment and social inequality would have proved politically sustainable. In other words, what we now refer to as Thatcherism would have been impossible in the absence of the Winter of Discontent.

Defrosting the Winter of Discontent: de-*myth*-ification

Thus far I have sought to limit my reflections on the Winter of Discontent to those which arise from a direct engagement with the argument and evidence presented in these two important studies. But there is another way of approaching the Winter of Discontent and the debates that it has generated in the light of the evidence that Shepherd and Martin López bring to bear upon it. That is not to confine oneself to the argument each presents, but to ask instead whether, to what extent, and how that evidence can be used to adjudicate between existing disputes in the wider literature on the period. That is my aim in this final section. There is much which could be said here, but I will confine myself to commenting on three key issues which have been widely debated in the existing literature and each of which is recast, at least to some extent, by the evidence Shepherd and Martin López unearth. I conclude with a brief discussion of the wider methodological implications of the opening of the public records and the reopening of the debate on the Winter of Discontent that it has generated.

The 'phoney' election episode

The first set of issues, which Shepherd and Martin López both explore in some detail, relates to the 'phoney' election campaign of autumn 1978. There are, in fact, three issues here: why did Callaghan not rush to the polls at the earliest opportunity in autumn 1978; was he wrong not to do so; and what difference would it have made anyway? Clearly the three questions are related but somewhat strangely, to my mind, Shepherd and Martin López both concentrate on the second – the judgement of Callaghan's conduct. And, perhaps more strangely still in the light of the evidence they present, they both conclude that Callaghan was wrong not to call an early general election. This, I fear, is the wrong answer to the wrong question.

In a book that is often frustratingly equivocal, Shepherd is in fact unchar-
acteristically forthright on the issue, suggesting that the Prime Minister's
decision to defer the election was 'astonishing' (pp. 15–16), and, later on,
that this was his 'single greatest error' (pp. 125–6). Martin López, too,
chastises Callaghan for his strategic ineptitude in ostensibly similar terms,
arguing that his actions throughout 1978, most notably his 'cancellation
[*sic*.] of the autumn election, illustrate his decision to have a showdown with
the trade unions over economic policy' (p. 61). But both judgements are, in
the end, too harsh on Callaghan, though Martin López's is perhaps more
easily explicable. For her concern is with rank-and-file union members.
And, from this perspective, as soon as there was no longer the prospect of
an autumn election, Labour's political and, indeed, electoral fortunes rested
solely on the government's capacity to hold wage inflation (particularly that
in the public sector) significantly below price inflation. Callaghan was, in
effect, gambling his political career and the electoral prospects of his party
on his ability to inflict continued suffering on (what he arrogantly assumed
to be) his core supporters in the public-sector unions.

Recast in such terms, Martin López may well be right. But the
underpinning logic of her argument is surely that Callaghan's error was
not the decision to postpone the election but, instead, the choice of the 5%
ceiling on wage inflation in the first place. Indeed the real problem here
is that both Shepherd and Martin López allow the benefit of their shared
historical hindsight to shape their judgement of Callaghan's conduct.
The key question here is surely not whether, with thirty years' hindsight,
Callaghan was right but why, *at the time*, he chose to defer the election until
at least the spring. Seen from his perspective, particularly in the light of
the advice that he received, it would have been 'astonishing' had he chosen
an autumn election which it was far from clear that he would have won.
One might even argue that if Callaghan's actions appear 'astonishing' to
Shepherd it is only because he has failed to understand them.

The irony is that, between them, Shepherd and Martin López provide
us with all the evidence we need to make sense of Callaghan's fateful
decision. He was unsure that his government would win an early election;
he retained the courage of his conviction that the 5% wage-inflation target
was the best means of controlling inflation; he remained no less certain that
his strategy would work, or would work at least sufficiently well, to show
that Labour was the only party capable of improving Britain's still parlous
economic condition after the IMF loan; and he was confident that this would
ultimately be rewarded at the polls, was his best chance of re-election and,
indeed, his only chance of achieving a working majority. Put in these terms
(and putting to one side our hindsight) it would have been remarkable had
Callaghan done anything else.

Indeed, there is one final piece of the jigsaw here. For, as Shepherd in fact shows rather well, Callaghan and his advisers were, at the time, unaware of an additional factor that was to prove crucial to the unfolding of the Winter of Discontent. They assumed that, as long as union leaders and the TUC general council supported (however reluctantly) the terms of the Social Contract, then ultimately so too would rank-and-file union members. With the benefit of hindsight this might appear naive; but this was a hindsight that Callaghan could not and did not enjoy.

If we pull all of these pieces of the puzzle together, then, I think it is actually quite clear that Callaghan's decision to defer the election until the spring – while inadvertently setting the government, union leaders and rank-and-file union members on a path that could only end badly – was not in any sense part of a deliberate strategy to confront the unions (as Martin López implies). It was, moreover, perfectly rational and intelligible given the situation in which Callaghan found himself and the advice that he received. Though this is not their conclusion, I think it is the logical inference to be drawn from the new archival material that Shepherd and Martin López assemble.

Why no declaration of a State of Emergency?

The second issue which, arguably, Shepherd and Martin López's fresh evidence allows us to resolve once and for all, concerns Callaghan's reluctance or failure to declare a State of Emergency in January 1979 at the height of the road haulage strike and the oil tanker drivers' overtime ban.

In a way the problem is not terribly different from the question of the phoney election of 1978 in the sense that to understand the Winter of Discontent is, I would contend, to understand why, from the perspective of the government, it was rational *not* to declare a State of Emergency. Yet, interestingly and although once again drawing on the very same sources, here Shepherd and Martin López reach profoundly different conclusions. Shepherd, though a little more equivocal, seems ultimately convinced by Peter Shore's suggestion (extemporizing on a comment in Callaghan's autobiography) that, 'The armed forces should have been deployed to clear the refuse, dig the graves, ensure the water and essential services', in other words, a State of Emergency should have been declared (p. 107).[10]

I think we need to be careful here. Though Shore was, of course, a Cabinet minister at the time, his comment comes from his own autobiography published in 1993. It develops a similar remark in Callaghan's own autobiography published in 1987. While it would be wrong to accuse either figure of retrospectively according to themselves a degree of foresight they lacked at the time, we should undoubtedly give precedence to evidence

---

10 Citing P. Shore, *Leading the Left* (Weidenfeld and Nicolson: 1993).

simultaneous to the events themselves. What is clear from the public record is that there is very little if any evidence of a cogent argument being made in Cabinet (by Callaghan, Shore or anyone else for that matter) for the declaration of a State of Emergency. Moreover, the Cabinet and Civil Contingencies Unit sought, received and considered reams of evidence showing that there was rather less of a threat to essential services than the media narrative of the time suggested, and that the logistical complexities alone meant that the declaration of a State of Emergency would almost certainly make matters worse not better. Even putting to one side the practical difficulties of bringing troops back from Germany and training them to drive oil tankers, the declaration of a State of Emergency could only further serve to antagonize the unions, galvanizing them into more co-ordinated collective action and thereby precipitating a greater problem of secondary picketing while offering the capacity to deliver, at best, a small fraction of the fuel that was already being supplied (in part through the co-operation of the Transport and General Workers' Union). In short, the Cabinet would have had to discount systematically the strategic assessment of the situation that it had sought in order to declare a State of Emergency. Finally, it might well also be pointed out that to act in such a way would, almost certainly, have been seen to accede to an agenda now being set by Margaret Thatcher and the Conservative Party, and to commit the party, in effect, just before an election, to some form of anti-union legislation in the immediate aftermath, should it prevail at the polls.

That Callaghan, looking back wistfully almost two decades later, might have wished that he had declared a State of Emergency is no reason for questioning Martin López's conclusion that, at the time, he had no alternative other than to heed the advice he had requested. As this suggests, here, just as in the case of the 'phoney' election, the combination of counter-factuals and hindsight (whether that of the historian or, as here, that of the participants themselves) is a potentially dangerous thing. In such situations we can do a lot worse than to recall the aphorism usually attributed to Eric Hobsbawm, 'ultimately things turned out the way they did, and because they did they couldn't have turned out any other way'. To understand the Winter of Discontent is to understand how things came to turn out the way they did, and that is to understand how the declaration of a State of Emergency was never really a possibility.

A 'constructed crisis'?

This brings us to a final consideration and one of a rather more theoretical nature. Both Shepherd and Martin López, albeit in different ways, take explicit inspiration from the idea of the Winter of Discontent as a 'manufactured' or 'constructed crisis' – with Shepherd's focus on the media's coverage of the events of the winter of 1978–79 and, indeed, his discussion of the 1979 general election owing much to this perspective (pp. 7–8, 112ff.), and with Martin López keen to declare the concept 'foundational' to her own analysis (pp. 10–12).[11]

As the author of this concept, I should perhaps just be grateful for the compliment and leave it at that. But, no doubt owing to my own infelicities of expression and not for the first time in the debate on the Winter of Discontent, I fear that both Shepherd and Martin López misinterpret in a non-trivial way the argument that I was seeking to develop. And, more significantly, I think this leads them to misinterpret the Winter of Discontent itself. As such, I hope I can be excused the indulgence of returning briefly to the idea of the Winter of Discontent as a constructed crisis in the light of the argument and the evidence both present.

To get at the issues involved here, it is perhaps best simply to cite (Lord) David Lipsey's clearly exasperated comments at the heresy of the suggestion that the crisis was 'constructed', which he delivered in response to my lecture to mark the thirtieth anniversary of the events at the British Academy in 2009. The passage from the transcript of the debate is repeated, tellingly, in full by Shepherd.

> I am not sure where you were Professor Hay, but I can tell you some of the places you weren't. You weren't in Manchester where for ten days people were getting water out of standpipes in the street. You weren't in Liverpool when the mortuaries were closed because the grave diggers wouldn't dig the graves, and serious consideration was being given to dumping bodies at sea ... and you certainly weren't in Downing Street, where I was, where hour by hour 'the newest grief of an hour's age doth hiss the speaker' ... I am sorry, this ['the Winter of Discontent'] was *not* a constructed crisis. It was a real crisis.[12]

Lipsey's remark is painful to read again and I can only apologize to him, as I did at the time, for any offence. His comment is entirely understandable and were my argument that these events never took place, it would surely be right. But that is not, nor ever has been, my argument, though I can see how the language of 'construction' might lead to such a confusion. What pains and surprises me more, though, is that the same confusion persists, if in a rather less acute form. For it characterizes both Shepherd and Martin López's comments on the subject too. Both authors use a reflection on the

---

11 On the Winter of Discontent as a 'constructed crisis', see Hay, 'Narrating Crisis', *Sociology*, pp. 253–77; *idem*, 'The Winter of Discontent Thirty Years On', *PQ*, pp. 545–52; *idem*, 'Chronicles of a Death Foretold', *Parl. Affairs*, pp. 446–70.

12 Cited in L. Black and H. Pemberton, 'The Winter of Discontent in British Politics', *PQ* 80:4 (2009), pp. 553–61, p. 556.

concept and the debate it has generated to open a discussion about the extent of the distortion or bias in the popular mythology and folklore of the Winter of Discontent.

That is, of course, an extremely important issue (and one that I have reflected on at length), but it is by no means the principal one issue raised by referring to the crisis as 'manufactured' or 'constructed'. For my argument is that *all crises are constructions* and that the construction of the (real) events themselves as symptomatic of a wider crisis is both what makes a crisis what it is (a crisis) and is integral to how the crisis is lived, experienced and responded to. This is as true of the global financial crisis as it is of the Winter of Discontent. Put simply, the construction of the events at the time *as symptomatic of a crisis* and symptomatic of a crisis *of a particular kind* (a crisis of a beleaguered state, or of Keynesianism, for instance) shapes the unfolding of those events over time as it does, crucially, the response to which they give rise. The Winter of Discontent is perhaps the clearest example of such a phenomenon in post-war British history, not least because the construction was, as Shepherd and Martin López show so well, based on an at times wild and wilful extrapolation and extemporization from the events that had already unfolded and those that were underway – and because the response was Thatcherism. But, crucially, the Winter of Discontent would have been no less of a constructed crisis had it given rise to a historically more credible mythology and to a response more appropriate to the events. The point is that, as with any other crisis, there is nothing inherent in the events of the winter of 1978–79 that makes them a crisis of a beleaguered and ungovernable state held to ransom by an all-powerful trade-union movement, or, indeed, a crisis at all.

The implication of this is that the Winter of Discontent was *lived and experienced through* a very particular construction of what was going on at the time. That construction was not a retrospective rationalization offered after the fact, as both Shepherd and Martin López assume, but was simultaneous with the events which it served to dramatize. Consequently, the question for analysts of the period, particularly those interested in its enduring significance, is not just about the accuracy of that construction, important though that undoubtedly is. For the construction came to have a life of its own. Put simply, how the events were understood at the time is crucial to how they were responded to and, consequently, to how the events of the winter of 1978–79 were to unfold. If the mythology of the Winter of Discontent was born contemporaneously, then it is crucial to our understanding of what that episode was.

This is illustrated by appeal to the witness testimony that we now have. Particularly valuable, here, is a paper written in 1984 by William Rodgers, Secretary of State for Transport between 1976 and 1979. Talking about the road haulage dispute, with which he was, of course, intimately involved, he states, 'like wartime bombing raids, the strike produced more warnings of shortages and more signs of damage than actual disruption'. He continues: 'the reporting of the strike by newspaper, radio and especially television was dramatic, and had much more impact on opinion than the public's own direct experience of the strike.' This is undoubtedly true and it is hardly remarkable. But what is perhaps remarkable – and certainly very interesting – are his final remarks on the subject:

> The demeanour of pickets – seen against a bleak winter landscape – caused anger and anxiety. *The Guardian* reported that the strike had cut the country's supply lines; that pigs and poultry might have to be slaughtered; that common vegetables were becoming a luxury; and that a shortage of newsprint might halt newspaper production. Ministers might have been tempted to treat this last possibility with equanimity. But in truth, most reporting of the strike was close to their own perception of events.[13]

The passage is perhaps slightly ambiguous. What it certainly seems to suggest is that, despite the close counsel of their civil service advisers that the road haulage dispute posed, at no point, any grave threat to the distribution of essential supplies,[14] ministers too lived and responded to the crisis through a media veil. Similarly, union leaders themselves may well have sought to broker an earlier deal on public-sector pay fearing the consequences that ongoing action was already having on workers not involved in the dispute – despite the now strong evidence to the contrary that we have.[15] If the fog of war descended on the direct participants in the elite-level politics of the unfolding crisis, then how much more pervasive must it have been for those with far less direct experience of the crisis to draw upon? As this suggests, the myths of the Winter of Discontent, and the very idea of the Winter of Discontent as a crisis, are crucial to its unfolding dynamic precisely because they provided the lens through which the events of that winter were to be experienced, responded to, and interpreted politically.

---

13 Rodgers, 'Government under Stress', *PQ*, pp. 177, 178. A former Fleet Street editor (at the time of the *Daily Star*), Derek Jameson, commented that 'We pulled every dirty trick in the book to get rid of Callaghan and Labour ... We made it look as if this [the strikes] was general, universal, eternal. In fact, it was only fragmentary, here and there. There was no big problem': T. Martin López, *The Winter of Discontent: Myth, Memory and History* (Liverpool University Press: 2014), p. 107. See also B. Jones, letter, *Guardian*, 23 April 2013.

14 See, for instance, PREM 16/1707, PREM 16/2128; CAB 128/65/3, The National Archives; see also Lopez, *Winter of Discontent*, pp. 101–4.

15 Hay, 'Chronicles of a Death Foretold', *Parl. Affairs*, p. 456; G. A. Dorfman, *British Trade Unionism against the Trades Union Congress* (Macmillan: 1983), pp. 84–5.

Conclusion: the opening of the archives

I want to conclude on a somewhat different note. As a political scientist and comparative political economist returning to the history of the Winter of Discontent through reading and rereading these two important works, I was struck by both authors' general silence on questions of methodology. Shepherd points, in the introduction to his chapter on the media, to the methodological issues raised by according to the media an independent role in the unfolding of the drama itself. But he then fails to discuss this further. And Martin López's book, as I have argued, could be seen as launching a profound methodological challenge to the conventional, archivally grounded, elite political history of the period. Yet that is not how she chooses to couch the challenge posed by her perspective-shifting oral social history. Even in terms of the simple conduct of the analysis both accounts are, certainly when gauged by the prevailing standards of mainstream political science, decidedly methodology-'lite'.

To be fair, I have no great problem with this. Indeed, I find it almost refreshing – not least because, even if they are not explicitly stated, there are subtle and sophisticated methodological choices being made in the work of each author. But, this notwithstanding, there are a series of broader methodological issues raised by these two books which warrant – indeed, arguably necessitate – more concerted and explicitly methodological reflection. Space does not permit an adequate treatment (though some are already hinted at in the preceding discussion), so I will merely list them:

- the place of oral history in post-war British political history;
- the perspectives, subject-positions, and vantage points from which our history is written and, in particular, the privileging within the archival record of certain of those perspectives, subject-positions, and vantage points;
- the extent of the need for 'triangulation' between contending sources, witnesses, and claims, and the most appropriate methodologies for achieving such 'triangulation';
- the reliability of interviews and other forms of witness testimony conducted or gathered two or more decades after the events themselves;
- the reliability and appropriate use of biographies and autobiographies typically also written many years after the events they purport to describe (and with the benefit of a hindsight not possible at the time).

There is much to be written on each of these points, and much of the preceding discussion could, indeed, be recast in terms of these more general issues. Rather than single out any one among them for further attention,

I want to conclude by discussing a different, if related, issue – the value added by the opening of the public records (under the thirty- (now twenty-) year rule).

When I read these two books for the first time I was struck by how *little* the opening of the public records has changed our view of the Winter of Discontent. This I attributed to the range, quality, and diversity of the biographies, autobiographies, and witness testimony already available to us. Indeed, I almost convinced myself that the opening of the archives was no longer a very significant moment. But on rereading these two studies and reflecting further upon this question, I have changed my mind in a way that raises serious methodological issues for contemporary British history.

Full access to the public record is important; indeed, it is crucial. But there is a danger here, a danger to which both of these studies ultimately succumb. It is that we do not make best use of such full access because we approach the archives seeking additional detail to supplement a pre-existing narrative. I want to suggest that, in future work on the Winter of Discontent, we need to strive to be both *more inductive* and *more deductive* (though not at the same time). By 'more inductive' I mean that we need to enter the archive, as it were, having put to one side (as best possible) the established narrative – seeking not verification, vindication or further detail but to reconstruct, as if for the first time, a narrative from the record itself. This we might later compare to the established orthodoxy. And by 'more deductive' I mean that we need also, quite separately, to enter the archive in the search for specific information which might help us answer a series of specific questions formulated in advance (the extent to which the government's thinking on the BBC dispute was similar to or different from that it exhibited in other public-sector disputes, for instance). Both perspectives, separately and together, can further augment our existing understanding of the Winter of Discontent – the moment, arguably, when 'then' became 'now'.

Sciences Po, Paris

HSIR 36 (2015) 205–218

doi:10.3828/hsir.2015.36.8

Striking Facts about the 'Winter of Discontent'

Dave Lyddon

J. Shepherd, *Crisis? What Crisis? The Callaghan Government and the British 'Winter of Discontent'* (Manchester University Press: 2013) xii + 205pp., £70, ISBN 978-0-7190-8247-4.

T. Martin López, *The Winter of Discontent: Myth, Memory and History* (Liverpool University Press: 2014) 252pp., £70, ISBN 978-1-7813-8029-1.

The recent publication of two books on the 1978–79 'Winter of Discontent' provides an opportunity to revisit the key strikes of that period. Colin Hay's essay in this issue of *Historial Studies in Industrial Relations* concentrates on the wider political argument and methodological issues, whereas my comment has a rather different focus, examining the experience and tactics of particular strikes. While both John Shepherd and Tara Martin López provide a pre-history for a number of the disputes they do not sufficiently emphasize the strong continuity with earlier strikes. Shepherd (p. 2) gives us the 'popular' image of the 'Winter of Discontent' as

> a familiar compilation of iconic media images and popular memories, such as the mountains of uncollected municipal rubbish in London's Leicester Square and elsewhere, union pickets at hospitals blocking entry to medical supplies and, probably above all, the refusal of the Merseyside gravediggers to bury the dead in Liverpool – with the rumoured possibility of interment at sea instead.

But mountains of rubbish and unburied bodies had occurred in the local authority strikes of 1969 and 1970, and many of the tactics used in the National Health Service (NHS) dispute had been prefigured in the earlier 1973 ancillary workers' industrial action.[1]

---

1 S. Williams and R. H. Fryer, *Leadership and Democracy. The History of the National Union of Public Employees, Vol. 2: 1928–1993* (Lawrence and Wishart: 2011), pp. 200–11.

The Winter of Discontent was, of course, much more than this and both Shepherd and Martin López devote a chapter each to the private-sector disputes at Ford and in road haulage. While Shepherd covers the public-sector strikes in one chapter (discussed by Roger Seifert in this issue), Martin López devotes individual chapters to the NHS and local authority strikes, with another specifically on the Liverpool gravediggers' dispute. These are the familiar landmarks. Hay draws our attention to the short but significant BBC strike. There are other disputes, only mentioned in passing, in one or both books, which deserve greater consideration – the bakers, water workers, and civil servants, for example. They will be among those disputes discussed in more detail below.

The account of the Winter of Discontent (and earlier) disputes presented here comes mainly from newspaper sources, especially the *Guardian* and *Financial Times* for 1978–79 as workers on *The Times* ('the newspaper of record') were locked out in their own industrial dispute from 1 December 1978 until 19 October 1979.[2] Martin López (p. 13) says her analysis is 'based on more than 60 interviews with participants' as well as other sources; investigation of these shows a narrower base than this. She interviewed four former Ford workers but these add little to standard accounts and her road haulage chapter only uses already existing testimony. Her interview sources are more powerful in the public-sector chapters, highlighting the nature of many of the low-paid and taken-for-granted jobs in essential public services and, especially, the centrality of women. Yet these interviews include only about five who were workers at the time in the NHS dispute and five in the local authority dispute – in both cases all were National Union of Public Employees (NUPE) members and several were shop stewards. This is supplemented by the important testimony of Ian Lowes, the Liverpool gravediggers' leader, of the General and Municipal Workers' Union (GMWU) but he seems to be the sole voice for this particular strike.

Before examining some of the individual strikes, this comment will first discuss the misleading use of strike statistics that tends to exaggerate the actual record of the Winter of Discontent.

Strike statistics

Shepherd makes the common mistake of conflating all the strikes of 1979 into the Winter of Discontent:

the 'winter of discontent' of 1978–79 witnessed a national outburst of strikes comparable with earlier years of industrial protest, in 1915–22 and 1972–74. In

---

2 *Employment Gazette*, August 1980, p. 871. See S. Meredeen, *Managing Industrial Conflict: Seven Major Disputes* (Hutchinson: 1988), pp. 98–134.

1979 alone, over 29 million days were lost as a result of around 2,000 stoppages involving nearly 5 million workers … During January–March 1979 – at the peak of the 'winter of discontent' – 5 million working days were lost. (p. 3)

In fact, the bulk of 'days lost' in strikes in 1979 was in the national strikes in the engineering industry, over the shorter working week, from 6 August to 2 October. Taking place under a Conservative government, these strikes directly involved a maximum of 1.5 million workers in three weekly one-day strikes and then, after a gap, five weekly two-day strikes.[3] A total of 16 million days lost were credited to this strike, the highest of any single dispute up to that point since the 1926 miners' lockout. The total days lost figure in September 1979 was also higher than in any month since 1926, which contained the General Strike and the largest-ever miners' lockout.[4]

Table 1 gives the monthly totals of days lost for 1978 and 1979, showing the peaks in the Winter of Discontent and the bulge of the engineering strikes. It is also helpful to separate out the 'pay round' year, which, at this point, was determined by when each new stage of incomes policy started, that is from the beginning of August.

Table 1: Working days lost by month, 1978–79

	1978	1979
January	836,000	2,966,000
February	571,000	2,425,000
March	377,000	1,333,000
April	595,000	867,000
May	527,000	485,000
June	452,000	613,000
July	379,000	662,000
August	472,000	4,103,000
September	878,000	11,716,000
October	1,857,000	3,508,000
November	1,918,000	606,000
December	542,000	190,000

Source: Department of Employment Gazette (1979); Employment Gazette (1980).

3 See reports in Financial Times from 7 August to 5 October 1979, and Meredeen, Managing Industrial Conflict, pp. 135–68. Employment Gazette, August 1980, p. 868, gives the date of the first one-day strike as the start date, 6 August, but the end date, 4 October (two days after the last national strike), as when the settlement was reached, probably because some workers were locked out.

4 Financial Times, 25 October 1979.

Table 2: Working days lost, 1974–80

Calendar year	
1974	14,750,000
1975	6,012,000
1976	3,284,000
1977	10,142,000
1978	9,405,000
1979	29,474,000
1980	11,964,000
Pay-round year (August–July)	
1974–75	9,934,000
1975–76	3,285,000
1976–77	5,842,000
1977–78	9,512,000
1978–79	15,018,000
1979–80	31,328,000

Source: Department of Employment Gazette (1974–79); *Employment Gazette* (1980–81).

Table 2 gives both calendar year and 'pay round' years and shows that days lost in August 1978–July 1979, while high compared to previous pay rounds, was only just half of the calendar year total for 1979, which figure is subsumed into most accounts of the Winter of Discontent.

Shepherd (p. 82) wrongly states that the public services' 'day of action' on 22 January 1979, with 1.5 million workers stopping, was 'the largest turn-out since the 1926 General Strike'.[5] According to the official count,[6] the largest such participation was the one-day strikes of 5 February and 5 March 1962 when an estimated 1.75 million (from the thirty-nine unions affiliated to the Confederation of Shipbuilding and Engineering Unions) were 'directly and indirectly involved' in strike action. The *Financial Times* even suggested that 'between 2m and 2½m' came out in February and that more came out in March.[7] Then on 15 May 1968, 1.5 million engineering workers went on a one-day strike.[8]

The claim that a particular strike is the largest since 1926 is made every time

---

5 The *Daily Telegraph* seems to have been his source. Williams and Fryer, *Leadership and Democracy*, p. 328, are among many others making this claim.
6 *Ministry of Labour Gazette*, April 1963, p. 144.
7 *Financial Times*, 6 February, 6 March 1962.
8 *Employment and Productivity Gazette*, May 1969, p. 440.

there is a very large strike (for example, recently, the local government pensions strike of 28 March 2006, and the 30 November 2011 public-services pensions strike).[9] We do not have an official figure for how many strikers there were on 22 January. The Department of Employment collapsed into one dispute all the strikes of several groups of workers with different bargaining arrangements: mainly local authority manual workers and NHS ancillary staff but also university manual workers (who seem only to have come out for one day, 22 January).[10] These strikes lasted from 22 January to, apparently, 17 April 1979, well after national settlements. Some 1,300,000 were estimated as having been directly, and another 200,000 indirectly, involved, between these dates with a total loss of 3,239,000 working days. On the face of it, this would suggest that each full-time equivalent worker took just over two days' strike action each; but the high proportion of part-time workers in these strikes (see below) means that the average number of shifts lost per actual worker was certainly higher than two. Ambulance workers (also partly out on 22 January but with some other stoppages) were only credited with striking between 21 February and 6 April 1979, with 6,300 workers directly involved and 34,000 working days lost.[11]

Three of the NHS ancillary unions ended the dispute on 7 March and the fourth, NUPE, on 28 March, followed the next day by the ambulance workers. The local authority dispute ended on 7 March though 'some local disputes continued ... over problems associated with the return to work, for example [as in 1970], payments for clearing the backlog of refuse collection and other work'.[12]

Private-sector disputes

Both Shepherd and Martin López recognize that the walkouts at Ford in September 1978 were spontaneous and that they were made official by the two main unions soon after. What is not appreciated is that this strike was also 'unconstitutional', in the sense that the existing agreement still had one month to run. This was almost identical to the sequence of events at Ford in 1971. While giving unofficial strikes official status was not unusual before the balloting laws made such practices unlawful, 'officializing' an

9 For example, *Financial Times*, 16 March 2006; *Independent*, 29 March 2006; *Daily Telegraph*, 4 November 2011.
10 Williams and Fryer, *Leadership and Democracy*, p. 329, seem to suggest 'selective action' took place in universities after 22 January.
11 *Employment Gazette*, August 1980, p. 873. Perhaps some figures in the published start date of the ambulance dispute were transposed and '21.2.79' should have been 22.1.79.
12 J. Gennard, 'Chronicle', *British Journal of Industrial Relations* 17:2 (1979), pp. 279–81.

unconstitutional strike was extremely rare. Yet there was a history of this at Ford, as it had also happened with the sewing machinists' 'equal pay' strike in 1968 and the 'penalty clauses' strike the next year. And the company, faced with a series of unofficial, sectional strikes on pay at a time of rapidly rising inflation in 1974, offered to scrap its existing agreement five months early and negotiated a new deal.[13] So the 1978 Ford strike, as with others at the company, was a movement from below and Ford, whatever its rhetoric about the 'right to manage', was used to dealing with such insurgency.

Before the Ford strike had finished on 24 November, the bakers' strike (mentioned only briefly by Shepherd and not by Martin López), had started. This lasted from 7 November to 15 December 1978, involving 20,000 workers directly and causing the loss of 370,000 working days and had the potential to cause bread shortages.[14] As with Ford, there was a recent history of lengthy national strikes: five weeks over pay in 1974 – after a spate of unofficial strikes – and three weeks over bank holiday payments in 1977, again starting unofficially.[15] And as with Ford, the 1978 strike was unconstitutional, starting a month before the existing agreement ran out.[16] This time the union was not so successful. On the third day there were arrests of pickets: thirteen at Walthamstow, six at Ipswich, two at Cardiff and three at Bradford. The next day, five pickets in Manchester and two in Cheshire were arrested and there were continuing incidents with police in several places.[17] There was another flurry of arrests in early December: six in Liverpool and two in Tewkesbury, followed by five in Reading.[18] A drift back to work undermined the strike, whose settlement was the least successful of all the disputes considered here.[19]

In the road haulage strike a driver picketing outside the London docks made a pointed remark: 'Two-thirds of haulage company drivers are not union members – without hitting the country's vitals we'd be about as effective as the bakers' strike'.[20] This stoppage, a series of area strikes, reflecting the structure of bargaining in the industry, started unofficially on 2 January but was made official by the Transport and General Workers' Union (TGWU) nine days later. As noted in the quote, secondary picketing was vital and was generally very successful. Shepherd (but not Martin López) gives extensive coverage to the oil tanker drivers' dispute, which did result in unofficial picketing by Texaco drivers and an unofficial strike in Northern Ireland.

---

13 See D. Lyddon, 'The Changing Pattern of UK Strikes, 1964–2014', *Employee Relations* (forthcoming).
14 *Department of Employment Gazette*, July 1979, p. 663.
15 *Guardian*, 3 December 1974, 9 September 1977.
16 *Ibid.*, 7 November 1978.
17 *Ibid.*, 10, 11, 15 November 1979.
18 *Ibid.*, 2, 4 December 1978.
19 *Ibid.*, 14 December 1978.
20 *Ibid.*, 13 January 1979.

Public-service strikes

According to the Clegg Comparability Commission, in 1979 there were about 1.1 million local authority manual workers; 63% (or about 700,000) were part time and mostly women; of the 400,000 full-time workers, about two-thirds were men. Of the 270,000 NHS ancillary workers, about half were part time (mainly women) and the full-time staff were split roughly equally between men and women. About 30% of the 31,000 university manual workers were full time.[21] Martin López is successful in emphasizing the largely part-time and largely female workforce and how the 1979 disputes were important as many women came to the fore, especially in NUPE. The variegated nature of the industrial action, particularly in hospitals, is difficult to catalogue and will not be attempted here. Stephen Williams and Bob Fryer do this to some extent in the history of NUPE[22] but this is hardly drawn on by either Shepherd or Martin López.

What does not seem to be recognized in either book is NUPE's early decision (March 1978) to go for 'a *common claim* across the public services' (emphasis added) in 1978–79.[23] The local government agreement was due to start on 4 November; university manual staff likewise had a November settlement whereas the NHS ancillaries' date was 13 December, with the water workers' also in December and ambulance staff on 1 January.[24] A common claim would avoid workers being split off from each other, though, in practice, efforts that were eventually successful detached the water workers. The 'day of action' on 22 January was a 'co-ordinated'[25] strike by the four unions with members in these services.

Local authority workers

Shepherd's image of 'mountains of uncollected municipal rubbish' is probably the most remembered aspect of the local authority strikes. Yet this was hardly new. This feature was present in the unofficial strike of mainly dustmen in 1969 (which started in London and was particularly strong there, though eventually encompassing some provincial towns) and the official 'dirty jobs' national strike of 1970.

---

21 Standing Commission on Pay Comparability (Clegg), *Report 1: Local Authority and University Manual Workers; NHS Ancillary Staffs; and Ambulancemen,* Cmnd 7641 (1979), pp. 3–4.
22 Williams and Fryer, *Leadership and Democracy,* ch. 11.
23 *Ibid.,* p. 311.
24 *Financial Times,* 19 January 1979; G. Kelly, *A History of the Local Authorities' Conditions of Service Advisory Board 1947 to 1991* (Centurion: 1991), p. 92; *Guardian,* 21 September 1978.
25 This term was used in the *Guardian,* 21 September and 12 December 1978.

The 1969 strike started in Hackney in late September and then spread very quickly to other London boroughs. Almost immediately it was reported that 'piles of rubbish are rotting in the streets in some boroughs'.[26] By 7 October, nearly 10,000 tons of rubbish was being added every day as all but two of London's thirty-two boroughs were affected. Fairly quickly a national deal was negotiated and then recommended by two of the three main unions, but not the TGWU.[27] Slowly strikers started to go back to work in London, while workers were still coming out elsewhere.

In 1970 the 'dirty jobs' strike was on a much larger scale. It started in London on 29 September and was extended very quickly to other parts of England. Most workers were out for up to six weeks, with dustmen in Kensington and Chelsea the last to go back, after eight weeks, having been denied a bonus to clear the backlog of rubbish.[28] As Guy Fawkes Night approached, there were fears of dangerous fires, particularly where children let off fireworks. One newspaper headline ran: 'Rubbish piles mount – new fire fears – LONDON – CITY OF SQUALOUR.'[29] The *Financial Times* ran a sober reflective piece, which now illuminates how much the equivalent experience in 1979 was sensationalized.

> Once again the Government and local councils are having to deal with a new situation of which they do not have past experience. This has happened several times during the five weeks since the local government unions started the strikes in sewerage plants, refuse collection depots and other council services which – apart from the dustmen's strike last year – have not been hit before by such industrial action.
>
> Because of this it has been easy for scares to be built up about river pollution contaminating water and killing fish, of blocked sewers flooding house basements, of serious diseases being spread by overflowing dustbins, and of colonies of rats breeding in the refuse.
>
> Each of these potential crises has been overcome or avoided by one means or another with considerable inconvenience to the public and to council operations, but without the wholesale disruption which had sometimes been feared.[30]

In 1979, sewerage was no longer under the control of local councils, while the Arctic conditions meant that the piles of rubbish posed less of an immediate health threat than they did in the autumn of 1970.

---

26 *Financial Times*, 30 September, 2 October 1969.
27 *Ibid.*, 7, 10 September 1969.
28 Cited in *ibid.*, 30 September, 21 November 1970.
29 *Ibid.*, 4 November 1970.
30 *Ibid.*

Gravediggers

Martin López based her chapter and later comments on gravediggers on the GMWU strike in Liverpool and the NUPE strike in Tameside. She cites the *Liverpool Echo* for other gravediggers' and crematorium workers' strikes in the Wirral, Sefton, Southport and Crewe, the *Guardian* for Sedgefield in county Durham, and a NUPE source for Woking and Guildford (pp. 127–8). The same *Guardian* report suggested that a strike was about to happen in Plymouth, while an article at the start of the dispute indicated there was action in Yorkshire and 'one or two crematoria in London were closed'.[31] But the national concentration on Liverpool was probably because of the higher number of bodies there waiting for burial. Lowes is quoted by Martin López (p. 123), saying 'This was the first strike in history involving this type of worker.' Perhaps that was so in Liverpool (though even this cannot be certain) but not elsewhere. Given how the press exploited the gravediggers' strikes at the time and how they have been used in subsequent accounts, it is important to correct this.

The precursors of the wider revolt of the low paid in 1979 were the strikes of 1969 and 1970, and it is these we must examine first. The 1969 unofficial strikes of (mainly London) council workers included gravediggers at three cemeteries in Lambeth (including Streatham) and the Hither Green cemetery in Lewisham.[32] Before the 1970 official 'dirty jobs' strike, the likelihood of gravediggers coming out was well flagged up; one newspaper pondered what might happen:

> It is possible by injection to preserve corpses without offensive smells or health hazards; but the use of communal graves in an absolute emergency, or burying them in private cemeteries (such as churchyards) has been discussed. Several London boroughs will suggest the use of a private cemetery if space has not already been reserved in one under local authority jurisdiction.[33]

In the 1970 strike of council manual workers, stoppages of gravediggers, cemetery and crematorium workers took place in Manchester (one-day strikes), Bexley, Newham, Southwark and Barking in Greater London, Luton, Birmingham, Sutton Coldfield, Bournemouth, Ipswich and Gloucester, and probably other places.[34] In early November, there were talks 'on resolving the "humanitarian problems" of the "dirty jobs" strike'

---

31 *Guardian*, 3 February, 24 January 1979.
32 *The Times*, 1 October 1969; *Guardian*, 7, 8 October 1969; *Financial Times*, 2, 7 October 1969.
33 *Guardian*, 5 September 1970.
34 *Ibid.*, 10 September, 1, 13, 15 October 1970; *The Times*, 1, 7, 13, 16, 19 and 27 October 1970.

in London, which included 'burial of the dead', suggesting this was still an issue.[35] Afterwards, the past president of the Institute of Burial and Cremation Administration wrote to *The Times*:

> The government knew from day one that fifty bob [£2.50] would settle the job. The unions certainly knew they could have ended it in a week ... if they had called out all cemetery and crematorium workers. There is only a three day capacity for the cold storage of human corpses! No calling in of troops could ever have coped with the very specialized and highly technical job of running a cemetery or crematorium.[36]

At the time there did not seem to have been any great outcry about gravediggers striking. The *Financial Times* even referred to 'the sympathy ... attracted' by the 1969 council workers' dispute, and this was probably carried over into the 1970 strike.[37] There were other occasional strikes – at least three weeks in Newtownabbey, County Antrim, in 1974 and six gravediggers were out for a week in Southwark, London, in 1975[38] – or strike threats.[39] Despite the bad press in 1979, there have been further instances since. Gravediggers and crematorium staff went on strike in the Wirral in 1983, the same year as gravediggers were part of a 500-strong strike at Merthyr Tydfil.[40] There were even threatened strikes in Liverpool in 1981 and 1982; an overtime ban (against compulsory redundancy) by cemetery and crematorium staff went ahead there in 1991, delaying funerals, but an attempt to include these workers in a wider strike ballot was withdrawn.[41] There will have been other, often short-lived, examples that could be unearthed. Gravediggers and crematorium staff will also have joined national one-day strikes of local government workers (for example, the local government pensions strike in 2006).[42]

In fact, while gravediggers' strikes have never been common they have always happened. Kenneth Knowles's comprehensive book on the years 1911–47[43] does not seem to have mentioned them but a perusal of some UK national newspapers disinters several (and local newspapers would undoubtedly add to these). Sometimes these were strikes of gravediggers on

35 *Financial Times*, 3 November 1970.
36 *The Times*, 10 November 1970.
37 *Financial Times*, 3 November 1969.
38 *Irish Times*, 28 June, 18 July 1974; *Observer*, 18 May 1975.
39 *Guardian*, 7 January 1970, 15 November 1973.
40 *Ibid.*, 15 November 1983; *The Times*, 27, 28, 29 June 1983.
41 *Guardian*, 3, 10 October 1981; 5, 6 May 1982; 17 July 1991.
42 *Scotsman*, 29 March 2006.
43 K. Knowles, *Strikes – A Study in Industrial Conflict, with Special Reference to British Experience between 1911 and 1947* (Blackwell, Oxford: 1952).

their own (Bolton, 1919; Belfast, 1947; Glasgow, 1952), sometimes as part of a wider movement of municipal workers (such as Derry, 1924; Barnsley, 1946; Swansea, 1950) or a mass municipal movement (such as the Leeds strike of 1913; Cardiff, 1920; City of London, 1947; the Rhondda, 1956; Jersey, 1970) or local general strikes (Belfast, 1919).[44] In some strikes, alternative labour was found or relatives of the deceased dug the graves.

Ireland has seen several, with strikes in Dublin recorded for 1890, 1915, three in 1916 and two in 1919.[45] The longest was a fifteen-week strike in 1921, followed by others in 1958, 1965 and 1971.[46] But the most substantial tradition seems to have been in the United States, particularly New York, where there have been many strikes of gravediggers, sometimes lasting weeks or months: for example, in 1929, 1938, 1948, 1949, 1953 and 1967. During the 1970s, there were long strikes in New York in 1970 and 1973 (with 7,000 unburied bodies), San Francisco in 1971 (with 1,800 unburied bodies), and Chicago in 1977. Since then, there have been further long strikes in New York in 1985 and 1998.[47] This weight of evidence dispels the notion that there is something unusual about such strikes and draws attention to the particular way the gravediggers' strikes (especially that in Liverpool) during the Winter of Discontent have been sensationalized.

Water workers and ambulance workers

While Shepherd gives two pages (pp. 98–9) to the water workers' pay negotiations, he only mentions (unofficial) industrial action in one area, yet there was significant unofficial action across the country which needs recounting for the record. Six hundred water and sewage workers in the Pennine division of the North West Water Authority started an unofficial strike on 11 January; others in the north west of England began an overtime ban six days later. In Stoke-on-Trent, 120 banned overtime, call-out and standby duties on 15 January.[48]

A 14% increase was recommended by the TGWU and GMWU but NUPE made no recommendation. 'The size of the increase, which includes a substantial efficiency bonus, reflects the enormous pressure on Government and employers to avoid a clash with the water workers.'[49] It was enough for the Pennine division's workers to call off their strike on 22 January, by 205 to 200 in a secret ballot. But 200 workers in Manchester rejected it and banned

---

44 All reported in national newspapers.
45 All reported in the *Irish Times*.
46 *Ibid.*, 21 January, 6 May 1921; 4 February 1958; 14, 22 June 1965; 20 January, 13 February 1971.
47 All reported in the *New York Times*.
48 *Guardian*, 12, 16, 18 January 1979.
49 *Financial Times*, 20 January 1979.

overtime, while another 600 in the Ribble division (Preston, Blackburn, Blackpool) started an unofficial strike. They were followed by 400 in the Southern division (Birkenhead, the Wirral, Macclesfield and Congleton) and other strikes in Mansfield, Worcestershire and Gloucestershire, and parts of south Wales. Workers from Crewe, Nantwich and Northwich then joined their Cheshire colleagues, though some in Lancashire returned to work.[50] At the end of January workers were coming out in Yorkshire and Merseyside. Threats of regional all-out strikes were no doubt a factor in the continuing improvement of the employers' pay offer, though Greater Manchester workers still struck on 9 February. Merseyside workers were probably the last to go back, with the action finishing on 16 February. This completely unofficial dispute had lasted five weeks at the height of the Winter of Discontent.[51]

The ambulance workers are also neglected by both Shepherd and Martin López. This group also engaged in significant unofficial action, starting with the 22 January mass strike, when it was reported that 'ambulance men' in Birmingham, Coventry, Solihull, Cardiff, Glasgow, Inverness, Strathclyde and Fife, but not London, were implementing a complete ban on calls.[52] In the event, 'the 2,300 ambulance men [in London] went back on a commitment to provide emergency cover, which was provided by only about 10 out of 76 ambulance stations'. On Merseyside, the day after 22 January, all 800 workers 'walked out after being told to work normally or not at all'.[53] Very soon, twelve Merseyside depots were answering emergency calls and another twelve were on indefinite strike, while west Glamorgan also struck.[54]

Early in February, NUPE (representing the majority of ambulance workers but opposing strike action) told members 'to keep strictly to 999 emergency work'.[55] Ambulance crews in Aberdeen were on strike from 19 February and in London there was a threat of a total 24-hour strike on 21 February. Although this was postponed, 'half the capital's ambulance men walked out on strike at midnight'.[56] Newcastle's ambulance men began an indefinite strike on 27 February.[57] In March, there were claims that several hundred were going on indefinite strike, particularly in west Yorkshire, while ambulance men

---

50 *Guardian*, 23, 24, 25 January 1979.
51 *Ibid.*, 31 January, 1, 2, 10, 14 February 1979. *Employment Gazette*, August 1980, p. 872, gave a total of 2,500 strikers (an underestimate, based on the evidence of newspaper reports), causing 25,000 working days lost, suggesting an average of 10 working days out per striker.
52 *Guardian*, 22 January 1979.
53 *Financial Times*, 23, 24 January 1979.
54 *Guardian*, 25 January 1979; *Financial Times*, 26 January 1979.
55 *Financial Times*, 9 February 1979.
56 *Ibid.*, 20 February 1979; *Guardian*, 21 February 1979.
57 *Financial Times*, 28 February 1979.

in west Glamorgan struck for 48 hours in support of colleagues locked out in the south of the county.[58] On 26 March, 250 NUPE members ended their seven-week strike on north Merseyside, and there were others still locked out in Manchester. Many of the strikes seem to have revolved around the exact definition of emergency work. Any account of the Winter of Discontent cannot ignore the importance of this action.

Civil servants

Shepherd relies on Michael Kelly's account of the civil service strikes[59] but this is not very detailed. This dispute lasted from the opening one-day strike on 23 February until 3 May, just before the general election. It involved a maximum of 278,600 employees, leading to 507,900 working days lost.[60] After 23 February, the two largest unions embarked on a programme of selective industrial action, 'directed at sensitive areas of the Government machine rather than the general public'.[61] As a result, it did not have the same high profile as the local authority and NHS strikes, but was nonetheless very effective. It was particularly targeted at the then 140 computers in government departments. Initially, some 1,300 union members were called out, and received from the unions their normal full net pay. VAT revenue was blocked, as were farm subsidies, payments to Ministry of Defence contractors and the government's own rent and utilities' bills. Companies House was paralysed, as was the distribution of coins from the Royal Mint and the stamping of share transfers. The Scottish court system was stopped for the first time in its history, while the GCHQ computer and the coding and decoding of confidential communications with overseas embassies were blocked.[62] Along with these and other targets, there was a series of lightning strikes by selected groups, such as customs staff and driving-test examiners.

In the middle of March another 1,600 members, again mostly computer staff, were brought out in hitherto unaffected government departments.[63] Almost immediately the Scottish Office went ahead with its threat to suspend thirty-nine employees who had refused to cover for striking computer staff. 'In an apparently spontaneous reaction, unprecedented in the Civil Service, officials closed down Government offices throughout Scotland.' A few days later more than 30,000 Scottish civil servants stopped work in solidarity and were joined by thousands from the rest of Britain.

---

58 *Ibid.*, 19, 20 March 1979.
59 M. P. Kelly, *White-Collar Proletariat: The Industrial Behaviour of British Civil Servants* (Routledge and Kegan Paul: 1980), pp. 114–18.
60 *Employment Gazette*, August 1980, p. 873.
61 *Guardian*, 24 February 1979.
62 *Ibid.*, 26, 27 February 1979.
63 *Ibid.*, 8, 16 March 1979.

A further fourteen employees were suspended by the Scottish Office, leading to more protest.[64] Another national one-day strike on 2 April was joined by five more civil service unions, including some members of the First Division Association (now the FDA), representing the top grades. The Prison Officers' Association instituted an overtime ban at 103 establishments.[65] While a pay offer was finally accepted in late April there were delays in restarting work, caused by the Civil Service Department's refusal to take into account for seniority and promotion purposes the period of striking for those workers out for up to nine weeks.[66]

Conclusion

While this comment has filled in some gaps, and identified the prevalence of unofficial action in many of the strikes discussed, its main contribution is to stress the continuity of the local authority (and NHS) disputes of 1979 with their antecedents. Evidence has been accumulated to show that previous instances of mountains of rubbish and unburied corpses did not attract much opprobrium (it is likely that earlier industrial action in the NHS was also generally tolerated). The sensationalization of events by politicians (of both hues) and by some of the media during what we have grown used to calling the Winter of Discontent was contingent on a particular set of economic and political circumstances.

Isolating disputes to study them singly – something this comment shares with Shepherd and Martin López – can dissipate the intensity of their experience in real time, particularly as in the last full week of January 1979 when several separate disputes intersected.[67] Individual strikes have their own definite features and rhythms and highly constrained outcomes. Yet the sustained assault on incomes policy limits during 1978–79 created an environment favourable to the cross-fertilization of tactics

Centre for Industrial Relations, KMS
Keele University, Staffordshire ST5 5BG

---

64 *Ibid.*, 17, 22 and 24 March 1979. According to *Employment Gazette*, August 1980, p. 873, a total of 62,000 civil servants took protest action between 16 and 23 March, leading to 74,700 working days lost.
65 *Guardian*, 29 March, 3, 4 April 1979.
66 *Ibid.*, 28 April 1979.
67 This includes the one-day strikes by train drivers which have not been covered here.

HSIR 36 (2015) 219–226

doi:10.3828/hsir.2015.36.9

Public-Sector Strikes in the 'Winter of Discontent'

Roger Seifert

J. Shepherd, *Crisis? What Crisis? The Callaghan Government and the British 'Winter of Discontent'* (Manchester University Press: 2013)

John Shepherd's book, in particular chapter 5: 'Public-Sector Strikes', represents another attempt to capture the series of strikes and their political reaction, collectively known as the 'Winter of Discontent'. Others have written about those events stretching from December 1978 through to March 1979. Such commentaries have varied from detailed accounts of a particular strike[1] through to the impact on the union movement,[2] the Labour Party,[3] the rise of Thatcherism,[4] and the political fallout in terms of

---

1   P. Smith, '"The Winter of Discontent": The Hire and Reward Road Haulage Dispute, 1979', *Historical Studies in Industrial Relations* 7 (1999), pp. 27–56; *idem, Unionization and Union Leadership: The Road Haulage Industry* (Continuum: 2001), ch. 7.

2   R. Taylor, *The Fifth Estate* (Pan Books: 1978); *idem, The Trade Union Question in British Politics* (Blackwell, Oxford: 1993); *idem, The Future of the Trade Unions* (Andre Deutsch: 1994); R. Taylor and A. Seldon, 'The Winter of Discontent', *Contemporary Record* 1:3 (1987), pp. 34–43.

3   L. Minkin, *The Contentious Alliance: Trade Unions and the Labour Party* (Edinburgh University Press: 1991); W. Rodgers, 'Government under Stress: Britain's Winter of Discontent, 1979', *Political Quarterly (PQ)* 55:2 (2005), pp. 171–9; W. Thompson, *The Long Death of British Labourism: Interpreting a Political Culture* (Pluto Press: 1993).

4   M. Greeson, 'Thatcher and the British Election of 1979: Taxes, Nationalization, and Unions Run Amok', *Colgate Academic Review* 4:1 (2012); C. Leys, *Politics in Britain from Labour to Thatcherism* (Verso: 1989); L. Black and H. Pemberton, 'The Winter of Discontent in British Politics', *PQ* 80:4 (2009), pp. 553–61.

public opinion and working-class sentiment.[5] While Shepherd's book adds nothing to these views, it does bring together in one volume many of the most relevant facts and factors associated with this strike wave. It is also a timely reminder of the lasting importance of those events as it resonates down the years, so that even in 2015 (the year of Richard III's reburial) journalists frequently ask the question whenever there are strikes: is this another 'season' of discontent?

It is a tribute to the political myopia and skewed analytical model derived from the Donovan Report[6] that the dominant academic industrial relations groups reduced and finally removed any coverage of these strikes from their consideration. Certainly mainstream textbooks on industrial relations only made limited references to these events. The most influential textbook on the subject edited by George Bain contains virtually no mention of the 'Winter of Discontent' at all.[7] Its successor volume edited by Paul Edwards has an explicit reference to it in the chapter by Richard Hyman.[8] In the 2003 edition of the book this becomes an even more limited reference in the chapter by Edwards, with no reference to any other works.[9]

Sid Kessler and Fred Bayliss produced a more historically minded textbook on industrial relations. In the 1992 edition there are several references to the 'Winter of Discontent', in which the strikes were seen as a major part of the defeat of the Labour government, but all in all the thirteen references say virtually nothing about what happened.[10] In the 1995 edition the same references more or less appeared unchanged. As with 'after two

5 C. Hay, 'Narrating Crisis: The Discursive Construction of the "Winter of Discontent"', *Sociology* 30 (1996), pp. 253–77; *idem*, 'Chronicles of a Death Foretold: The Winter of Discontent and Construction of the Crisis of British Keynesianism', *Parliamentary Affairs* 63:3 (2010), pp. 446–70; *idem*, 'The Winter of Discontent Thirty Years On', *PQ* 80:4 (2009), pp. 545–52; J. Thomas, '"Bound in by history": The Winter of Discontent in British Politics, 1979–2004', *Media, Culture and Society* 29:2 (2007), pp. 263–83; T. Martin, 'The Beginning of Labor's End? Britain's "Winter of Discontent" and Working-Class Women's Activism', *International Labor and Working-Class History* 75:01 (2009), pp. 49–67.

6 Royal Commission on Trade Unions and Employers' Associations, 1965–68 (Donovan), *Report*, Cmnd 3623 (1968).

7 G. Bain (ed.), *Industrial Relations in Britain* (Basil Blackwell, Oxford: 1983).

8 R. Hyman, 'The Historical Evolution of British Industrial Relations', in P. Edwards (ed.), *Industrial Relations: Theory and Practice in Britain* (Blackwell, Oxford: 1995), p. 47.

9 P. Edwards, 'The Employment Relationship and the Field of Industrial Relations', in *idem* (ed.), *Industrial Relations: Theory and Practice in Britain* (2nd edn, Blackwell, Oxford: 2003), p. 22.

10 S. Kessler and F. Bayliss, *Contemporary British Industrial Relations* (Macmillan: 1992).

years of trade union restraint, pressure mounted, culminating eventually in the so-called Winter of Discontent in 1978–9 which resulted in the general election of 1979 and the return of a Conservative Government'.[11] In the 1998 edition of their book, Paul Blyton and Peter Turnbull make seven references, but as above, mainly in passing. A typical comment throughout would be 'a popular (mis)conception of industrial relations is that the entire subject can be reduced simply to the Winter of Discontent (1978–9)'.[12]

There are equally limited references in books on strikes. The most authoritative analysis of strikes by Hyman, in the book of the same name, even in the 1989 edition, only discusses 'the winter of discontent' in passing as part of a revolt against incomes policies and as an example of powerful discontent. Like others his main reference is condensed: 'continued restraint was first passively deprecated (1977–8, when only the firemen offered a sustained and large-scale challenge), then actively resisted (1978–9, the winter of discontent)'.[13]   In Peter Hain's book, published in 1986, he gives the usual limited twist on 'the winter of discontent'.[14] Authors such as Ken Coates and Tony Topham refer to the Winter of Discontent as a mutiny by low-paid, public-sector workers.[15] In other words, there was and remains a need for a book that covers all these strikes.

One reason for the paucity of comment on the strikes is that these are predicated upon a state-sponsored system of wage control which fitted mainstream labour doctrines.[16] Incomes policies in any guise, including that of the Social Contract, were both an abject failure of the academic analysis presented by Hugh Clegg and his colleagues in the Donovan Report, and a failure of Labour Party policies for sustainable economic growth and social justice. Once Thatcher was elected, the appetite for Labour renewal from a left perspective diminished until the advent of the Blair governments in the late 1990s.

Political biographies and autobiographies have some references to the strikes but tend to be self-serving, whereas more general accounts remain very limited. James Callaghan as the Prime Minister gives remarkably little coverage in his autobiography to these events, and Kenneth Morgan's

---

11 *Idem, Contemporary British Industrial Relations* (2nd edn, Macmillan: 1995), p. 19.

12 P. Blyton and P. Turnbull, *The Dynamics of Employee* Relations (Macmillan: 1998), p. 7.

13 R. Hyman, *Strikes* (4th edn, Fontana: 1989), p. 222.

14 P. Hain, *Political Strikes: The State and Trade Unionism in Britain* (Penguin: 1986), p. 120.

15 K. Coates and T. Topham, *Trade Unions in Britain* (Spokesman, Nottingham: 1988), p. 293.

16 G. Dorfman, *Government versus Trade Unionism in British Politics since 1968* (Macmillan: 1979).

biography of him says not much more.[17] Memoirs by leading political figures such as Margaret Thatcher, Denis Healey, Richard Crossman, Barbara Castle, Harold Wilson, and Tony Benn collectively add very little to our knowledge and understanding of these months. Shepherd makes extensive use of such sources to throw additional dim light into this corner of British history.

Of the over sixty sources cited from (auto)biographies and diaries, only two (maybe three) are from the trade-union side or those to the left of the Labour Party. This suggests an overly narrow focus on political-insider stories and the relative neglect of the view from below. In other words, this is not a study of the workers, rank-and-file leaders, and trade-unionists involved in the strikes. Shepherd's book over-relies on such sources which are inadequate generally, but particularly so when dealing with the strikes – their causes, conduct, and consequences on a strike-by-strike basis. This point is made more eloquently by Colin Hay in this volume. A collective political shyness by the political leaders involved, as the whole series of events, from wage restraint to strike wave, left exposed a serious failure of Labour politics and programmes.

The strength of the book is mainly in its effort to bring all the facets from that winter under one roof. Its other main feature is to examine in detail the debates inside the leadership of the Labour government, and to use that as the prism with which to view the disputes. Its weaknesses include a lack of original material on the strikes themselves, and an inadequate appreciation of the industrial relations' dimensions involved. In particular, there is little understanding of the nature of collective bargaining in each sector, the neglect of left politics and the role of the Communist Party of Great Britain,[18] and the nature of strike action itself. The real problem with the book remains its failure to come to terms with the role of the state as an instrument of class oppression.[19]

That said, the treatment of the strikes in the public sector is well worth a read and will assist a new generation of students and labour-movement

17 J. Callaghan, *Time and Chance* (Collins: 1987); K. Morgan, *Callaghan: A Life* (Oxford University Press: 1997).

18 G. Andrews, *Endgames and New Times: The Final Years of British Communism, 1964–1991* (Lawrence and Wishart: 2004); C. Andrew, *The Defence of the Realm: The Authorized History of MI5* (Allen Lane: 2009); W. Thompson, *The Good Old Cause: British Communism, 1921–1991* (Pluto Press: 1992); J. McIlroy and A. Campbell, 'Organizing the Militants: The Liaison Committee for the Defence of Trade Unions, 1966–79', *British Journal of Industrial Relations* 37:1 (1999), pp. 1–31.

19 L. Panitch, 'Trade Unions and the Capitalist State', *New Left Review* I/125 (1981); *idem*, *Social Democracy and Industrial Militancy: The Labour Party, the Trade Unions, and Incomes Policy, 1945–1974* (Cambridge University Press: 1976); R. Miliband, *The State in Capitalist Society* (Quartet: 1973).

activists in their understanding of what happened. The Labour government under Wilson and then Callaghan was still engrossed with the reform of industrial relations because they saw it as the key to unlocking the persistent problem of low productivity. Still partly influenced by the Donovan prescriptions and deeply embedded in anti-communist Cold War politics, the Labour leadership sought to hold back the rising tide of militancy of the trade-union movement, reflecting a wider and deeper mood of public discontent.

The Social Contract (the immediate cause of the strike wave, but itself a symptom of Labour's failures to deal with structural economic and social reform) was seen by the left as a means to hold down wages, stem the wave of strikes, and buy off union leaders.[20] The right-leaning social democrats at the heart of government and elsewhere saw it as part of a deal to control, through the state, labour costs, reduce inflation, and maintain order. The latter was a requirement of both the bailout by the International Monetary Fund and to reassure inward investors of the stability of the British economy. It was a crucial test for traditional Labourites: a test they failed. The political context therefore was dangerously muddled, and from the ashes of ruined government policies came the simplistic nostrums of Thatcherism built upon a crude mixture of traditional right-wing Toryism, little Englander posturing, and a decisive shift to the power of finance capital. This was made real by the financial deregulation symbolized by the 'Big Bang', October 1986, when the London Stock Exchange was deregulated, part of the wider financial deregulation and privatization.[21]

Shepherd ignores much of this, and does not deal with the intricacies of the strikes in the public sector. His general neglect of the economics of wages and the wider economic forces is a major omission in his account. In chapter 5 he provides an unevenly breathless account of some of the five public-sector strikes. Generally he is sympathetic to the plight of the low-paid manual workers, especially in local government. There are some vivid moments when the pitiless attacks on these groups from the

---

20 B. Ramelson, *Bury the Social Contract: The Case for an Alternative Policy* (Communist Party: 1977); R. Seifert and T. Sibley, 'Communists and the Trade Union Left Revisited: The Case of the UK, 1964–1979', *World Review of Political Economy* 1:1 (2010), pp. 112–26; K. Halpin, *Memoirs of a Militant* (Praxis Press, Glasgow: 2012); J. Campbell and B. Ramelson, 'British State Monopoly Capitalism and Its Impact on Trade Unions and Wages', *Marxism Today* (January/February 1968), pp. 7–14; T. Cliff, *The Crisis: Social Contract or Socialism* (Pluto Press: 1975); R. Tarling and F. Wilkinson, 'The Social Contract: Post-War Incomes Policies and Their Inflationary Impact', *Cambridge Journal of Economics* 1:4 (1977), pp. 395–414.

21 See R. C. Michie, *The London Stock Exchange: A History* (Oxford University Press: 2001).

right-wing press are displayed as the heartless and class-ridden account that they were. Shepherd is also sympathetic to most union leaders from the National Union of Public Employees and the General and Municipal Workers' Union, sensing the pressure they were under and the frustration they felt on behalf of their desperate members with the failings of the Labour leadership. He captures the splits in the government, the careless arrogance of Callaghan and Healey, and the indifference of senior civil servants.

There is a strong sense, once one has read the chapter, that these strikes were justified given the pay levels and the nature of the jobs undertaken. As he notes, 'the principal cause of these public sector strikes was in fact chronic low pay' (p. 89). What is missing of course is why, after Labour being in power for eleven of the last fifteen years, this was the situation. Shepherd's failure to deal with the politics of incomes policy in any guise, for example the Social Contract, creates the illusion that economic failure and low pay were something that happened to the Labour governments, rather than something caused by their policies.

What is missing throughout this chapter is any feeling for the collective-bargaining processes and systems, for the dynamic inside unions as between the militancy of most members born of a genuine and genuinely experienced injustice of inadequate pay, the leadership trying to force a negotiated settlement, and the political left seeking to win the battle and develop strategies to win the war. Shepherd is shy of confronting the class realities of the strike wave, unwilling to confront the deeper inadequacies of the government's social-democratic economic programme based largely on acceptance of the emerging monetarism of the day, and negligent of the influence of Communists and other non-aligned Marxist sympathizers in the struggle.

Of the strikes themselves, despite a list of those involved (p. 84) and some comment on the actual wage demands (pp. 86, 89, 99), there is nothing on what happened inside the separate negotiating groups. The coverage is thin despite quotes from a handful of activists and leaders, too much depending (as throughout the book) on hindsight of key political players, including Callaghan himself. The chapter is organized and largely driven not by the realities and relative importance of each strike but by the media and political agenda. Hence the small-scale strike by Liverpool gravediggers is given substantial coverage (pp. 90–2), whereas more important action is treated with less concern.[22]

On the strikes in the National Health Service, for example, there is

---

22   This contrasts with other books on strikes, such as Foner's account of the 1877 railway strike in the USA , a model of historical writing from the perspective of those involved: P. Foner, *The Great Labor Uprising of 1877* (Pathfinder, New York: 1977).

virtually nothing worth comment (p. 97),[23] and the civil service strikes receive slightly more attention (pp. 103–4). This by-passing of the white-collar strikes fits Shepherd's thesis that the low-paid manual workers deserved a pay rise, were right to strike when all other avenues were closed, and exposed the Labour government's anti-working-class sentiments. But his failure to deal with the non-manual discontent shows a lack of awareness of the wider class issues, of the coming shift in unionization and union politics, and fundamental weakness at the heart of Labourism.

Shepherd is rightly impressed with the day of action involving 1.5 million workers on 22 January 1979 (pp. 82–5). But as he notes 'after the National Day of Action, there was little effective co-operation between the different public sector unions' (p. 92). The reasons for this are not explained. There is an account of how the government paid off the water workers (p. 99) but all tends to be *post facto* rationalization. When dealing with underlying problems, Shepherd notes that 'despite five years in office, the Labour government by and large did not possess a comprehensive strategy for remedying low pay in the British economy' (p. 100). This is true but begs the question as to whether the government wanted to remedy low pay at all given that it accepted the need to hold down wages as a cure for inflation, seen as the number one enemy. Further, Shepherd fails to explain the deeper commitment of the Labour leadership to orthodox economic policy and a class-stratified society. The Social Contract is not sufficiently explored as a device to hold down wages and therefore creating pressure for a wages explosion at some time. Buying into Clegg's solutions of regulation and investigation to placate the unions as time ran out for the government was never convincing. It is telling that Shepherd gives Clegg the last word on these strikes (p. 107) and shows the extent to which they both misunderstood the role of the state in the modernization of British social and economic life, and neglected any analytical framework founded on the class nature of the system.

The chapter flits between strikes, the day of action, and the political response of the Labour leadership. It is sympathetic to the low-paid workers on strike, exposes the reactionary fury of the press (matched at times by some in Cabinet) that workers could cause so much disruption, and tries at times to express the feelings of those involved at the time. This style makes it difficult to fathom the exact nature of the strikers' demands, the collective-bargaining machinery involved with separate employers, the internal union political struggles, and the reasons behind the government's miscalculations and then mishandling of the strike wave. A lack of knowledge of union politics, collective bargaining, and the wider failure to

23 F. Pethybridge, 'Whitley and the Winter of Discontent', *Health Social Service Journal* 6:89 (1979) (4649), pp. 840–1.

reform the labour market, alongside a neglect of the function of state power and the historic purpose of European social democracy, makes his account somewhat diffuse. It is not a book about the strike wave, but about how the political leadership of the Labour government reacted to the strikes and the strikers.

Business School, University of Wolverhampton
Wulfruna Street, Wolverhampton WV1 1LY

doi:10.3828/hsir.2015.36.10

The Neoliberal Labyrinth

John Eldridge

Pierre Dardot and Christian Laval, *The New Way of the World: On Neoliberal Society* (Verso: 2013), 352pp., handback £20, ISBN 978-1-78168-176-3.

Colin Crouch, *The Strange Non-Death of Neoliberalism* (Polity, Cambridge: 2011), 224pp., £15.99, ISBN 978-0-7456-5221-4.

Philip Mirowski, *Never Let a Serious Crisis Go to Waste: How Neoliberalism Survived the Financial Meltdown* (Verso: 2013), 384pp., £20, ISBN 978-1-78168-079-7.

George Monbiot, the well-known environmental campaigner, began a lecture in July 2014 melodramatically: 'Ladies and gentlemen we are witnessing the death of both the theory and practice of neo-liberal capitalism. This is the doctrine which holds that the market can resolve almost all social, economic and political problems. It holds that people are best served, and their prosperity is best advanced, by the minimum of intervention and spending by the state. It contends that we can maximise the general social interest through the pursuit of self-interest.'[1]

Monbiot went on to tell the story of Matt Ridley (now Lord Ridley) who, as a *Daily Telegraph* journalist in 1996, had asserted that taxes, bailouts, regulations, subsidies, and interventions of any kind were an unwarranted restraint on market freedom. The same Ridley inherited from his father the chairmanship of Northern Rock. When it collapsed in 2007 he had to look to the government for help to the tune of £27 billion. In very difficult

---

1 G. Monbiot, *The Price of Everything*, SPER Lecture 2014, p. 1. I should add that the substance of his lecture does not altogether accord with this view as when he rails against neoliberal attempts to 'monetise and financialise nature' and the ways in which cost–benefit analyses are always rigged. If neoliberalism is dead then it must be neoliberal zombies who are disempowering the environmentalists, and which Monbiot documents when he talks about giving the natural world to the City of London.

circumstances the government had to guarantee all the deposits of the investors in the bank and later nationalized it. This, of course, subsequently happened to other British banks such as the Royal Bank of Scotland.

It was not only environmentalists such as Monbiot who took this position. The noted economist Joseph Stiglitz argued that neoliberalism was dead in most Western countries.[2] It could not be supported as an economic theory or justified by historical experience. Rather, neoliberal market fundamentalism had to be understood as a political doctrine serving certain interests. Indeed, he claimed, learning this lesson might constitute the silver lining of the cloud hanging over the global economy.

So far so straightforward, we may think. Yet if the three books under review have anything in common it is that they all deny that neoliberalism is dead. This is exemplified in the title of Colin Crouch's book, *The Strange Non-Death of Neoliberalism,* parodying George Dangerfield's famous study, *The Strange Death of Liberal England.*[3] Surely, one would have thought, with Monbiot, that the spectacular collapse of major banks and institutions in the USA and the UK in 2008–09 would have sounded the death knell for neoliberalism. It is here we begin to enter the labyrinth. How indeed does it come about, asks Crouch, 'that neoliberalism is emerging from the financial collapse more politically powerful than ever? Whereas the financial crisis concerned banks and their behaviour, resolution of the crisis has been redefined in many countries as a need to cut back, once and for all, the welfare state and public spending' (p. viii). 'Austerity' becomes the only game in town.

So, like the premature obituary of Mark Twain, the death of neoliberalism has been announced too soon. Indeed, Pierre Dardot and Christian Laval at the conclusion of their magisterial study issue a warning: 'the belief that the financial crisis by itself sounds the death-knell of neoliberal capitalism is the *worst* of beliefs. It is possibly a source of pleasure to those who think they are witnessing reality running ahead of their desires, without them having to move their little finger ... At bottom, it is the least acceptable form of intellectual and political abdication. Neo-liberalism is not falling like a "ripe fruit" on account of its internal contradictions; and traders will not be its undreamed – of "gravediggers" despite themselves' (p. 321).

It is Philip Mirowski who offers intriguing answers to this question in an approach that borders on the sociology of knowledge. He refers to the Mont Pelerin Society, founded in 1947, where the intellectual foundations of neoliberalism were laid and writes of the movement as the Neoliberal Thought Collective. This network of thinkers, while they might argue

---

2 J. Stiglitz, *Freefall: Free Markets and the Sinking of the Global Economy* (Penguin Books: 2010).

3 G. Dangerfield, *The Strange Death of Liberal England* (Paladin: 1970, first published 1935).

among each other, according to Mirowski, 'eventually produced a relatively shared ontology concerning the world coupled with a more-or-less shared set of propositions about markets and political economy' (p. 50). On this reading, neoliberalism has to be seen as a comprehensive world view and not just an economic doctrine.

The Neoliberal Thought Collective project, claims Mirowski, was an overriding political project which sought to reform society by subordinating it to the market. As an invisible college it is somewhat elitist, seeking to sustain its position by the manufacture of ignorance. Thus Friedrich Hayek, a pioneer of neoliberal thinking in his much quoted *Road to Serfdom*,[4] saw 'knowledge' as very significant for economic thinkers while asserting that 'Probably it is true enough that the great majority are rarely capable of thinking independently, that on most questions they accept views which they find ready-made, and that they will be equally content if born or coaxed into one set of beliefs or another. In any society freedom of thought will probably be of direct significance only for a small minority' (Hayek cited in Mirowski, p. 79). This, of course, is profoundly anti-democratic in spirit. It rests on the core conviction that the market knows what is best for us and our society. Yet, for Hayek, it is this ignorant submission to the impersonal forces of the market that has made possible the growth of civilization. In place of the holy Mother Church, which had once held doctrinal sway over the minds of millions, it is now this reified object – the market – which commands our allegiance.

But what happens when faith in the market is severely tested, when financial collapse occurs on a massive scale? It is here that Mirowski refers to Leon Festinger *et al.*'s, famous study, *When Prophecy Fails.*[5] This was an account of how a group of people (the Seekers) committed to an apocalyptic prophecy that their city was to be engulfed by a great flood but they would be rescued by a spacecraft ahead of that on a precise date. This was a strong absolutist ideology so what happened when the ideology was falsified and the events did not take place as forecast? They had to deal with what Festinger termed cognitive dissonance – the gap between belief and empirical reality. While some abandoned their faith most held on, reinterpreting their doctrine and continuing to proselytize. In fact most people did not shift their allegiances in the face of contravening evidence. This, argued Mirowski, is how the Neoliberal Thought Collective reacted. Indeed, they 'persisted in being richly rewarded by many constituencies for remaining stalwart in their beliefs' (p. 36). Their faith was big enough to move mountains in the face of a negative media and public.

---

4 F. Hayek, *The Road to Serfdom* (University of Chicago Press: 1944).
5 L. Festinger, H. Riecken and S. Schachter, *When Prophecy Fails* (University of Minneapolis Press: 1956).

What the Neoliberal Thought Collective has done, according to Mirowski, is to fill the public sphere with fog. Its many layers of organizations (Mirowski refers to its 'Russian doll structure') are eminently suited to this task (pp. 43–50). This is a way of manufacturing ignorance by claiming that everything is uncertain and too complex to understand. In such circumstances the general public will tend to tune out.[6] So it is that the peddled 'solution' to market failures is more markets! For employment, this entails more privatization, contracting out, anti-union legislation, and deregulation of the labour market (including health and safety, and employment protection). From the standpoint of neoliberalism, Mirowski comments: 'The beauty of the manufacture of ignorance is that it has proven an ideal short-term response to unanticipated surprises: when disaster hits, and reformers propose to strike while the iron is hot with their nostrums and antidotes, the Neoliberal Thought Collective can stymie them and can buy time by filling the public sphere with fog' (p. 344).

The French scholars, Dardot and Laval, provide us with a very fine nuanced treatment of the European roots of neoliberalism and its spread throughout the twentieth century and beyond. They are at pains to differentiate neoliberalism from laissez-faire liberalism, arguing that neoliberalism allows much more scope for state intervention. Here it is good to see them paying tribute to L. T. Hobhouse's somewhat neglected classic on liberalism, first published in 1911.[7] Hobhouse was concerned with the ways in which the state could, through legislation, create the conditions for social freedom, and by tackling inequality enhance the possibilities for effective and inclusive citizenship within the social and industrial spheres of society. This embodied concerns for social welfare and a recognition of the role of trade unions. This form of new liberalism still finds advocates. It was well expressed in Ralf Dahrendorf's Reith lectures. It is worth pointing out that both Hobhouse and Dahrendorf made strong and approving references back to J. S. Mill's writing on liberty.[8]

But neoliberalism, Dardot and Laval argue, has gone in a different direction from this, almost socialist, form of new liberalism. What neoliberalism at root set out to do was to give the state a political role to fashion a society in which economic and social relations were governed by competition. Dardot and Laval quote a passage from Karl Polanyi's *The*

6 See O. Jones, *The Establishment: And How They Get Away With It* (Allen Lane: 2014).

7 L. T. Hobhouse, *Liberalism and Other Writings* (Cambridge University Press: 1994).

8 R. Dahrendorf, *The New Liberty: Survival and Justice in a Changing World* (Routledge and Kegan Paul, London: 1975)

Great Transformation[9] which they regard as particularly significant, even prescient:

> There was nothing natural about *laissez-faire*; free markets could never have come into being merely by allowing things to take their course ... The thirties and forties [1830s and 1840s] saw not only an outburst of legislation repealing restrictive regulations, but also an enormous increase in the administrative functions of the state, which was now being endowed with a central bureaucracy able to fulfil the tasks set by the adherents of liberalism. To the typical utilitarian, economic liberalism was a social project which should be put into effect for the greatest happiness of the greatest number; *laissez-faire was not a method to achieve a thing, it was the thing to be achieved.* (cited in Dardot and Laval, p. 43, emphasis added)

Dardot and Laval are clear that what certainly came into the foreground with the advent of neoliberalism was an attack on collectivism, with the fear of a drift into totalitarianism. This meant opposing policies of redistribution, social security, planning regulation, and protection, all of which had been part of the new liberal project of the Hobhouse variety. They argue that the origin of the neoliberal project predated the Mont Pelerin Society, which first met in 1947, to the Walter Lippmann Colloquium, which took place in Paris 1938. Lippmann himself was an American journalist well known for his studies of public opinion but it was his newly published book, *An Inquiry into the Principles of the Good Society*,[10] which underpinned the Paris conference. Here he made the case for 'liberal interventionism' in which the state, through the law, provided the conditions for free competition and used its authority to resist the pressure of special interest groups. This advocacy of a new mode of government implied the construction of a strong state. As Dardot and Laval put it: 'The exercise of this new mode of government had increased the field of interdependence, bringing more and more individuals into the network of transactions and competition, to the point where it was possible to imagine a "Great Society" on a world scale, the logical outcome of the global division of labour' (p. 71). This was a vision no less of a new kind of civil society.

Now if we fast forward to the Thatcher era in the UK, from 1979 onwards, we can readily see how much was foreshadowed by Lippmann. Here we had the advent of what came to be called the New Right. Given that Margaret Thatcher became leader of the Tory Party in a surprising and

9 K. Polanyi, *The Great Transformation* (Beacon Press, Boston, MA: 1944).
10 W. Lippmann, *An Inquiry into the Principles of the Good Society* (Little, Brown and Co., Boston, MA: 1943).

unexpected way[11] we may suggest that she could be seen as a cuckoo in the nest. Encouraged by Hayek and Milton Friedman, and also by 'think-tanks' such as the Institute of Economic Affairs and the Adam Smith Institute, she developed a political practice that fused together the concepts of the free market and the strong state. The notion of freedom became the centre-piece of the analysis. The people, individuals, need to be set free, so that they may become citizens in a property-owning democracy. The stress is on hard-working individuals exercising choice in their lives and getting the right rewards for the efforts they put into their jobs. However, the concept of 'freedom of choice' on inspection becomes something of a neologism.

What all this is predicated upon is a hierarchical inequality of rewards. Indeed, individualism in this context is based not only on the fact of inequality but of its desirability as one of the engines of capitalism. After all, the notion of the free market carries with it the importance of competition as a driving force. In the world of early capitalism that might be seen as embodying competition between small firms, but in today's world of multi-nationals and large corporations it is a very different story. It is indeed this corporate takeover of the market which Crouch traces out so well in his book (particularly chapter 3). He rightly points out that large corporations are not as subject to consumer sovereignty and market forces as neoliberal rhetoric claims. However, it was the overriding concern with competition that led the drive for privatization and attacks on the public sector. The very concepts of the public good or the public interest were rendered problematic in a blanket attack on collectivism.[12]

So it was that public institutions – the trade unions, local government, the civil service, the BBC, the bureaucracy of the welfare state – all came under attack from the Thatcher government. This led to what Stuart Hall called 'authoritarian populism'. This was the idea that the state – in the form of the Prime Minister and the coterie of people around her – appealed to 'the people' over the heads of the institutions they disapproved of. In such a way was the strong state developed. This could be supported by the army and the police when thought to be necessary, as in the case of the miners' strike of 1984–85.

It was in this context that something like a cold war developed between the government and the Trades Union Congress (TUC). Incomes policies and social contracts were discarded; unions were defined as obstacles to economic regeneration because of their 'irresponsible' and 'restrictive' behaviour. The possibility for what Crouch called 'bargained corporatism'

---

11   J. Campbell, *Margaret Thatcher: Vol. 1, The Grocer's Daughter* (Cape: 2000), ch. 10.

12   J. Eldridge, *Industrial Relations and the New Right* (Trent Polytechnic, Nottingham: 1983).

between the government, the Confederation of British Industry and the TUC,[13] whereby intelligent discussion concerning economic and industrial strategy could take place, was set aside. Trade unions were seen as 'over-mighty subjects', which needed to be brought to book by legislation. The Employment Act 1980 was explicitly represented as redressing the balance between unions and employers. This required ever more fine-tuning, hence the five more statutes enacted between 1982 and 1993.

According to Naomi Klein, neoliberalism rests on three pillars: privati-zation of the 'public sphere', deregulation of the corporate sector, and the lowering of income and corporate taxes, paid for with cuts to public spending.[14] By these criteria, Thatcherism passed the neoliberal test with flying colours. It stood on the axiom that there is no alternative (TINA). The same of course could be said for Reaganomics which paralleled the Thatcher years.

But, as all three authors under review show, the philosophy of neolib-eralism can cross political boundaries. This was manifestly true in the case of the UK. The New Labour government of Tony Blair explicitly adopted much of the neoliberal legislation on industrial relations enacted under Thatcher, as Paul Smith and Gary Morton have argued. They maintain that

In nine years of government, New Labour has developed a distinctive form of neoliberalism in which Conservative legislation on trade unions and industrial action has been integrated within a more subtle discourse of social partnership and collective and individual rights, and carefully defined intervention in the labour market and the employment relationship is designed to promote efficiency.[15]

But, as they point out, this left the UK in open disregard of international standards on workers' rights to organize and take industrial action, with the right to picket vulnerable to legislation on anti-social behaviour and harassment. They conclude that 'the widespread and embedded hostility to anything other than a narrow role for trade unions means that a campaign to restore and entrench trade unions' liberties will be long and arduous'.[16] And so, thus far, has it proved to be.

Again, all three authors argue that the progressive left has not been

13 C. Crouch, *Politics of Industrial Relations* (2nd edn, Fontana: 1982), pp. 212–22.

14 N. Klein, *This Changes Everything: Capitalism vs. The Climate* (Simon and Schuster, New York: 2014).

15 P. Smith and G. Morton, 'Nine Years of New Labour: Neoliberalism and Workers' Rights', *British Journal of Industrial Relations* 44:3 (2006), pp. 401–20, p. 414.

16 *Ibid.*, p. 415.

effective in mobilizing an effective and practical response to the relentless march of neoliberalism. Mirowski, for example, claims that the economics profession was caught off guard when the financial crisis happened, and that the language of neoliberalism was culturally embedded into popular consciousness so that it was difficult to think outside the box. Call to mind such ugly sounding terms as privatization, marketization, incentivi-zation, and monetization, of management by objectives, and performance indicators, not to mention 'doing more with less' – the mantra for austerity. He is sceptical of the effectiveness of the Occupy Movement in the USA, claiming, perhaps a little harshly, that such movements can be co-opted into neoliberal takeovers and that the political practice of protest can itself be subjected to marketing.

In November/December 1998, the journal *Marxism Today*, which had closed in 1991, reappeared for one last issue. On the cover was a picture of Tony Blair and emblazoned across it one word: WRONG. Over the years the journal had placed some faith in Blair's embracing of the modernity project since it showed, *pace* Thatcher, there was an alternative. Surely this heralded the New Times they advocated? But disillusion had set in according to Martin Jacques: 'New Labour did not herald the end of neolib-eralism; on the contrary, for the most part it acquiesced in its nostra because it believed – politically and intellectually – that nothing else was possible.' He continued:

> Although one cannot but be impressed by the sheer energy and *élan* of Tony Blair, there is, at the heart of New Labour, a profound pessimism. The fundamental architecture inherited from the neoliberal era cannot be disturbed: globalisation cannot be controlled or tamed: growing inequality can only be at best modified. We are, in short, at the mercy of nature and the market.[17]

The journal brought out its prominent intellectuals – Eric Hobsbawm and Stuart Hall – to reflect on all this. Hobsbawm claimed that holding on to the doctrine of the free market, as Blair did, was the neoliberal equivalent of the old Marxist belief in historical inevitability. Yet some kind of political intervention was called for: 'if the market is to work adequately, its systematic tendency to generate acute inequality and maldistribution needs to be regulated and controlled.'[18] This, of course, is in line with the recent influential work of Thomas Piketty.[19] For his part, Hall forcefully argued that

---

17 M. Jacques, 'Good to be Back', *Marxism Today* (Nov./Dec. 1998), p. 3.
18 E. Hobsbawm, 'The Death of Neo-Liberalism', *Marxism Today*, pp. 4–8, p. 8.
19 T. Piketty, *Capital in the Twenty-First Century* (Harvard University Press, Cambridge, MA: 2014).

The framing strategy of New Labour's economic repertoire remained essentially the neo-liberal one: the deregulation of markets, the wholesale refashioning of the public sector by the New Managerialism, the continued privatisation of public assets, low taxation, breaking the 'inhibitions' to market flexibility, institutionalising the culture of private provision and personal risk, and privileging in its moral discourse the values of self-sufficiency, competitiveness and entrepreneurial dynamism.[20]

So, he concluded, the Blair New Labour (Third Way) project was framed by, and moving on, terrain defined by Thatcherism.

It is the pervasiveness of neoliberalism which fascinates and challenges all three of our authors. Crouch, for example, confronting the question of what is left of neoliberalism after the financial crisis, answers 'virtually everything'. He writes:

The combination of economic and political forces behind this agenda is too powerful for it to be fundamentally dislodged from its predominance. Already we have seen how a crisis caused by appalling behaviour among banks has been redefined as a crisis of public spending. Bankers' bonuses are returning to their pre-crisis level, while thousands of public employees are losing their jobs. (p. 179)

There is a pleasing bluntness about this. But what is to be done? Crouch offers a solution that is essentially pluralist and which looks to the strengthening of civil society. For him, it is the role of churches, voluntary organizations, and professional associations to challenge the role of both states and corporations. This, he claims, allows citizens to win back some power and offers grounds for hope through the development of campaigns and such like. This approach, as he acknowledges, takes us back to the work of J. K. Galbraith in the 1950s.[21] It seeks to confront the world of fragmented values and the ethical questions which this throws up.

What is particularly interesting is that this kind of analysis has strong parallels with Emile Durkheim's *Professional Ethics and Civic Morals*, the product of lectures delivered in 1898, 1899 and 1900.[22] It is there that Durkheim wrestled with the problem of the relation between the state and the individual, and advocated the development of secondary groups and professional associations as a check on state power. He attacked unjust

---

20 S. Hall, 'The Great Moving Nowhere Show', *Marxism Today* (1998), pp. 9–11, at p. 11.
21 J. K. Galbraith, *American Capitalism: The Concept of Countervailing Power* (Brunswick, NJ, Transaction Press: 1952).
22 E. Durkheim, *Professional Ethics and Civic Morals* (Routledge and Kegan Paul: 1957).

contracts that were based on inequalities of power. A just society demanded the eradication of such relationships. Ultimately, he argued, true human solidarity called for the exercise of charity – the deep feeling of sympathy towards one's fellow humans. This principle should no longer be seen as an optional extra but become what he called 'the spring of new institutions'.[23]

In like manner Crouch refers to the role of *caritas* and the altruism it embodies. He emphasizes that 'In very recent decades, when risks of environmental damage have begun to threaten the planet itself and its climate, there has been a return to charitable concern for that most extensive entity of all: the natural world, taken for granted for so many centuries as civilization looked to an urban and social expression of itself' (p. 158). By contrast, it can be added, Mirowski spends time discussing how and why neoliberals are among the ranks of climate change deniers (pp. 334–42).

So it is that the vision of a new civil society under neoliberalism, proposed by Lippmann and his ilk, is directly challenged by Crouch. The growth of citizenship which had been sketched out by T. H. Marshall, with the extension of civil rights in the legal, political and social spheres, was actually being pushed back, ironically in the name of individual freedom.[24]

It is, as it seems to me, this concern for citizenship and its erosion in a neoliberal world that accounts for the interest shown by Mirowski as well as Dardot and Laval in Michel Foucault, particularly his treatment of 'governmentality'. Thus Foucault spotted early on that neoliberalism involves a reconstruction of the ontology of what it means to be a person in modern society. 'In neoliberalism,' Foucault wrote, 'Homo Economicus is an entrepreneur, an entrepreneur of himself' (Mirowski, p. 58). But what about the market itself? Mirowski writes: 'Neoliberals seek to transcend the intolerable contradiction of democratic rejection of the neoliberal state by treating politics *as if* it were a market and promoting an economic theory of "democracy". In its most advanced manifestation, there is no separate content of the notion of citizenship other than as a customer of state services' (p. 58).

Yet, for all his recognition of Foucault's significance, notably his treatment of biopolitics and the way in which power operates at the micro-level, Mirowski parts company with him. 'If I had to summarize where the otherwise prescient Foucault took a wrong turn, it was in too readily swallowing the basic neoliberal precept that the market was an information processor more powerful and encompassing than any human being or organization of humans' (p. 98). But, argues Mirowski, neoliberals do not practise what they preach. 'Their version of governmentality elevates

23 *Ibid.*, p. 220.
24 T. H. Marshall, *Citizenship and Social Class* (Cambridge University Press: 1950).

ELDRIDGE: THE NEOLIBERAL LABYRINTH 237

the market as a site of truth *for everyone but themselves*. If Foucault had taken this to heart, he would have had to revise his portrait of how regimes of truth validate power' (pp. 98–9). What Mirowski does is to challenge the idea of 'the market' as a monolithic entity and argues, crucially in my opinion, that markets do not 'validate' truth but are themselves the product of struggles over truth. This is to bring human agency back into the reckoning, which suggests that the manufacture of fog, which is a kind of false consciousness, needs to be challenged and dispelled.

For their part, Dardot and Laval use Foucault in their attempt to 'invent a different governmentality' (p. 311). They claim that neoliberalism has become the dominant rationality of today and global in its reach. In the light of this, they claim that 'the only question that is really worth posing is whether the left can counterpose an alternative governmentality to neoliberal governmentality' (p. 312). Foucault, in *The Birth of Biopolitics*, had argued that an autonomous socialist governmentality had never actually existed.[25] What might such a governmentality look like? It must be invented, said Foucault. However, quite where this takes us is unclear to me, despite their excursus which references Jean-Jacques Rousseau, Henri de Saint-Simon, and Karl Marx: 'To lead human beings is neither to make them bend under the inflexible yoke of the law, nor to make them acknowledge the force of a truth' (p. 315). What do we do after we have ticked that box?

The question Dardot and Laval end up by posing is: How do we escape from neoliberal rationality? They point out that if we understand that *the subject is always to be constructed*, then the issue becomes how to articulate subjectivation with resistance to power. This, they say, is precisely what was at the heart of Foucault's thought. This leads them to advocate forms of counter-conduct against neoliberal rationality, for example 'a refusal to conduct oneself towards oneself as a personal enterprise and a refusal to conduct oneself towards others in accordance with the norm of competition' (p. 320). And they point to the practices of 'communization of knowledge', mutual aid and co-operative work as delineating features of a different world of reason. But for those critics of neoliberalism and those appalled at the damage it has inflicted on the world and its peoples, they end on a note of hope: 'The genealogy of neo-liberalism attempted in this book teaches us that the new global rationality is in no wise an inevitable fate shackling humanity. Unlike Hegelian Reason, it is not the reason *of* human history. It is itself wholly *historical* – that is, relative to strictly singular conditions that cannot legitimately be regarded as untranscendable' (pp. 320–1).

Each of the books reviewed here is marked by a deep concern for the ways in which neoliberalism has spread itself into our globalized modern world. They are all infused with a generous humanism and offer hopeful

---

25 M. Foucault, *The Birth of Biopolitics* (Palgrave Macmillan, New York: 2008).

approaches to challenging, resisting and overcoming this hydra-headed monster. For that we owe them thanks.

After all the theoretical reflections are done and dusted, it is surely important to come down to earth and remind ourselves that we live in a world of contending and competing interests. It is a world in which markets are rigged in favour of the powerful and sometimes corrupt owners of capital. No one knew this better than Richard Tawney who, in his day, was more than a match for Hayek. Let us give him the last word:

> The plutocracy consists of forceable, astute, self-confident and when hard pressed unscrupulous people who know pretty well which side their bread is buttered on and intend that the supply of butter should not run short. If their position is threatened they will use every piece on the board, political and economic, House of Lords, the Crown, the press, financial crises, allegations of disaffection in the army, international complication, in the honest belief that they are saving civilisation.[26]

School of Social and Political Sciences
University of Glasgow
Glasgow G12 8QQ

---

26 R. H. Tawney, 'The Choice before the Labour Party', *Political Quarterly* 3:3 (1932), pp. 328–45.

HSIR 36 (2015) 239–253

doi:10.3828/hsir.2015.36.11

Book Reviews

John Tully, *Silvertown: The Lost Story of a Strike that Shook London and Helped Launch the Modern Labor Movement* (Monthly Review Press, New York: 2014), 267pp., $28.95, ISBN 978-1-5836743-4-5.

In the late 1880s, a wave of strikes swept across Britain. The end of a prolonged economic downturn, in combination with technological change and speed-ups, released old grievances while fuelling new ones. A new layer of largely unskilled and unorganized labour was drawn into confrontation with employers. Many of these rebellions were spontaneous, and the main participants tended to be non-craft male and female workers. John Tully's book offers valuable insight into the cause, effects, and consequences of one of these revolts. Set against the backdrop of the emergence of New Unionism in 1889, his dramatic story of the twelve-week strike of 3,000 workers employed at Silver's India-Rubber Company, in the East End of London, reveals the class character of a revolt against exploitation, which was initiated by rank-and-file workers.

In his introduction Tully places the strike in the context of an upsurge in industrial action led by socialists, such as John Burns, Tom Mann, Eleanor Marx, Will Thorne and Ben Tillett, who saw the trade-union struggle as part of a continuous process in developing the fight for socialism. It also marked a shift in women's participation. Tully recognizes the importance of the 1888 Bryant and May matchwomen's strike in providing an early and successful example of rank-and-file militants in rebellion against their employer, a dispute which attracted the support of the socialist Annie Besant, who was able to publicize the strikers' demands (p. 38). He also highlights the significance of the National Union of Gas Workers and General Labourers (NUGW&GL) in opening its doors to female workers at a time when most trade unions excluded them from membership. Under Eleanor Marx's guidance, Silver's women workers founded the first women's branch of the NUGW&GL during the Silvertown dispute (p. 42).

Tully charts the growing tension between the company and the largely unorganized and unskilled section of its workforce; the class contradictions were sharp. He describes the company as constantly striving to maintain profitability in a high-tech industry, which required huge amounts of capital investment on the one hand, while on the other saw an impoverished workforce struggling to make ends meet amid a smoke-blackened, cheerless environment. He graphically depicts Silvertown's poor, plagued by 'liquid filth' and 'unliftable black smog' (pp. 70–1). Problematically, Tully's examples draw on a long time-span; Brunner Mond munition's factory explosion in 1917, housing conditions in the 1930s, and the Great Flood of 1953. Moreover, some of his images are drawn from London in general rather than Silvertown in particular. Nonetheless, Tully leaves the reader in no doubt about Silvertown's high rates of infant mortality, poor health, overcrowding, poor sanitary conditions, and poisoned atmosphere.

Inspired by the London dock labourers' fight for the famed "dockers' tanner", industrial action began at Silver's in earnest on 19 September, just one day before the successful conclusion of the dockers' dispute. Building on Yvonne Kapp's account of the strike, in her biography of Eleanor Marx,[1] Tully explores the workers' demands, the company's demands, its reaction, and the course, form, and organization of the strike. Making good use of primary sources, such as company minutes, reports of the NUGW&GL, and contemporary newspaper articles, he provides an engaging account of the role of the rank and file, the strike committee, and its leaders, which explores the breadth and depth of the broad support that strikers received from their community and beyond.

Tully also examines the strike's Achilles' heel – the refusal of craft workers and their unions to make common cause with their fellow workers and join the strike. Such divisions were not new, and Tully gives a brief history of these divisions, based largely on skill and gender, before evaluating the impact disunity had on the course of the strike (pp. 139–56). Skirmishes at the factory gates resulted, as the pickets clashed with non-strikers; inevitably these encounters led to confrontations with the police, and the appearance of pickets, charged with intimidating non-strikers, in the courts.

Strong-arm police tactics, however, did not materialize until early November when, according to the Metropolitan Police Commissioner, a period of 'firm' action by the police caused the strike to collapse. As Tully describes, it was the 'hunger and cold', as well as the refusal of craft workers to join the strike, that contributed hugely to the eventual defeat of the strikers rather than beatings suffered at the hands of the police, and prosecutions of pickets (pp. 165–76).

By the end of November a significant number of strikers had given up and gone back to work. Tully reports that the strike leaders and diehard activists had no realistic option of returning to work, as they would have been subject to victimization. Despite their heroic stand, dejection set in and the strike crumbled. On 9 December the dispute was declared officially over.

In an epilogue Tully briefly traces the demise of the NUGW&GL Silvertown branch, and the involvement of Silver's engineers in the 1897 Amalgamated Society of Engineers' national lockout that ended in defeat.

This study of the 1889 Silver's strike provides an important contribution to the literature on New Unionism, a relatively neglected area of research. However, I have a few concerns. First, particularly in the early chapters of the book, the account does not proceed from one event to another or follow on chronologically. It is easy to lose the thread. Second, Tully overplays the significance of the strike. In concluding his account, he argues 'that the employer's victory at Silvertown stiffened the resolve of the capitalist class as a whole to face down the New Unions' (p. 192). One cannot formulate such a conclusive result based on a single case study.

Such a huge claim ignores many of the other disputes that occurred around this time, outside, as well as inside, London; some ending in victory, others in defeat. Sheila Rowbotham, in her book, *Hidden from History,* drew attention to reports in *Commonweal*, the organ of the Socialist League, of a series of strikes and disputes around the country involving women in 1888 and 1889. For instance, in April 1889, 130 women weavers at Alverthorpe, near Wakefield, rejected a move to reduce their rate of pay and struck for five weeks.[2] From 1888 to 1890, a wave of strikes hit provincial cities such as Leeds and Bristol. In Bristol, the NUGW&GL threw open its doors to around 1,200 women cotton workers in their hard-fought, month-long stoppage in October and November 1889.[3]

A third area of concern is Tully's tendency to make suppositions, which are not backed with specific evidence. His inference that cash-strapped women strikers were tempted into prostitution is one example of this tendency. While acknowledging that Eleanor Marx denounced such rumours, Tully argues that these women 'were only human' and close to starvation 'so it is possible that some did succumb to the temptation' (pp. 166–7). He thus falls into the Victorian middle-class stereotyping of working-class women as prostitutes and reproduces the categorization by the state, which equated their social and political rebellion with being unrespectable fallen women. These reservations aside, this book is a welcome addition to the literature on the experiences of workers' militancy in this period of New Unionism.

Michael Richardson
University of the West of England

Notes

1 Y. Kapp, *Eleanor Marx, Vol. 2: The Crowded Years 1884–1898* (Lawrence and Wishart: 1976), pp. 336–63.
2 S. Rowbotham, *Hidden from History* (Pluto: 1973), p. 61.
3 S. Bryher, *An Account of the Bristol Labour and Socialist Movement in Bristol, Part 2* (Bristol British Labour Weekly: 1929), pp. 6–7.

Alison Heath, *The Life of George Ranken Askwith, 1861–1942* (Pickering and Chatto: 2013), ix + 283pp., £60, ISBN 978-1-84893-379-8.

George Askwith was a well-known figure in Edwardian Britain, often in the newspapers because of his success as a conciliator and arbitrator on behalf of the Board of Trade during industrial disputes. The satirical magazine *Punch* drew attention to his importance when it ran an article in 1911 entitled 'Askwith On Strike!' which jested 'It is felt by ministers that if Askwith does not return to work, no strike in England will ever end' and joked that if the man himself went on strike the Cabinet would have to make him a blackleg by nominating him as 'arbitrator in his own strike'.[1] From comfortable origins, Askwith had studied at Brasenose College, Oxford, and been called to the Bar in 1886. He joined the Board of Trade in 1907, working initially in the Railways Department. Appointed head of the Labour Department in 1909, he became the main official used by the Board to mediate in the numerous disputes during this period. Thus he played a significant role in the trend whereby his department gave increased attention to strikes, building on its role established by the Conciliation Act of 1896. He was appointed Chief Industrial Commissioner in 1911, chairing the Industrial Council (a body set up after the major transport strike in 1911 to mediate during disputes) and also went on to chair the Committee on Production, the main wartime arbitration tribunal, from 1915 to 1917. In 1916, the responsibility for involvement in industrial relations was transferred to the newly established Ministry of Labour, after which Askwith lost much of his influence and position, leading him to resign in 1918.

Given his renown and position at the Board of Trade during the expansion of that department, amid the reforms of the Asquith government, the growth of unskilled trade-unionism and a rise in industrial unrest before the war, a biography of Askwith seems well overdue. He has received little attention, mostly referred to in passing by historians concerned with the strikes of the period.[2] Alison Heath has sought to combine an account of Askwith's personal life with his professional experiences and achievements in a book that traces his life from his childhood to his death (in 1942, at the age of 81). With access to the private Askwith family papers, including the diary of his wife, Ellen, Heath provides an account that covers the detail of family life and draws on Askwith's own memoir, a selection of secondary works, and a range of material from the time – both political and bureaucratic – to write a chronological account of his life and work. Her interpretation is based to a large extent on information from the family papers, or, when discussing Askwith's department, on material from the Board of Trade.

Coverage of Askwith's family life is based mostly on Ellen Askwith's diary, supplemented occasionally by other material, and generally offers all the detail a reader might need about this aspect of his life. Praise is also due for the detailed coverage given to the major developments within the Board of Trade and the increased role it had in providing conciliation and arbitration to help mediate in industrial strikes. Some of Heath's research sheds interesting light on the development of Askwith's role in this: chapter 2 examines the younger Askwith's work under the well-known lawyer, Sir Henry James, and his first experiences of conciliation and arbitration work. She also notes his friendships with Sir Charles Dilke and Lord Dunraven, both of whom took a keen interest in labour questions. This detail about his early experiences offers insight into his success in later years, when he grappled to bring together the hostile parties in some of the most difficult strikes of the period before the war. Another strength is the insight provided by drawing on Ellen's diary and private letters between her and George, which comment on the reactions of members of the government, Askwith and his colleagues, and even the King (George V), to the dramatic strikes in 1911 and 1912. Askwith, who, at that time, had at least limited access to all these parties (the King singled him out for discussion on industrial matters on at least two occasions), was well placed to report on such matters.

A limitation of the book is that beginning in the early chapters, Heath has a tendency to jump between Askwith's personal and professional life with little or no link between the two. This somewhat interrupts the flow of the text, although it is, one supposes, a frequent reminder of the busy and well-known professional's family commitments, which he found difficult to balance at times. The details of his social engagements can also be informative of the link between his social and professional connections.[3] Heath's decision to write chronologically sometimes results in a jumping between topics: thus chapter 6 moves abruptly from George and Ellen's social engagements to an in-depth account of Askwith's role in the Copyright Conference held in Berlin in October 1908 (called to clarify international copyright law and agreements) which requires quite an adjustment on the part of the reader. Another shortcoming is that, at times, complex developments in the world of labour and trade-unionism lack analysis: the preface refers to the 'comparatively civilized' negotiations between employers and craft unions before the new unionization of the 1890s, and seems to accept the view that the unskilled or semi-skilled unions that came later were inevitably more militant, although later discussions of Askwith's dealings with these unions illustrate the fact that this was not necessarily the case (p. ix).

There are certain topics to which Heath gives considerable attention, furnishing the reader with well-researched detail. Chapter 3 covers Askwith's early dealings with labour matters at the Board of Trade, providing details of the general economic and labour situation and the increased involvement of the Board of Trade in strikes. Here, and indeed throughout the text, there is rather an over-reliance on Askwith's own account or on the Board of Trade files. The book explores the difficulties that faced Askwith, including hostility from employers and trade-unionists, and also the departmental jealousies within the Civil Service, particularly between the Home Office and Board of Trade, about the responsibilities affecting labour and the workplace. Askwith had strong opinions about the responsibilities of the state, particularly as potential providers of industrial education, and Heath's account helps to explain the influences on his opinions on this matter.[4] Chapter 7 develops the theme of bureaucratic competition, offering some valuable insight into the relations between civil servants such as Askwith and ministers, illustrated by evidence she offers for Askwith's difficulties adjusting to working under Sydney Buxton after the latter had replaced Winston Churchill as President of the Board of Trade (pp. 161–2). Although offering little analysis, Heath does present a detailed narrative of the development of the department and its expanded role in this period, as well as detailing some of the major strikes that required intervention led by the Board of Trade, particularly the major transport strikes in 1911–12.

The chapters that discuss some of the major strikes, such as the Belfast dock strike in 1907 and the complex negotiations involving the rail companies during the same year (chapter 5), or the national transport strikes in 1911 (chapter 9), provide admirable detail and evidence of Askwith's personal skill at bringing parties together to encourage compromise, although explanation of the causes or implications of the strikes is lacking. Similarly, treatment of the Industrial Council (chapter 10) narrates the process of its birth and demise but accepts Askwith's own analysis of its failure (that, essentially, it was not supported robustly enough by the government). The credence given to Askwith's version of events permeates the text, and the unquestioning acceptance of key evidence, such as the assertion that Churchill's report of the Tonypandy disturbances is 'almost certainly the most detailed and accurate account', limits the analysis of key events of the period, and the controversy that has surrounded them since is not discussed (p. 104). In discussion of the problems Askwith experienced after his transfer to the Ministry of Labour (chapter 15), Heath accepts Askwith's criticism of John Hodge (Minister of Labour 1916–17) and David Shackleton (Permanent Secretary in the Ministry of Labour). There is limited discussion of the former's failings; Heath notes only that 'he was arrogant and lacking in tact' (p. 199).

Despite these limitations, the book's treatment of the war years is a particular strength: it is here that Heath presents complex developments clearly, covering the problems between departments, industry, the government, and Civil Service at the start of the war, and the obstacles of taming a labour force wary of profiteering. These chapters detail the establishment of the Committee on Production, initially in engineering and shipbuilding, an important co-ordinating body during the war, in which Askwith played a key role as chairman, and the hasty agreements made with employers and workers to avoid strikes, as well as the limited success of this strategy. Askwith's work and the challenges he faced are contextualized by explanation of the increasing cost of living and the government's response to it, emphasizing Askwith's call for a second cycle of wage increases which, he said, was needed to address the worst effects of inflation. The problems caused by dilution in the workforce are also discussed, giving greater context to the labour unrest during the war. These chapters are also praiseworthy in their discussion of the difficulties in communication between departments of the Civil Service, the Committee on Production and the Admiralty (p. 191). Discussion of Askwith's wife, Ellen, and her untiring work for various committees during the war is a touching aside from the main narrative and an interesting insight into the life of an educated, middle-class woman with political and social links which enabled her to participate in providing and co-ordinating relief efforts.

Heath narrates the changes to the Committee on Production, of which Askwith had been chairman, and his eventual resignation from his department under pressure from his superiors (to which he would only agree with the promise of a pension and peerage). Assigned against his will to the new Ministry of Labour in 1916, Askwith was forced to retire after proving himself incapable of working satisfactorily with others in the department and opposing the government's increased intervention in industrial relations.[5] His retirement resulted at least partly from his inability to adapt or accept changes to his department after the war, which saw his position and influence diminish. Heath, accepting Askwith's own version of events, notes only the 'ruthless way in which Wilson and Shackleton combined to remove Askwith from Office' (p. 210).

What Heath offers is a detailed biography of a man who was a central figure in the industrial relations of the period before the First World War. She weaves together an account of George Askwith's life, pulling together the many threads that influenced his ideas and work into a text that would benefit any reader interested in the bureaucratic or labour history of the Edwardian period, as it provides detail of the major events and changes affecting the development of the Labour Department of the Board of Trade, (reflecting the general expansion of the bureaucratic state) and of industrial unrest, and of methods to mediate strikes. As the first, and possibly the only, 'celebrity arbitrator', George Askwith's working life was a reflection of these trends which had repercussions well beyond his own lifetime, and this detailed biography does a great deal to illustrate his role during this turbulent period.

Lydia Redman

Notes

1 *Punch* cartoon and article in G. R. Askwith, *Industrial Problems and Disputes* (Murray: 1920), p. 173.
2 The only notable exception is Rodney Lowe's review of Askwith's memoir, in which he gives a great deal of attention to the man himself: R. Lowe, 'Review of G. R. Askwith, *Industrial Problems and Disputes*', *British Journal of Industrial Relations* 13 (1975), pp. 115–20. Élie Halévy also referred to Askwith's position and influence in industrial relations, calling him a 'secret dictator': É. Halévy, *A History of the English-Speaking People in the Nineteenth-Century,Vol. 6: The Rule of Democracy, 1905–1914,* translated by E. I. Watkin (2nd edn, Benn: 1952), p. 265.
3 Ellen kept meticulous records of with whom they dined or socialized and Heath notes those who were particularly relevant to Askwith's work or political connections. See, particularly, p. 80, which details their engagements with leading Liberal politicians, including David Lloyd George and Winston Churchill. Askwith also had a social, as well as working, relationship with the Prime Minister Herbert Asquith and a range of educated radicals, such as Sidney and Beatrice Webb.
4 Askwith discusses his views on these matters in his memoir, *Industrial Problems and Disputes*, p. 23
5 For details see the letters between Lloyd George, Bonar Law and their secretaries about the matter between December 1918 and February 1919, LG/F/29/3/10, LG/F/79/5 and LG/F/79/5, Parliamentary Archives.

Lewis Minkin, *The Blair Supremacy: A Study in the Politics of Labour's Party Management* (Manchester University Press: 2014), 864pp., hbk £90, ISBN 978-0-7190-7379-3; pbk £26.99, 978-0-7190-7380-9.

In 1999 the *Independent on Sunday* quoted Tony Blair's description of New Labour: 'It is the newest political party on the scene and the smallest. It has membership of about five people' (p. 118). The five were Blair himself, Gordon Brown, Peter Mandelson, Philip Gould and Alastair Campbell (p. 115). As part of what Mandelson called 'The Project' and Gould called 'The Revolution',[1] these five aimed to change the Labour Party in all its aspects – policy, structure, membership, and management of the party.

Lewis Minkin is the foremost scholar of the Labour Party's organization and practice.[2] In *The Blair Supremacy* he examines the way Blair managed the party during his decade in power. Minkin's analysis is compelling, many of his revelations are startling and some are shocking. Others have suggested that Blair was not interested in the details of Labour Party management, only in the outcomes. Minkin disagrees. He shows that Blair was not only the driving force behind the changes in party rules and conventions but would often intervene directly to achieve his purpose. Blair's personality dominates every page of this book – his brilliance, his personal charm, his determination and his great disregard, often amounting to contempt, for anything and anyone who got in his way.

Blair was not interested in leading through consensus or by consent. He said with disarming directness that he intended to be 'in charge' (p. 120). He had monumental self-confidence. Ignorance did not deter him. Knowing next to nothing about trade unions, he went to the annual Trade Union Congress in 1997 and lectured the delegates on the need for modernization: 'I will be watching you carefully', he added (p. 290). It sounded like a threat, and it was.

Blair often said that he was not 'born into the Labour Party' and he certainly had none of the tribal loyalty that binds many of us to it. He accused me of opposing his policies in order to gain publicity. I explained with absolute and misplaced honesty that fighting the Labour Party held no joy for me. It was, I said, as miserable as falling out with my mother. Blair looked at me as if I had gone mad. He could never understand the emotional attachment that some of us had to a party that, in his view, had so many imperfections.

Blair regarded the leadership style of his predecessor, John Smith, as twenty-five years out of date (p. 85). He thought that party activists were 'too impulsive and irrational' (p. 139) and that the trade unions were old fashioned and obstructive. The trade unions also interfered with Blair's wish to move Labour closer to the Confederation of British Industry (CBI).

Minkin reveals that early drafts of the revised Clause IV approved by Blair failed to mention trade unions but he was forthright about the need for Labour to be close to business (p. 181).

Minkin describes the changes made to the Labour Party as a rolling *coup d'état* by New Labour (p. 664). The aim was to extract the power from each of the party's institutions and concentrate it in the hands of the Leader. The national executive committee (NEC) was reconstituted and lost its right to make policy (chapter 8). The national policy forum was constrained and the policy commissions were taken over by ministers (p. 309). The annual conference was redesigned as a public relations showcase for Blair (p. 345), with little opportunity for delegates to challenge the content of lengthy policy reports and with a much diminished opportunity to generate policy initiatives (p. 220). Members of the Parliamentary Party lost their involvement in the preparation of election manifestos.

Sometimes the changes required by Blair were enacted in accordance with the constitution but, as time went on, the formal procedures were bypassed or ignored. Without the agreement of NEC or conference Blair appointed a chair of the Labour Party (p. 485). The manifesto for the 2001 general election was written in the Leader's Office without the involvement of the NEC or much input from the Parliamentary Party (p. 479).

The thoroughness with which the Labour Party rules were suborned and party conventions were brushed aside was breathtaking. Party officials were traditionally regarded as Labour's civil servants, honouring the constitution and applying the rules (p. 155). Blair wanted none of that. The party's general secretary was replaced (p. 146). New officials were recruited, younger, middle class and with a clear political purpose: deliver what the Leader wants (p. 165). Awkward members were vilified (p. 240). Favoured candidates were supplied with lists of voting members and party officials helped them get elected (p. 372). The NEC and Labour MPs were bypassed. 'Unhelpful' committee members were not told of meetings. The verbatim conference report, recording commitments and the details of policy, became very difficult to obtain and eventually was not produced at all (p. 169). By 2007 the position of the NEC was so reduced that Dianne Hayter's official report on NEC governance contained this extraordinary recommendation: 'The NEC must be communicated with so that it knows what is taking place in its name' (p. 651).

Blair often talked about policy being based on 'what works'. In this new and amoral world of centralized control the party's officials learned a new mantra: 'what works is what works for Tony' (p. 137). Minkin's interviews with party managers reveal that they were impatient with arguments about due process. The Tories would use dirty tactics and that justified a tough response from Labour. To win elections the party had to unite behind Blair. The Tory media would seize on any suggestion of division or ill-discipline.

Central control was essential. One phrase was used repeatedly: party officials said they were engaged in 'serious politics'.

For most of this period of high-pressure management of the Labour Party, the high command of New Labour managed to convince themselves that they had the support of the party's ordinary members. As far back as 1992, Blair, Mandelson and Brown had agreed that the Labour Party needed a new decision-making structure. Ideally trade unions would be on the outside, with no rights or votes. However, it gradually dawned on the true believers that pushing the trade unions out of the party would cause massive disruption. So a new strategy was developed for mobilizing the support of party members. As far as possible, members would decide policy by voting individually, sidelining the trade unions and minimizing the influence of unreliable activists.

This was the one-man-one-vote (OMOV) solution, vigorously advocated by Gould, the pollster for the inner circle. He insisted that relying on the good sense of Labour Party members to vote the right way would 'complete the revolution' that New Labour had started. OMOV would free the party from the trade unions and other remnants of Old Labour (p. 280). However, as Minkin makes clear, Gould was wrong. Individual party members tended to share the beliefs of their trade-union colleagues, and the activists were often speaking with the support of their local constituency party. Eventually even Blair recognized that Gould was perpetuating an illusion. He says wryly in his autobiography 'how extraordinary' he found the similarity between Gould's own beliefs and what the focus groups seemed to tell him (p. 61).

Unable to exclude trade unions, and reluctantly aware that OMOV would not deliver the support he wanted (p. 238), Blair came to rely more and more on excessive methods of control. His behaviour took him a long way from the promises he had made as a newly elected Leader, to bring a new 'ethical dimension' to politics. He had spoken of creating an 'unbroken line of accountability' from the Prime Minister to the Labour Party and the people. Minkin argues that Blair's method of control was in direct contradiction of these ethical ambitions. Blair's manner of party management ensured that accountability would not happen (p. 688).

Spin and dissembling became second nature. Labour owed no allegiance to the Tory media so feeding them inaccurate information was easily justified (p. 360). Misleading party members was more difficult to defend but the process began very early. In 1996 the Labour Party had voted on the election manifesto, but unknown to party members a second document, the 'Business Manifesto', was being drafted. This second manifesto contained commitments to the CBI and to business that were never publicized and which undermined many of the policies that party members had voted to support (p. 439).[3]

Two unsuccessful interventions by Blair into the election of party candidates illustrate the crude and arbitrary nature of his methods. The first was in Wales. When Ron Davies resigned as Welsh Party Leader, the popular choice to succeed him was Rhodri Morgan. But Blair preferred Alun Michael and, in effect, promised him the job. Encountering opposition in Wales, Blair abandoned OMOV and all thought of democratic processes, and authorized what Number 10 insider, Lance Price, called 'an old style Labour stitch-up' (p. 386). Michael won but the resentment of Morgan supporters dogged him during his short period in office. He resigned in February 2000 and six days later Morgan was elected unanimously.

The attempt to prevent Ken Livingstone becoming London Mayor was more public and more damaging. After a series of senior Labour figures declined to stand, Frank Dobson was persuaded to run against Livingstone for the Labour nomination. The London Labour Party wanted the election to be conducted as an OMOV ballot of party members and it soon became clear that Livingstone would win by a large margin. So Blair and his allies looked for a voting method that would 'stop Livingstone' (p. 389). Gould of all people, the arch supporter of OMOV, proposed a specially constructed and much-derided college voting system. The methods used to deliver Dobson the victory made the candidate himself distinctly queasy (p. 393) but a narrow victory was achieved. It was, as Chris Mullin MP recorded in his diary, 'a result that stinks' (p. 394). Denied the Labour nomination, Livingstone stood as an Independent and won convincingly. He was expelled from the Labour Party but in due course was accepted back on his own terms.

Trade unions suffered most from New Labour's duplicity. After Labour came to power in 1997 the trade unions began discussions with the government to deliver the promised improvements in employment rights. An important element was a new statutory right to trade-union recognition. It was not until the discussions became bogged down in apparently irrelevant arguments about the status of in-house staff unions that it became clear, and was then admitted by the minister, that Blair would not agree to any proposals that Rupert Murdoch thought might put News International under any pressure to recognize independent trade unions at Wapping (p. 436). Blair would not give up what was effectively a Murdoch veto and the law that was eventually passed gave recalcitrant employers many opportunities to deny union recognition (p. 456).

Minkin records many other occasions where promises were broken (p. 464). In exchange for the withdrawal of a popular but inconvenient motion to the annual conference, the Transport and General Workers' Union was guaranteed a national debate on the future of the welfare state. It never happened (p. 319). Under pressure from Unison and the GMB, Blair promised a review of the private finance initiative. No review ever took place (p. 538). The Warwick Agreement, reached in the National Policy Forum of 2004, was hailed as a breakthrough in Labour Party–union relationships. In the event many of the elements were never implemented (p. 598). The trade unions were the target for continual criticism and abuse. Assistance to Blair never produced gratitude and was usually followed by an attack. Trade-union votes gave Blair his Clause IV victory but the outcome was immediately spun as a victory of the Labour Leader over the unions (p. 185). Differences of view were not tolerated. When doubts were expressed about Blair public-service reforms, union leaders – much to the delight of the *Daily Mail* – were labelled as 'wreckers' (p. 517).

Why did the trade unions and the wider Labour Party put up with it for so long? Minkin's explanation is subtle and convincing. For decades the relationships between the various sections of the Labour Party were regulated not just by the constitution but by a number of unwritten conventions. As Minkin has explained elsewhere,[4] the trade unions accepted that they should not try to unseat the Leader and that they should not use their financial power to force policies on the Labour Party; without these conventions the party would quickly become ungovernable. In exchange the trade unions expected respect for their position in the party and hoped that reasonable consideration would be given to trade unions' policy proposals. Blair delivered neither. He gave the unions no credit for their restraint and used the manoeuvring room provided by the conventions to press forward with his project.

However, that is not the whole story. Blair was also much admired. He won elections, he had mastery of the Tories in the House of Commons, he was a brilliant communicator and his presence on the conference rostrum commanded respect. As time passed the admiration began to dim but it was only after the invasion of Iraq that many in the Labour Party wanted Blair to be gone. Until then, most people felt a mixture of pride and discomfort. As Robin Cook put it, party members were 'regretful rather than angry' (p. 355). But regret turned into disillusionment. Many members left the party: by 2007 membership was well below 200,000 (p. 639). Participation dropped. The number of votes cast in NEC elections fell by over 70% (p. 243); fewer constituency parties sent delegates to conference (p. 618). Labour was becoming a hollow shell. Mandelson recognized the trend and made light of it. 'Welcome to the virtual Party', he joked (p. 254).

Disillusionment also depressed Labour's support throughout the country. In 2005 Labour had the lowest level of support for a winning party since the beginning of universal suffrage. Significantly, the decline was greatest among the working class (p. 484). Especially after the Iraq invasion, trust was the problem (p. 655). Control freakery and spin came to be the defining feature of Blair's leadership. Polls showed that between 1997 and 2007 the proportion of the public who thought Blair could be trusted had fallen from

63% to 22%. Blair responded by promising to change: 'No more spin', he declared (p. 681.) He then insisted that he would hold a 'big conversation' with the British people (p. 570). Little came of it as Blair could not reinvent himself as a consensual politician. Alastair Campbell records that Blair continued to call for 'more communication' (also known as spin) at the same time as he was telling the British people that the era of spin was over (p. 514). After two years of intermittent crisis and much criticism, it all ended in tears. And those tears were shed not just by the lost Leader as he was forced from power, but by many Labour loyalists as they realized what had been done in their name.

Minkin's book is meticulously researched and engagingly written. He has conducted many thousands of interviews, some formal and lengthy but often of short duration to check a fact or a statement. He has sat in on many of the meetings he describes in the early part of his book and is so familiar with the people involved that he always knows whom to go to. His authority is unquestioned. Although I sometimes thought I could have added a fact or two, never once in this lengthy book did I encounter what I thought was a mistake.

Not everyone will agree with all of Minkin's judgements. Perhaps the trade unions are treated more kindly than they sometimes deserved; perhaps John Prescott's role was less significant than it is portrayed here; perhaps the demoralizing effect of the Iraq 'dodgy dossier' damaged Blair more deeply than even Minkin concludes; perhaps Blair's eviction from office was more the result of Brown's relentless pressure than Minkin sometimes seems to suggest. But these are minor quibbles about emphasis. The book is a masterpiece. Almost every page contains a revelation and, although Minkin avoids outrage and gratuitous criticism, the logic of the narrative adds up to an awful indictment of Blair's management of the Labour Party.

Minkin's book deserves to be read by everyone interested in politics. More important, it *needs* to be read by anyone who seeks high office in the Labour Party.

John Edmonds
Durham University Business School
Mill Hill Lane
Durham DH1 3LB

Notes

1 P. Mandelson and R. Liddle, *The Blair Revolution* (Faber: 1996); P. Gould, *The Unfinished Revolution: How the Modernisers Saved the Labour Party* (Little, Brown and Co.: 1998).
2 See L. Minkin, *The Contentious Alliance: Trade Unions and the Labour Party* (Edinburgh University Press: 1991).
3 J. Edmonds, 'Positioning Labour Closer to the Employers: The Importance of the Labour Party's 1997 Business Manifesto', *Historical Studies in Industrial Relations* 22 (2006), pp. 85–107.
4 Minkin, *The Contentious Alliance*.

doi:10.3828/hsir.2015.36.12

Abstracts

German Codetermination without Nationalization, and British Nationalization without Codetermination: Retelling the Story (pp. 1–27) Rebecca Zahn

Codetermination – workers' participation in management – forms part of the industrial relations traditions of a number of European countries. Among these, the German system of parity codetermination (*paritätische Mitbestimmung*) which was first introduced in the iron and steel industries by the British military command after the Second World War provides the greatest level of involvement for workers. Similar debates which are often overlooked over the introduction of codetermination were taking place in the UK in the late 1940s. This article provides a new perspective on the history of codetermination in the UK and Germany in order to explain why codetermination was introduced in its current form in Germany but not in the UK. The article questions whether the failure to institute a system of workers' participation in management in the UK should be considered a missed opportunity.

Spheres of Justice in the 1942 Betteshanger Miners' Strike: An Essay in Historical Ethnography (pp. 29–57) Ariane Mak

This article seeks to refresh the understanding of the 1942 Betteshanger strike, the famous symbol of the failure to enforce Order 1305, which was introduced in 1940 to ban strikes during the Second World War. The analysis is based on an ethnographic survey carried out at Betteshanger by Mass Observation during the conflict, a key primary source which has not been exploited before. It allows for a study of the conflicting descriptions and framing of the dispute by the strikers, their families and neighbours, union representatives and rank and file, coal owners and colliery managers, conciliation officers from various departments, and the press. The contention is that the complex connections between three spheres of justice – patriotism, social justice, and legality – are a central issue in reassessing the reasons for the failure to enforce Order 1305 in Betteshanger colliery.

Arms'-Length Bargaining or Nose to Nose? Eric Batstone and Bargaining in 1970s France (pp. 59–71) Steve Jefferys

This contribution provides the context to French employment relations and Eric Batstone's illuminating description of the French worker–employer, plant-level interface in the 1970s. The 1970s represented a transition decade between the post-war boom and the significantly lower levels of growth and higher levels of unemployment that set in from the 1980s. In France, as in Britain, the 1970s was a decade of trade-union growth. The numbers of private-sector strikes are shown from 1960 to 1999, as is the evolution of the wage-share of GDP in both France and the UK. The article discusses why French workers have never joined French trade unions in the same numbers as occurred in Britain, and yet are ready to accept the use of minority direct action and to support mass strikes.

Arms'-Length Bargaining: Industrial Relations in a French Company (pp. 73–136) Eric Batstone (1944–87)

A review of the French literature on industrial relations demonstrates marked contrasts to the English literature. This paper seeks to understand the broader pattern of industrial relations in two French plants and, where possible, to assess the typicality of the findings. It focuses upon what will be termed "arms'-length bargaining", by which is meant that at plant level, bargaining in terms of negotiations around a table, in other words, of an institutionalized form, is of limited significance. Nevertheless, the two parties have a considerable impact upon each other; that is pressures are imposed at the workplace rather than at the bargaining table. In such a situation, the crucial factor from the union point of view is to prove to management that the demands put forward are strongly felt by the workforce. It is in this respect that the strike and other forms of collective action assume particular importance. Arms'-length bargaining therefore involves two crucial types of strategy for both employers and the unions: the first is issue-specific, while the second seeks to influence the broader background conditions in one's own favour.

In Praise of Collective Bargaining: The Enduring Significance of Hugh Clegg's Trade Unionism under Collective Bargaining (pp. 137–158) Keith Sisson

Hugh Clegg's *Trade Unionism under Collective Bargaining* was published nearly forty years ago. It is far from being just a work of antiquarian interest, however. Its core argument, that the main influence on trade-union behaviour is the structure of collective bargaining, which depends on the role of employers and their organizations, remains as challenging as it ever was. Its approach, comparative and historical, is a watershed in the theoretical development of industrial relations, paving the way for an emphasis on theory 'in' rather than theory 'of'. It also implicitly raises two questions of enduring significance. The first is the wider contribution of collective bargaining and what its decline means not just for trade-union members but also society as a whole. The other is the conditions necessary for the survival of collective bargaining. The policy implication is that, if society wants to have the benefits of collective bargaining, there will be a need for legislation to boost collective bargaining's 'legitimacy power' to make up for the decline in its 'coercive power'.

The Trade Disputes Bills of 1903: Sir Charles Dilke and Charles Percy Sanger (pp. 159–180) Paul Smith

No paper trail exists in The National Archives to cast light as to how the Trade Disputes Act (TDA) 1906 emerged in its final form. The succession of private members' bills, many sponsored by the Trades Union Congress, and the Liberal government's bill, and associated parliamentary debates, are very useful but the process of negotiation within Parliament that produced the finished statute is obscure. The reports of the Parliamentary Committee of the Trades Union Congress are a valuable source, but they are cryptic at times. The documents published here for the first time thus have an importance that belies their brevity in that they provide evidence of Sir Charles Dilke's position in 1903 on the reform of trade-union law, which came to fruition with the TDA, his radicalism, and that Labour MPs were too modest in their ambitions.

The Trade Unions and the 'Winter of Discontent': A Case of Myth-Taken Identity? (pp. 181–203) Colin Hay

Three decades after the events themselves and with full access to the public record, historians and political scientists are now well placed to revisit and re-evaluate the 'Winter of Discontent'. This article reflects on the first book-length studies of the period published since the opening of the archives. I argue that although neither study profoundly alters our view of this crucial episode and its place in the pre-history of Thatcherism, taken together the evidence they uncover might provide the basis for an alternative assessment. Ultimately, however, such an assessment requires more attention to methodology and, above all, an approach to the archives and to witness testimony that is both *more inductive* and *more deductive* than that exhibited in the existing literature. In the process I hope to clarify what we now know and we have still to learn about the winter of 1978–79 and the popular mythology to which it gave rise.

Striking Facts about the 'Winter of Discontent' (pp. 205–218) Dave Lyddon

The recent books by John Shepherd and Tara Martin López on the Winter of Discontent of 1978–79 provide an opportunity to examine the experience and tactics of several of its strikes and to challenge standard statistical views of its strike record. The main conclusion is to stress the continuity of the local authority and National Health Service disputes of 1979 with their antecedents from 1969 to 1973. Evidence is provided to show that previous instances of mountains of rubbish and unburied corpses did not attract much opprobrium (it is likely that earlier industrial action in the NHS was also generally tolerated). The sensationalization of events by politicians (of both hues) and by some of the media was contingent on a particular set of economic and political circumstances.

Public-Sector Strikes in the 'Winter of Discontent' (pp. 219–226) Roger Seifert

John Shepherd's chapter on public-sector strikes provides a useful overview of what happened, giving due weight to the plight of both the low-paid manual workers and their trade-union leaders. However, he tends to ignore the sector-by-sector negotiations; he lacks understanding of the politics inside each union; and he ignores the vital role of left groupings (especially the Communist Party) in the strikes. He is over-reliant on accounts by political leaders, with the benefit of hindsight, and fails to appreciate the nature of struggle, in particular the difficulty of striking against the state.

The Neoliberal Labyrinth (pp. 227–238) John Eldridge

The three books under review all deny that neoliberalism is dead and that it remains pervasive as a comprehensive world view and not just an economic doctrine. Its vitality, notwithstanding premature death-notices, is due its role as a political doctrine serving certain interests which sought to reform society by subordinating it to the market. Support for neoliberal values and policies crosses political boundaries. The role of the state is limited but important: a strong state to create and supervise the market. The response of neoliberals to crisis, some directly of their own making, is additional neoliberal measures. For employment, this entails more privatization, contracting out, anti-union legislation, and deregulation of the labour market (including health and safety, and employment protection). Each of the books reviewed is infused with a generous humanism and offer hopeful approaches to challenging, resisting and overcoming the hydra-headed monster that constitutes neoliberalism.